HERE LIES AMERICA

HERE LIES AMERICA

Buried Agendas & Family Secrets at the
Tourist Sites Where Bad History Went Down

JASON COCHRAN

WELL HALL
BOOKS

COPYRIGHT © 2019 JASON COCHRAN

HERE LIES AMERICA

Buried Agendas & Family Secrets at the Tourist Sites Where Bad History Went Down

ISBN   978-1-5445-0366-0 *Hardcover*

978-1-5445-0365-3 *Paperback*

978-1-5445-0364-6 *Ebook*

Illustrations by Josh Koll.

For my family, here and gone.

CONTENTS

"The present state of things is the consequence of the former."

—SAMUEL JOHNSON, *RASSELAS*

INTRODUCTION

A Tragedy

IT STARTS, AS ALL STORIES DO, WITH WHAT WE don't know yet. I wasn't there, and neither were you, but you should trust me that this is how it happened.

In rural west South Carolina, near a town that isn't there anymore, in the middle of the night, a faraway train approaches on tracks laid through a deep gash in the fields. It is February, between 2:30 and 3:00 in the morning. Stand on the rails and wait for history to happen. The churn of the locomotive grows louder and more insistent, nine minutes late through the farmland.

As it approaches, you discern more. The distant chug becomes layered with a steam hiss, and beneath that, the arrhythmic creak of carriages in tow. The peace of the farmhouses in slumber now bellows with industry as the grinding of the train assumes control over the landscape. And then, at 2:47, in a time and place that all people have forgotten, you see the headlight of the locomotive as it rounds the bend and into your sight. The rails shine in the light, the steam billows proudly in the air, and as it gains speed, you can barely make out the engine number: 1233.

But then it tips. The headlight beam unexpectedly slouches against the embankment, spotlighting weeds, and before you understand what's happening, the locomotive is somersaulting sideways. Metal screams, steam plumes gush in every direction, and a burst nest of scattered sparks casts crazy fleeting shadows over land that only one second ago was silent and dark. Rails jump from their beds and flutter in the air like charmed snakes. Through the cacophonous molten flicker, you can see the trailing carriages tipping, too, collapsing behind in strobe, window glass twinkling as it shatters. The tumbling kaleidoscope of machinery drags a scar through the earth for twenty, thirty, forty feet, spitting steam and sizzling water, before finally halting, just short of you, under its own dead, groaning weight.

The jumbled train curls like a felled beast, steam deafeningly blasting from somewhere within its tangled guts. It curls, as if pausing to calculate how to spring forward into an escape. A moment passes, with no sign of movement except clouds of gas. But then, a human stirring. An arm appears in a blackened depression that you now realize was a window of the locomotive cab. Then another arm, joined by a head, joined by a man. He is dragging himself out of the wreckage, wheezing, gasping. You cannot see him well, but you think he might be somehow unbroken, because he is crawling.

His movements are painstaking and erratic, first in

one direction, then another, perhaps disoriented, but moving insistently toward the embankment. And now you hear other voices, too, from the rear of the train, both male and female calling out to each other. Some are sobbing. Signs of life increase, and another body drops from the crushed locomotive window, slower than the first one, tentative with effort, pausing too often to pull itself from the hot spattering cloud.

The first man has found the bottom slope of the embankment, but now he doesn't seem able to stand. Instead, he is laboriously trying to clamber up. His shoes can't secure a grip, and stones roll from his failing grasp as he feebly leans into the hill. In the dark, in the distance, he disappears against the earth, but you can hear his ghastly struggle for breath.

"It was set," he gasps.

A long time passes. It's hard to know how long, but long enough for reality to set in. This wreck really just happened. Passengers in their nightclothes are coming from the rear of the train now, picking their way around debris to view the mangled condition of the locomotive. There is more sobbing, some embraces, the dusting off of clothing, the inspection of light wounds. The hissing has subsided, and now the cooling metal clicks and pongs in aftereffect. And then someone cries out that someone is over there, "Look, on the embankment!"

A man shouts out and three human shapes rush away from the wreckage and halfway up the slope to meet him. "It's the engineer!" cries a voice. "Sir, we're here."

A man bends down to help him. He looks in the engineer's face. He freezes.

"Oh, dear God," he says.

That was the main event, but it's also how it started, in 1909.

Here's how it goes now.

It's slightly over a century later. Like the train, I'm also in rural South Carolina, on the cusp of the Blue Ridge Mountains, but I am whole and standing, and it's daytime. I need to find the place where the wreck happened. I'm on a half-overgrown gravel road with logs slung across it, well past the signs that plainly informed me that I was in a position to get shot if I was discovered. Although my story went through this place in 1909, I'm a city boy now, so I instinctively locked my rented Nissan Versa when I left it, even though there isn't a soul in this empty wilderness, only kudzu and grinding insects. Whoever hung that sign has a shotgun loaded because they're probably just as gripped by baseless fears, and that's all it takes to end everything. Step by step, tempting the wrath of my countryman, I push into denser greenery, the shifting rocks giving me away to my murderer with every inch gained.

But this road is the road, I think. I've studied the satellite images, I've pored over maps from the era, I've worked against the laws of entropy in archival materials to locate the few source materials that anyone cared to preserve. This was always an ignored backwoods, even in its unnoticed heyday. The era's newspapers said the crash happened at a bend in the railway at a flag stop at

"Harbin's," which, based on a hand-drawn map I'd found, seemed to correspond with a crossing at the modern-day Idlewild Drive. This blocked gravel road hasn't even merited pavement in the one hundred years since that map, but if I'm right, it leads on for a few hundred yards, I surmise, and then it crosses the old railroad on a wooden bridge. Within sight of that bridge, I'll find the bend where the No. 1233 crumpled right by the whistle stop. That's no longer there. As long as I could spot it based on its no longer being there. And as long as nothing has changed. Or so I think.

I spent the early afternoon trying other roads that I triumphantly concluded were also about to lead me there before they would veer into other directions, routed in antiquity around homesteads that no longer existed. I went down six or eight failed roads like this, miles from town, the only driver, perhaps ever, to slowly cruise suspiciously in an economy car past the occasional sullen houses with their rusting railings and shifting curtains.

So this road, the last of my options, has to be *the* road, Idlewild Drive. When the train crashed, in 1909, it was probably rutted with farm carts that shuttled down to the railway to pick up supplies. This place was rolling farmland where electricity wasn't a guarantee and where the approaching whistle meant the mail, your only proof of the world beyond, had arrived.

Society's regard for this corner of America hadn't changed much; my GPS is useless because this corner of South Carolina isn't deemed worthy of mobile service.

Now, instead of streaming with sunshine and waving with crops, the land, gone wild with gnarled trees, envelops me in ever-greener darkness the more I dare to move into it. Between the rustles and the sticks, I can almost imagine the ghosts of cows that once wandered this patch, the long-faded calls of farmhands across fields, the clang of a dinner bell that surely lies rusting somewhere under soil.

I nearly trip over a fallen tree. Beyond it, a construction bracket braced by a reflective sign: ROAD CLOSED. Somewhere beyond, the bridge must be out, and out for a long time, because someone—perhaps the person who so demonstratively wishes to perforate outsiders—is using the erstwhile Idlewild Drive to store a shoulder-high pile of mulch. There is no passing without fighting the Carolina jungle.

I stand and listen to where I am, trying to make the most of getting this far. I try to invoke a feeling of homecoming even though I am at the end of my road. I could force myself on, I think. I could hurl myself into the bushes, clamber over the mulch into darker forest yet, and hack my way to the railway with flailing arms. Torn and spent, I could clamber down the same embankment that the engineer, grievously scalded, tried to scale with flayed fingers in his final pitiful moments, bleeding my DNA into the dirt to mingle somehow with his, shouting for anyone who could run for help. I could commune with anguish in the place where his train lay tangled and hissing as he deliriously clung to life.

But there I stand, staring into a landscape that has

swallowed everything, and for a moment exactly as long as I can quell my anxieties, I allow the silence that engulfed my past to engulf me next. If I stand here long enough, die on this dirt, I would be erased within a few weeks, too. Like kudzu, this land is always creeping in to overtake anything that holds still, even its own, like me. It does so in increments so subtle and slow that you don't notice until you're already gone.

A SILENT BELL RINGS

Oakland Historic Cemetery

My peculiar plan to see America's greatest death tourism sights was inspired by that lonely South Carolina train wreck from 1909. It was an unlikely catalyst, I know, but getting stewed by a belly-flopping train was also an unlikely way to go, and the best stories are born from the accumulation of a series of unlikely events. The dying engineer was cooked by escaping steam. It was a terrible way to go, and he didn't last until dawn. Within the week, he was lying cold in Atlanta's Oakland Cemetery, the city's most prestigious graveyard. And that's where I actually started my explorations, a few months before parking my rental car at a dead end. Oakland Cemetery is the only place in the world where the engineer, whom in my mind I call my engineer, *The* Engineer, can definitely be found.

Strange as it is, some graveyards are always prestigious, as if money still matters after your final exit. In 1900, the Engineer, pre-accident, had needed a plot for his newly deceased daughter, Urdis, and it says something about his success with the Southern Railway that he was connected enough and cool enough to secure a plot in Oakland even if he hadn't been cool enough to think twice about naming a little girl Urdis. He also obtained plots for his wife, his parents (such a good Southern boy) and himself, because once you got your foot into Oakland, you brought the whole clan. The Engineer, whose name was Will O'Neal, also knew that his train life was dangerous and tended to derail without warning, as it indeed did just nine years later, when he joined Urdis as his plot's second occupant.

I walked around Oakland now, just as Will had done in 1900 with a combination of grief and social pride, not purely because I was paying respects to my poor, scalded great-great-grandfather—poor Will was my grandfather's grandfather—but also just because Oakland is a fun place to go. It's what you might call a dark tourism attraction. That is an actual type of attraction, common around the world. People like to go to certain places just because they're associated with death and suffering. Oakland shares the same neighborhood as the Jimmy Carter Center, Martin Luther King, Jr.'s home and tomb, and Ebenezer Baptist Church. The savvy vacationer makes a circuit of them all, guided through the sightseeing ritual by Atlanta's taxpayer-supported *Things to Do* brochures.

"A hidden treasure, a secret sanctuary, welcomes you," it beckons. Oakland's popularity among Red Hat Society types supports a gift shop, cell phone tours, seasonal signs announcing which flowers are blooming, and popular concert events such as—I kid you not—"Tunes from the Tombs." It's an Old South deathgasm. People go.

Oakland delicately skirts accusations of poor taste by billing itself today as Oakland Historic Cemetery. With a permanent population of 70,000, it's the graveyard of your fantasies, but if you plan on dropping by to enjoy death for its own pleasures, you'll find it impossible, because if you have any social awareness at all, every inscription is soaked with political subtext. If you're a native white Atlantan, being buried in Oakland gives your lineage the imprimatur of continuity because it was where they honored the loftiest Confederates—to be dead in Oakland meant you finally arrived. If Scarlett O'Hara had existed, you'd find her in in Oakland for sure. In a way, she is there: Margaret Mitchell, who wrote *Gone With the Wind*, became one of its most illustrious residents after a 1949 rendezvous with a taxicab on Peachtree Street officially made her a one-hit wonder. Former mayor Maynard Jackson is there, too, but guides don't usually dwell long on the man's accomplishments, but rather on the fact that his body was misfiled—he was placed in the whites-only section in 2003, a scant thirty years after the cemetery gave up segregation, and that's usually why the man gets pointed out at all, as if in grudging congratulations. Racial politics reign forever in Atlanta. Old-timers hint that Oakland is where you'll find the "real" Atlanta, which is to say the one before Bravo reality shows and Tyler Perry movies, which is to say the white one. People have told me I should be proud to have a family plot there. Whatever; I just think the place looks cool.

Oakland is a graveyard with a lived-in look. Its sloppy jumble of mismatched grey spires and slouching crypts compete for attention and eternal esteem. Gravestones are sad by definition, but here, vandalism and entropy have honed a crowd-pleasing dolor worthy of a John Berendt yarn. Stone angels are decapitated and melted by acid rain and brick pathways buckle; in 2008, a rogue tornado trashed the place to art-directed perfection. Trees and flowers make the dignified decay appealingly atmospheric, and now and then, it's possible to peer directly into the fissure of some broken-down family tomb and imagine you saw something slink toward the darkness. Oakland is the kind of place where Scooby-Doo would leap into Shaggy's arms. It's hard not to love it.

One of its landmarks is the "Lion of Atlanta" sculpture, plump and coiffed like the one in L. Frank Baum, cuddling a Confederate flag as he sleeps—that Southern hybrid of mourning and obsession persistently on display. The Lion, a gift of the Atlanta Ladies Memorial Association (there'll be more on Ladies Memorial groups later on) in 1894, presides over a section containing nearly 7,000 Confederate dead, 3,000 of them unidentified, which is a polite way of saying "in a heap." Some Atlantans embrace the Lion as a symbol of proud antebellum ways, but some others benignly regard it as a stalwart, vaguely medieval emblem that validates the heritage of their hometown. None of them seem aware their mascot is actually an uncredited rip-off of the Swiss *Lion of Lucerne*. My mother uses a miniature one as a doorstop, which says all you need to know about our generation's ambivalence about certain aspects of our Southern identity. I can say Georgia is undoubtedly where I'm *from*—my lineage goes back at least eight generations there, deep into the 1700s—but since I have lived my life elsewhere, from New York, to Los Angeles, to Chicago, it's not who I *am*. My family moved away from Atlanta when I was in diapers, but in true Southern fashion, we always claimed to be Georgia Peaches out of a vague assertion of pride, even though none of us has a trace of an accent. I am a Southerner who assimilated with, or perhaps, more precisely, who emigrated to the nation as a whole; I have only ever considered myself to be "American."

Which explains why I never bothered to visit the grave of Will O'Neal before. But having a Southern heritage is like having herpes—you can forget you have it, you can deny it, but it inevitably bubbles up and requires attention. I was in town for some work—I write travel guidebooks and features—and while I was checking out Oakland on its merits as a tourist attraction, I thought it might be nice to locate the grave of the family's legendary wreck victim, to check in with my Georgia heritage, sort of like the way you slowly cruise past an old apartment building to see how it's changed before speeding off again.

My ancestral connection would dovetail nicely with my journalistic compliance and I could bone up on another Atlanta attraction for my readers.

Will O'Neal suffered the most extravagant end of anyone in my family, which gave him a certain celebrity cachet among his descendants. His likeness earned the coveted spot above the fireplace in my grandfather's basement: gazing upon his offspring in an 1890s double portrait with his blank-faced wife, Rosa. Will wore a thick wool-looking coat, vest, and tie, with a Teddy Roosevelt brushstache, modest sideburns, and slightly receding hair. She looked vacant and pinched in her high, white collar, like someone with something better to do. They didn't touch. Neither smiled, like two prisoners lingering in limbo before receiving a verdict.

I headed to the middle of the cemetery, in what was once the parlor of a groundskeeper's house, into what is now a rose-scented gift shop. By a crackling hearth, a well-dressed elderly woman perused a cookbook called *Drop Dead Delicious* containing "memorable epitaphs and 250 tested recipes" that are "sure to become undying favorites." While a steward fetched the card catalog of interments, I browsed ghoulish gewgaws such as sixty-cent erasers shaped like human skulls, fancy soaps, shot glasses, and novelty signs reading HARD WORK MUST HAVE KILLED SOMEONE. I selected, for purchase, Oakland's twist on that old souvenir staple, the collectible miniature spoon. This one, though, was shaped like a gravedigger's spade with the Oakland logo on the handle.

It was delightfully disrespectful, a death-defying lark, and I couldn't wait to find the most inappropriate use for it, like feeding an infant.

The card catalog recorded, in long-unconsulted writing, Will's spot, well away from the tonier plots on the edge of the cemetery in Lot 791, an area once nicknamed Hogpen Corner. How appropriate, or perhaps how profane—it was near some train tracks by the northern wall. If you could cross them and walk just a few hundred yards north into East Atlanta, you'd find yourself in the National Park Service campus devoted to the life and resting place of Martin Luther King, Jr. Will and my great-great-grandmother Rosa's shared stone was sturdy and speckled with silvery facets that looked as if they could flake away in a hard rain. Carved into it were their birth and death dates, two Masonic-looking symbols that looked typical for the period, although in Atlanta it feels like everything old has a Masonic lilt, and "A loving husband, an/affectionate father/and a true friend." It was exactly the kind of gravestone I would carve if I had to bury someone I didn't know: plain, genial, completely devoid of identifying detail. Beside Will and Rosa, their Urdis Milo (the paperwork misspelled it as Verdis), my ill-fated great-great-aunt—a toddler who died at age two and a half—was also laid. Her stone was topped by a carving of a sleeping infant, but a century of urban rain had melted it like butter in a saucepan.

At their feet was Will's dad, Joshua, another train engineer (a luckier one) born into a slave-owning family, and his wife. Here was Joshua, the Confederate veteran, who fought to preserve slavery, lost two brothers in the effort, and died at age ninety-three. He rests almost exactly 2,000 feet south of the body of MLK. My ancestral defender of bondage (one of many) molders in an ant-infested patch that his own descendants couldn't even find until ten minutes earlier, while the civil rights giant he tried to prevent from existing is entombed with respectful elegance above a water feature as inviting as a Playa del Carmen swim-up bar. I have tried to tell myself that Rebels were only doing the best they could with the little information they had about the outside world and the true depth of other people, but I still have to admit I love the karmic contrast.

Satisfied that I'd found Will O'Neal, poor bugger, I paid my respects, vague as they were—*sorry about the train*—and went back to exploring more interesting tombs.

I wandered alone down a shady side path. Always at these cemeteries, you see lots of grand stones belonging to people who are of no distinction to our lifetimes, although their elaborate carved vaults try in vain to argue the opposite. Maybe a Southerner from a hundred years ago would have known the names, but the relentless trudge of graves, once intended to eternalize their occupants, has absorbed their identities now. Wandering these rows was like scanning a box of jacketless novels in the final desperate moments of a picked-over garage sale.

Just as monotony was mortally eroding the intrigue of my visit, a plot caught my eye. It was poorly tended, essentially a few patches of degraded grass struggling through worn-out sand. But it was one of the only graves that gave a biographical hint of its contents beyond names and dates.

ORELIA KEY BELL

POET

APRIL 8, 1864

JUNE 2, 1959

I took out my iPhone to see if the internet had ever heard of her.

If you know me, and you're slowly getting to because you're reading this, you know this is not unusual for me. I have made my living diving into crash research on spots I have just stumbled across. I'm a travel writer. I go to places where I've never set foot before, take an appraising look around me, and instinctively find out everything I can about it. I go into a timeless, altered state when I do it, in the way I imagine Jackson Pollock might have started painting at noon and realized at midnight that he forgot to stop for dinner. I absorb the truth of things so that when my readers buy my books, listen to my radio show, or read my articles, I can hand them the best and easiest way to follow my footsteps and experience other places for themselves. I am a professional tourist. I am not simply trained to step back and see—the impulse to learn is who I am. When old friends come to town, my phone rings, because everyone in my circle wants me to show them around, whether it's the streets of literary Greenwich Village, the shortest waits at Disneyland, or the Dickensian remnants of London's West End. Some people have a knack for recipes or baseball scores. My gift is listening to places. I can get off a bus in a strange European city and instinctively know the route to the best hostel.

Right then, I was finding my way to this woman using all the primary sources I could click up. Indeed, there was a free Library of Congress copy of *Poems of Orelia Key Bell*, published in 1895, when she wasn't yet thirty years old. I downloaded a PDF and began reading it right there at her feet. I was fully aware that being able to do this is a miracle of our age, and it probably gratified her ghost.

I hope it's not disrespectful to say there's little wonder why her stuff isn't published today. Her style of writing didn't fall out of fashion so much as it was yanked down and clubbed to death by Hemingway and Fitzgerald. Orelia was given to soggy, overwrought classicism, saddled with prep school invocations of Diana and Calliope and Lebanon. One poem began, "She held life's dulcimer, and carelessly/Brushed 'er its diapason." One century plus two lines on, and her poetry still had the power to bore. Isn't technology wonderful?

If the revelations had stopped there, it would have been a warm moment: a forgotten poet had been resurrected by AT&T, which normally can't raise a signal much less the dead. But I kept probing. Near the front of the book's PDF was a photograph of Orelia herself. Here she was, young and beautiful with light eyes, coquettishly glancing back at me across the years from her left shoulder. I could see the nape of her pretty neck. The antique copy the library scanned for the e-book was inscribed in cursive: "Yours truly, Orelia Key Bell"—and that took my breath away. That actual neck, the hand that drew out that script, were lying here under my shoes. They would be within reach if it weren't for the deterrents of biting ants and a half-century of decomposition.

Next I found a review of Orelia's work by a doughty old reviewer, Mildred Rutherford—I didn't know it, but she would reenter my death tourism tale, too, much later—who compiled a contemporary textbook called *American Authors*. Orelia, she wrote, was a relation of Francis Scott Key, the accidental lyricist of our national anthem. Her thumbnail bio was mostly told in terms of the men who groomed her. "[She] is the daughter of Marcus A. Bell, a man of sterling worth and integrity of character...When General Sherman was in Atlanta, he used her father's home on Wheat Street for a stable and his horses ate corn from her cradle...Called a 'Tartar' when a child because she was such a 'fighter,' she continues to fight, but it is with the weapons of humility, faith, and love... She is truly practical and really enjoys 'turning a sonnet into a bonnet'...Miss Bell's poems will probably not reach the heart of the multitude, for they are too spiritual, too ideal.'" (Even in her time, a lukewarm review.)

In Orelia's own book, the acknowledgments page sounded as vague as the gravestones I was standing among. The first was "to the memory of my father, Marcus A. Bell, in loving reverence." Sure enough, there was Marcus, two graves to the left of her. But the longest and the most effusive inscription went to someone else: "Ida Ash, whose affection and encouragement have been among the chief sources of my inspiration." And there was Ida Jane Ash, lying exactly beside my ignored Orelia. Ida died in 1948, some fifty-three years after this book's dedication. The longevity of that relationship was heartwarming.

Then it clicked. The "practical" Orelia Key Bell and Ida Ash, her muse, must have been a couple. The idea of a good old Boston marriage here in Rebel Atlanta—in the heart of one of its most racist Confederate cemeteries—was scandalous! Reading on, I found an Orelia poem titled "A Word for Sappho." (Of course.) It went, "A word for Sappho. Not to paean/Her suicide for love of Phaon—. A slanderous myth! research will prove—/Not but sweet Sappho died of love,/But died as Hugo says to do it:/'To die of love is to live tho' it.'" Translation: If you die from the difficulty of love, you have truly lived. Isn't that just the sort of sly, self-aggrandizing thing a closeted lesbian would say if she had to live in Old Atlanta? Orelia, I love you. You're a proud dyke!

And indeed, as I discovered through online census records, she and Ida had moved together across the country, far from Georgia's reach, and settled in Pasadena,

California, where they lived out the rest of their days in the same home. With a little smartphone gumshoeing, I had deciphered an enduring lesbionic relationship hidden in plain sight in the middle of Atlanta's staunchest Rebel cemetery. It was like a gay *Da Vinci Code*! I headed back to the steward in the gift shop to ask about his female poet resident. He rifled through his handbook of Oakland's famous interments. "No. No. She's not here. Where did you say her grave was again?" Clearly, her anonymity remained unconstrained by the passage of time.

"And I'm pretty sure she was a lesbian!" I announced excitedly. A woman sampling the gift soaps pretended not to have heard. The steward definitely did, but didn't care. And why would he? Oakland is not that kind of cemetery.

And then, a few yards away, I thought of Will. Poor Will, whose story was also retold only by a rock. I walked back over to my people. Over the wall, MARTA trains rumbled past, which meant my great-great-grandparents were gently vibrating deep underground along with them. It seemed beautiful somehow, since Will gave his life to the railway in every sense. The constant rhythms of the passing trains commented more on him than the gravestone his loved ones put there. His epitaph offered only dates and a compliment about his fatherhood, which counted for nothing since no grave insults its occupant.

And so, like Orelia, poor Will O'Neal was Googled on his grave.

Clip One: ORPHEUM ACTORS MINISTER TO DYING, from the *Atlanta Journal* ("Covers Dixie Like the

Dew"). The train had entirely rolled off the tracks. The scalding steam flayed the skin from Will's body, but he didn't die right away. As it happened, a troupe of vaudeville actresses was traveling on his train on its way to a week's engagement at the Orpheum Theatre in Atlanta. The actresses were shaken, but not badly hurt, and they grabbed Vaseline and powder from their cosmetics bags and gathered on the rail bed around Will O'Neal, where they slathered his burns with theatrical makeup to ease his agony while they waited for someone to come find them in the blackness. There was a photo, but it wasn't of Will. It was of Miss Edna Dorman, the actress, in one of her acts, wearing white trousers and a sport coat like a man, her face fogged with printing dots. The caption calls her "the dainty little lady" although she's clearly not. "He was the most determined injured man that I ever saw," said the dainty Miss Dorman, who apparently had seen enough distressed expressions during her performances to make a sound comparison. "He seemed not to be in the least pain, though of course he was, and did not utter a word to show that he was suffering." (Across the centuries, the highest praise one can offer the deceased has always been that they took it like a champ.) Dorman was the most famous of the troupe of nubile actresses who rushed to the front of the wreck to soothe Will and "his fireman, Joe Clay, a Negro"—who, it bears noting, merited only a side note despite the fact that he was not expected to survive. When rescuers finally found them, they rushed them to Toccoa, Georgia, the nearest town, a few miles over the border from South Carolina. There, Will O'Neal's fate teetered.

Clip Two, also from the *Atlanta Journal*, shifts cinematically from the crash scene to the devastating impact eighty-five miles away in Atlanta, at early dawn. A telephone rings in the home of, as breathlessly reported, "Mrs. William J. O'Neal, of 135 Cherokee Avenue, who was waiting eagerly to hear the footsteps of her husband." The newspaper hinted at some kind of illness in the O'Neal household, describing her as "groping her way feebly from her sick bed" to pick up the fateful phone call. The prose is as purple as funeral bunting. "As the message of disaster came to her over the phone, she fell prostrate to the floor in a death-like swoon, and lay there, herself hovering between life and death, until other members of the family bore her again to her bed of sorrow." The paper said she remained unconscious for hours after hearing the news, "and her condition was regarded as most serious." Family lore fills the medical gap left by oblique turn-of-the-century reportage—Mrs. O'Neal, or Rosa, was hooked on over-the-counter paregoric, a tincture of opium. Rosa was a junkie, although in the most Southern, most polite way to be one.

Meanwhile, the *Journal* reported, Will's three young sons—including my eight-year-old great-grandfather— hastened from the side of the incapacitated Mrs. O'Neal to attend to their father in Toccoa, but "as the sons were swiftly speeding on their way, the father breathed his last."

The children reached him two hours after he died. My

great-grandfather Tracy, just a boy, stood over the ruined body of his father as it cooled and stiffened in a makeshift casket. He asked who did this. He wondered what was going to become of them.

Finally, Clip Three: DELIVERED MESSAGE AS SHE PROMISED, from the *Georgian*. It also took the celebrity angle, but left Will as a cypher. "Faithful to the promise made Engineer W. J. O'Neal as he lay dying from injuries in the wreck near Harbins, SC, Monday morning. Miss Edna Dorman, the young actress playing the Orpheum this week, called upon the wife of the dead engineer at her home in this city Wednesday afternoon and delivered his dying messages." The *Georgian* did not share those messages, stalwart they no doubt were. "...The young actress became deeply interested in Mrs. O'Neal, who is an invalid and who has been pronounced incurable by physicians. Believing that thru [sic] the medium of Christian Science she can find a cure, Miss Dorman, who is a Christian Scientist herself, has urged Mrs. O'Neal to try that method of treatment." Neither Edna nor the Christian Scientists make further appearances in family lore, but the wrinkle made me think Edna still would have slathered Will in theatrical makeup even if she had located a proper first aid kit. (Within a few years, Dorman's variety career carried on with enough renown that her name wound up in a 1913 advertisement that ran in both *Variety* and *The Billboard*. She was listed with seventeen other stage performers who landed an endorsement deal for a product called Rozalia Cream. The fifty-cent formula, made in Brooklyn, promised to possess "special medical values and therefore removes facial blemishes," especially when paired with "Dainty Rouge," which "adheres to the skin." I wonder if Rozalia Cream was the cosmetic Edna smeared on Will to ease his anguished final moments. There's a strong chance my ancestor met his maker with two round red cheeks caked with Dainty Rouge.)

Miss Dorman and the crash survivors, powerless to truly help the shattered O'Neals, chipped in for "a beautiful floral pall" for Will's casket, which was placed in Oakland Cemetery at the very grave now in front of me, and they took up a collection of $100 amongst themselves to give to the despairing Mrs. O'Neal, the closet drug addict who had been unexpectedly placed in the daunting position of raising three sons without a husband or a social safety net.

Yes, I thought again. *No grave insults its occupant,* and at the same time most graves don't sing a real story at all. I looked in the direction of the Lion of Atlanta's war-fixated Swiss rip-off, of the black mayor disrupting the white section, of Orelia's marathon partnership that was lost to time despite loud clues that had been carved to be read. Our predecessors are leaving clues for us, all the time, that we mostly ignore. Just a few decades after they were gone, I could only recall the first name of three of my eight great-grandparents. There's something profoundly wrong with that.

This is my America. This is your America, too. We

stand on a ground pocked with the scars of those who came before us, and shreds of their bodies which gave us ours, slumber everywhere underfoot. We might be inspired by our roots if only we knew where they were buried, but the markers are so poor. But if anyone is good at unforgetting worthwhile places, it's me. I'm a travel writer. I hook people on the true nature of places for a living. I'm also a reluctant Southerner who lives among Yankees, a curious graveside Googler, and a modern descendant of America's two cleaved worlds looking for common ground in an era of newly splintered division. There are few people better for the job than I am.

So I would visit my country's many death-related attractions to unbury things (if that's the phrase). Behind every gravestone, there's a story, and I would dig it up. (Again, strictly metaphorically.) It would be fun, in a weird way. It's a very strange habit we have—to make a point of visiting places where grisly events transpired way before we were born. This time, I would travel not to review hotels or name the least-crowded rooms at the museums, but to explain to America what it gets out of revisiting its worst moments. To do that, I would have to stick to spots my fellow citizens have already agreed are important. That means I wouldn't seek every forgotten plaque (there are thousands of those), but only to the tourist draws that, year in and year out, rack up attendance numbers. If it had a busy parking lot, a snack bar, and a gift shop, I would go. To the visitors, I would ask: "Why is this place so important?" To the dead, I would ask, "Have we become everything you hoped when you died?" And to the staff I would ask, "Coke please, and this magnet. And how much is that little souvenir spoon that looks like an undertaker's spade?"

This was going to be epic, this journey of grave expectations.

THE MOMENT THAT CHANGED AMERICA

HERE LIE THE REASONS FOR REMEMBERING

"But monuments themselves memorials need."

—GEORGE CRABBE, *THE BOROUGH*

"It is more of a job to interpret the interpretation than to interpret the thing."

—MICHEL DE MONTAIGNE

"Chaos is a great factor in making art happen."

—DEBBIE HARRY

POUR IT DOWN YOUR MUZZLE

Manassas
Chickamauga
Petersburg
Antietam

YOU CAN'T TALK ABOUT AMERICA'S STRAPPING
death tourism industry without dwelling on the Civil
War. In fact, you can't talk about pretty much anything
political in America, from the culture war, to states' rights,
to racism, without tracing the wires back to a socket on
the side of our largest national calamity. Its scars remain
everywhere, but on the bright side, they make for some
rip-roarin' vacationin'. America is crawling with Civil War
stuff. So for the first chunk of my odyssey, I decided to
nail down all the banner attractions of the War Between
the States. Fortunately, each one revealed something a
little different about how American likes its pain served.
There's been plenty more misery to go around in the fifteen decades since—not all of it self-inflicted—and there's
no way I was going to finish this tour without some of the
greatest hits that came after John Wilkes Booth's flying
leap from a theatre box, but those come afterward. You
can't build a tomb without laying some foundations. For
America, that's the Civil War, and in a big way.

I decided to start at the beginning, which proved to be
fortuitous, because I soon learned that the very first battle
of the Civil War was the only one in its four-year stretch
that you could have truthfully called a tourism attraction.

On Sunday, July 21, 1861, Rebels and Federals did
something they had never done before: They met. A
skirmish had been brewing for months, and as troops
converged near Manassas, a railroad supply depot in rural
Virginia, people sensed the climax was nigh. Hundreds of
rubbernecking civilians packed wine and picnic baskets

and paid $25 to hire double carriages from Washington for the fun. Unlike at the Battle of Lexington, which kicked off the American Revolution eighty-six years earlier, this time there was no expectation of casualties, only some testosteroned saber rattling to scare the Rebels back into obedience. Everyone expected a pleasing weekend sojourn while this little uprising was quickly put to bed.

William Howard Russell, a celebrity correspondent, was the one selected to cover it for the London *Times*. He encountered the battle-peepers as they completed the twenty-nine-mile trip deep into Virginia, which had recently become a *de facto* foreign land by seceding. The sightseers collected on a rise near a house owned by a woman named Mrs. Spindle, and it was here they strained to get an eyeful of the anticipated rout through the distant smoke and clatter. Russell related their giddiness: "The spectators were all excited, and a lady with an opera glass who was near me was quite beside herself when an unusually heavy discharge roused the current of her blood, 'That is splendid, oh my! Is not that first rate?'"

The looky-loos had no idea that they were viewing the passing of an epoch through a lorgnette. They had never seen so much as a photograph of a battle because no such images existed yet. Most of them had no concept of what war really meant, or what modern weapons were making it. Rapidly the day descended into a ferocious, limb-rending cataclysm that would drag on for eleven relentless hours and yield at least 5,000 casualties, probably far more. Within minutes, the tourist party was chased from its viewpoint and overtaken by a stampede of shattered troops shrieking in agony. By the end of the day, 900 soldiers would be dead, or half of the casualties racked up during the entire Mexican War thirteen years before.

Many of the men had never fired a gun in their lives, except maybe at a squirrel or a deer. More than a few dropped their weapons and ran bawling for the hills. For all its cockiness, the heralded Union army had never been taught how to retreat, and the pandemonium was magnified by the fact many of the Confederates who *had* been trained were still wearing the Union uniforms they'd received before Virginia seceded. No one knew with confidence where to aim.

"The striking of a rifle-ball near where I was standing admonished me of the danger of my position," recalled one of the observers, Alfred Ely, with a mildly composed report considering the bone-shredding predicament. The tourists soon found themselves huddled in terror behind trees being mulched by a relentless onslaught of lead Minié balls. The traumatized Union troops abandoned their supplies so they could flee even faster, crushing each other with their rolling caissons, and the stupefied tourists fled with them.

All except Ely, who had the distinction of serving as a Congressional representative from the state of New York. When he foolishly identified himself as such to the Rebels, they clapped him in chains and hauled him to prison in Richmond for five months. At the very least, he was able to cash in the following year by publishing a popular memoir, one that stands tall in a long literary heritage of travel-writing braggadocio. In it, he made conclusions that modern readers would probably think common sense to anyone with five firing brain cells, but which in 1862 were revelatory to the naïve inhabitants of our country: "To visit battle-fields as a mere pastime, or with the view of gratifying a panting curiosity...is neither a safe thing in itself, nor a justifiable use of the passion which Americans are said to possess for public spectacles." Even after his ordeal, Ely still couldn't quite bring himself to forbid such tourism entirely, because in closing his book, he advised his readers they would be better served "to study such things somewhere *north of the Potomac*"—or in other words, if you enjoy a military bloodbath, make sure it's in your neighborhood.

The South hosted an encore of the slaughter in 1862. We now call it the Second Battle of Manassas, and by then, would-be tourists knew enough to clutch their pearls in the safety of their parlors. But against the odds, another tourism clusterfuck went down at Manassas exactly one hundred years later, only this time, it was intentionally orchestrated by Uncle Sam.

Someone got the idea, back in the 1950s, to assemble a federal committee to throw a big ol' four-year-long kumbaya to commemorate the centennial of the Civil War from 1961 to 1965. The government decided that it would be grand to fund the program that would include reenactments, picnics, exhibitions, and galas, many to be held at our finest death tourism attractions. It sounded splendid on paper, but this is America. The party to honor national unity above sectional pressures quickly fractured because of our sectional pressures. Robert J. Cook chronicles the unraveling debacle in his book *Troubled Commemoration*, but this letter from a wealthy Washington doyenne who was against the plan encapsulates the fight that would doom it: "The South is only just recovering from northern devastation after ninety years...Congress is struggling with the problem of States' Rights. That was exactly the same in 1861. The negro will just be further inflamed."

In the late 1950s, as the anniversary planning advanced, the so-named Civil War Centennial Commission selected as its chairman Major General Ulysses Grant III, elderly veteran of two World Wars and the grandson of none other than the famed Ulysses Grant himself. Unfortunately, Grandson Grant's political skills were as feckless as his grandfather's. This Grant was no grizzled commando. He was Mr. Magoo with epaulettes. He spent most of his tenure muttering about the threat of Communist infiltration and writing fretful letters. He became obsessed with making this centennial celebration a huge conflict-free event to send those Reds a message about what a strapping democracy we ran. Above all, he wanted to use the Civil War not to dwell on the true tale of brutality and its wages, but to convey a consoling homily that America had moved, united and with clasped hands, into a bright new day.

Today we instantly recognize this as bald fantasy.

Nonetheless, he notified the esteemed historians serving in the commission that any nit-picking—like, say going much into slavery—would not be required, so they should shoot for something uplifting instead. Mentioning racial issues would only serve to enrage Southern powers that were resisting desegregation, and the CWCC needed the South's support for ticket sales since they were the ones with most of the battlegrounds—three out of five of them are located in Virginia, where colored-only fountains and bathrooms were still a thing—and it wanted to deliver a healthy return to the organizers who participated. Grant thought each state should take the lead on its own celebrations, because far be it from the government to pass judgment on a state's internal affairs. That stance was a lot like President James Buchanan's toward slavery, the stance that got us in the Civil War to begin with, but never mind. Besides, as one CWCC bigwig told *The Nation* in 1959, "A lot of fine Negro people loved life as it was in the Old South."

It got worse from there. The plan was so spectacularly ill-advised that it's a head-smacker even today. Grant and the federal CWCC convened an assembly of the states' planning commissions in Charleston on April 1961, the hundredth anniversary of the uprising that triggered the Civil War apocalypse. It was supposed to be one of those luxury junkets filled with gourmet meals, fireworks, and pageants, but a problem arose. Charleston was still segregated, and Madaline A. Williams, one of New Jersey's delegates, was African-American. This was like inviting a rabbi to a pork barbecue cook-off. Another roadblock: the host hotel, the Francis Marion, didn't accept reservations from black people. New Jersey's white delegates begged the CWCC to force the hotel to make an exception, but Grant, a born appeaser, shrugged in the face of fraudulency as his grandpa did during his presidential administration.

His only guidance was to tell New Jersey he dearly hoped it would find someone else to send. As one might expect, cries for a boycott of the commemorations immediately flew from Northern states. Southern newspapers accused then-President JFK of dishonoring states' rights; Northerners called it redneck racism; Southerners implied Williams was too snobbish to consort with members of her own race. President Kennedy shot Grant a brisk letter reminding him that the CWCC was a federal operation and so "the Constitutional rule of equal treatment for all Americans, regardless of race or color, should of course apply to all its operations." Finally, someone conceived the compromise of holding the confab across the water from Charleston on a US naval station, which, being federal, was by law desegregated. The solution was accepted half-heartedly by delegates who had been banking on feather beds and filet mignon.

That's where the Manassas morass comes in. Two months after the Charleston kerfuffle, in late July, the CWCC mounted its first major test: a full-scale recreation of the war's first big battle. Although today, reenactments support a robust subculture (see Tony Horwitz' superlative *Confederates in the Attic*), they were a novelty in 1961. This pioneering reenactment, an oxymoron for sure, was ordered to be authentic, expensive ($170,000 or $1.3 million today), and most important to the organizers, profitable. Over the protests of scholars who bemoaned the commodification and the glorification of a heinous tragedy, the CWCC, Virginia's state commemorative commission, area counties, and the Defense Department used the full force of their authority to descend on the actual battlefield for the inaugural bash of their four-year "commemoration." They had the National Park Service's enthusiastic blessing—rangers even threw camouflage over the visitor center and statuary to pretend everything looked like it did in Stonewall's era.

The weather on reenactment weekend was sweltering 101 degrees, with not enough water, parking, and facilities for the 50,000 to 70,000 people (no one is quite sure, even now) who clogged the rural Virginia lanes and trampled the historic soil with their death carnival. The crowd dug up relics, peed on graves, contracted poison ivy, left rubbish everywhere, and mashed grass to mud. Despite the organizers' lip service that the spectacle would honor American sacrifice and underscore unity, people got rowdy, cheering the Confederates and booing the Union men. A dummy corpse was accidentally lit ablaze by cannon fire. Some participants brought one-hundred-year-old weapons that exploded in their faces. One fake Rebel was pegged by a cannonball, a Yank was sent to the hospital when his coat buttons somehow got embedded in his chest, someone else collapsed and was evacuated by helicopter. "Casualties off the battlefield were higher than those on it," quipped the Associated Press, which tallied the fallen: more than a hundred for heat exhaustion, and "the civilian toll was swelled by seven bee stings, eight stomach upsets, and one dog bite." The one saving grace, at least to the organizers, was that tourists managed to leave a profit behind.

The National Park Service, apoplectic, reflexively prohibited any more fake battles from its sacred land, a ban that remains in force today. "Even the best-researched and most well-intentioned representation of combat cannot replicate the tragic complexity of real warfare," reads the regulation with a palpable scorn that still sears. "Respect for the memory of those whose lives were lost at these sites and whose unrecovered remains are often still interred in these grounds precludes the staging of inherently artificial battles at these memorial sites." That was the curatorial reason. The unpublicized motivation for the ban was that President Kennedy refused to give Southern hard-liners the satisfaction of again using Department of the Interior property to glorify the pro-slavery cause.

There went the rest of the CWCC's plan. Major General Grant resigned the next month. The CWCC's obsession with weaving profit and history wrapped around its axle and its grand plans for four years of epic pageantry fizzled into nothing but an innocuous four-year drone of lectures and wreath-layings.

The CWCC did contribute one major event to American history, but only obliquely, and only out of protest. By 1963, progressives were pushing it to do something meaningful to honor the anniversary of the Emancipation Proclamation, but the only thing the staunch old capitalists on the CWCC could muster was a program, in September 1962, at which only white men were invited to mount the dais. The CWCC, craven to its piteous end, lived in apprehension of antagonizing Southerners, and that cowardice was repaid with yet more public protest. Chagrined again, it hastily recruited an obscure federal judge named Thurgood Marshall to join the white men to provide some token remarks. President Kennedy, wisely distancing himself, only appeared by videotape.

Outraged by an event that did not reflect the America they knew, thousands of angry people decided they would hold their own Emancipation Proclamation anniversary march on the National Mall the following August. Today, most of us don't realize the reason for the legendary March on Washington was in protest. But we do remember who spoke: it was there, as a cosmic middle finger to the CWCC, that Martin Luther King, Jr. stood on the steps of the Lincoln Memorial and delivered his masterful "I Have a Dream" speech, an undisputed masterpiece of world oratory. King started that speech with a clear reference to the Civil War, that white men continue to bungle a century later: "Five score years ago, a great American, in whose symbolic shadow we stand today, signed the Emancipation Proclamation...In a sense, we've come to our nation's capital to cash a check." (On a spot within sight of that speech, MLK is permanently enshrined in his own clumsy granite memorial. I'll visit that eventually, too.)

At the 150th anniversary of the first fight, when the opportunity arose for yet another Battle of Manassas, I was powerless to restrain myself, much like those clueless day-trippers over a hundred years ago.

"The moment that changed America..." tempted the brochures put out by Prince William County. It had rented some farmland a few miles from the National Park site to mount a hearty slate of amusements over four days, including the Blue and Gray Civil War Ball, the Civil War Baseball Game, and temptingly, a reenactment of a 1911 reenactment of the original battle, like *Inception* for hopeless history geeks. But the undisputed highlight promised to be the full-scale reproduction of the battle to be held on July 23, two days after the actual anniversary, but on a Saturday so kids could participate. So many people wanted to play Confederates that organizers scheduled a duplicate scrimmage on Sunday. Everyone would get their chance to fake-shoot a Yankee.

On the 22nd, I started my day in the National Park visitor center. Of the 392 National Park units in 2011, about seventy primarily concerned the Civil War. More than any other historical parable, Americans cherish the one about the time we ripped the guts out of each other, and attendance reflects it. This one was thronged with people who were about to celebrate the start of the war's 150th anniversary. The nation was on the precipice of slogging through four long days replicating our brother-on-brother massacre, and you could really sense the giddy excitement in the air. Despite temperatures that pressed toward one hundred, the park bustled with people—easily the unit's highest numbers of the year, typically hitting about 800,000—most of whom shambled among the tents where costumed interpreters showed parents and small children the intricacies of loading period guns. Firing cannon for pleasure is a long-cherished tradition at American battlefields, and if you think about what those weapons did to necessitate the memorials to begin with, it's a lot like honoring the *Titanic* with an ice sculpture. Still, in the museum, the park's permanent exhibits were, as National Park exhibits often are, heavy on the guns. The allure of bullet and bore was strong. Middle-aged men in period-appropriate soldier garb gathered around a plastic display case of portable cannon, conferring with each other in lurid fancies about how easy they might be to carry.

A large topographical map of the battle's progress was laid out in little embedded lights, a sort of penny arcade version of the battle. A gravelly recorded male voice narrated with stern, Biblical importance, droning a timeline that phrased everything as if the generals were the only people who did anything that day—McDowell and his dotted line went this way with his charge, Jackson did that with his twinkly flank—all as if they were engaged in a gentlemanly game of chess. The little lights chased each other across the board, indicating with Christmas-tree harmlessness the fateful locations of gory regret and events that snuffed lives. I confess I was gratified when the narrator lightly touched upon the people "who came from Washington to witness the spectacle of war," but then he lapsed back into Militaryese about positions and retreats and whatnot. He wrapped momentously by announcing, "War is no longer the entertainment of a Sunday afternoon." Which was rich, considering everybody around me was there to enjoy war entertainment this very Sunday, and C-SPAN trucks were on hand to broadcast five hours of it live from coast to coast.

The first usage of the word *souvenir* in English dates to 1782, meaning it's about as old the American nation itself, and it owes its birth to the French, too—*memory* or *to remember*. And in this gift shop, there were many strange things to make an impression, although not of what war is really about. A sweaty teenager in a Ford baseball cap stood at the register. He carried a board game based on the Bull Run movie *Gods and Generals* (save the download time; it's terrible) and a 150th anniversary T-shirt with the flag of the Confederate States of America conspicuously positioned across it. As he reached to pay the equally sweaty cashier, I caught sight of a tattoo on his arm: the letters C.S.A. done in script, in red, white, and green, like the Italian flag; either the artist was short of blue ink or he had confused the Confederacy with Italy. I picked up some inappropriate souvenirs of my own: a baggie of Sutler Cyrus' Original Musket Ball Candy and a cylinder of Cyrus Wakefield's Original Fruit Flavored Cartridge Candy ("Pour it down your muzzle! $0.95"), which was wrapped and banded to resemble a packet of gunpowder (because so many people were killed by gunpowder here, get it?). I considered buying a matching set of "authentic" Billy Yank and Johnny Reb Beeswax Lip Balms (in "U.S. mint" or mint julep, respectively), but there are limits.

In the fields out back, where much of the original battle had taken place, one memorial in particular caught my eye. It was the one that was intended to: Thomas J. "Stonewall" Jackson: preternaturally mighty, muscles rippling like Superman's, cape flying, astride a daunting horse with a sort of stiff-backed lunacy. He looked like a man fearless enough to wear Speedos while chopping wood. "THERE STANDS JACKSON LIKE A STONE WALL" proclaimed the side, reminding bystanders in perpetuity that the general earned his nickname here. One version of the story, the one in every textbook, picture book, and coloring book about the Civil War (many of them on sale in the gift shop), claims another general by the name of Bee remarked that Jackson's resolve against the enemy was as solid as a stone wall. However, another version has Bee delivering it as a sneering insult, since Jackson should have been moving into the action and doing some fighting instead of parking himself stubbornly in one place like that. We'll never know the truth because Bee bit the dust right after saying it, and Jackson's fans eagerly ran the first version up their flagpole as a compliment and used it as an emblem of their demigod of choice.

I asked one of the rangers about that 1938 statue. Without hesitation, he said it was in the wrong spot on the crest of Henry Hill. Jackson actually had hunkered down somewhere behind it. I won't say he spoke of Stonewall's puff-chested likeness with resentment, but I did get the impression he spent his workdays waiting to issue this correction to anyone who approached him without asking him where the toilets are. Another problem with the statue, he gladly told me, is that far from standing tall after Manassas, Jackson departed a bloody wreck. He had a peculiar habit of raising his left arm, palm facing front, in the heat of hostilities, as if he was testifying to Jesus during the climax of an Alabama sermon. Raising your hand high for the enemy to find you and shoot at you is not ordinarily held as the mark of a brilliant soldier, especially if you also insist on remaining as immobile as a stone wall, and indeed, at Manassas, Stonewall was shot in the left hand and narrowly escaped amputation of his finger. (Two years later, a doctor would finally consummate the amputation—and dramatically.)

Regardless, the ranger said, the heroic statue will

never be moved to the correct location because the "Confederate park" that originally preserved and donated the land—seventy-seven years after the battle—had stipulated that Jackson must forevermore be given the place of honor in it, irrespective of the truth. Now, far be it from me to tell people how to deify the man who thought all glory should go only to God, but forcing the keepers of the historical record to mark the wrong spot simply because it was grander seems out of bounds. In the same period of time, the monuments honoring the New York regiments, which suffered the most casualties of any, were rusting and used for target practice. The problem statue wasn't the post-Confederates' only demand, either, the ranger said. The land's donors had another irrevocable condition: the national park must always be called Manassas, the Southern name for it, and never Bull Run, which is what a Yankee would say. To this day, the federal government is required to call the national park by its Rebel name because Southerners donated the land. Both names are correct, but there was a definite bias to why one was chosen over the other.

("It's an old saying that the Union won the war, but the Confederacy won the public relations battle," NPS director Jonathan B. Jarvis pointedly told the press over the reenactment weekend. I was beginning to see what he was getting at.)

When this enthusiastic ranger realized that my questions had nothing to do with the men's room, we bonded. "I want to show you something," he said conspiratorially, and produced an oval button badge printed with a stylized eagle and flag. DISNEY'S AMERICA it said.

I felt my face light up. This was a relic that excited me the way a smoothbore cannon thrills a gun nut: it was the logo of a 3,000-acre theme park that the Walt Disney Company had tried to build in nearby Haymarket in the early 1990s. Instead of showcasing animated characters or the future, this park was to cover our stirring national journey. It got as far as unveiling plans in a local preview center. The Hall of Presidents would be moved from Orlando; kids could pilot simulated World War II fighters for giggles; and an area was to be set aside for daily reenactments of key Civil War clashes, including a regularly scheduled aquatic battle between the *Merrimac* and the *Monitor*. Plus, you know, Mickey Mouse in a tricorner hat.

The ranger explained that local preservationist groups killed it with their outrage. Ken Burns, the 1860's designated spokesman, penned a politely necrotic editorial in *The Potomac News*:

> This project has the possibility of not only sanitizing and making 'enjoyable' a hugely tragic moment of our past, but of physically destroying, through subsequent development, the exquisite landscape where the ghosts of our collective past still have the power to mesmerize us with the palpable fact of our often sad history.

Burns, whose flowery prose had clearly been infused by years of Lincoln gazing, wrote his pitch against Disneyfication in May 1994. Four months later, Disney CEO Michael Eisner surrendered. Ken Burns had rebelled and defeated the Mouse.

"It's good the land was preserved," I volunteered hopefully.

"Naw, it got developed anyway," the ranger said.

The next morning at Pageland Farm, the site chosen for its proximity to the part of the battlefield the National Park Service successfully protected, the air was 105 degrees—twenty-five degrees higher than on battle day in 1861—and soupy with sinister humidity. Some 8,700 reenactors, each assigned to a state regiment, slogged under sweat-soaking layers of wool. They had paid $20 each to participate in ways that were "authentic with no anachronism present to the eye," as the FAQ had requested. With one exception necessary for today's audiences—at this Manassas, players were permitted to be older than thirty-two and heavier than 165 pounds, although, the FAQ warned "those that meet or exceed these standards" should be careful not to overexert themselves. In this sham battle, Confederates also outnumbered Federals—the historic name for Union that the organizers preferred—by 500 or 600. The original fight engaged the same number per side, 18,000. We were about to enjoy a battle (strange words for something so picnic like) less than a quarter as large, but we would make up some of those numbers with audience members. The reenactors, termed "interpreters"—as if they knew a language the rest of us didn't—were joined by 11,000 plainclothed spectators, each of whom had paid at least $30, and we all slogged in a forced march from motor coaches to bleachers.

On the walk, two participants, a father and son, passed me as I paused to wipe condensation from my zoom lens.

"I don't wanna be in the war!" the son complained. "I don't *wanna* get killed!"

Once we were seated, the stultifying heat paralyzed us while fake soldiers pretended to murder each other under high-capacity power lines. The report of cannon and rifles was more relentless and chaotic than many of us anticipated, but at least the smoke from the blanks gave us intermittent cloudy shade. Row by row, according to an agreed-upon plan ordained by blue and red bars in history books, moist woolly men walked forward, a thicket of rifles on their shoulders, and killed each other in an orderly fashion. They would take a minute to pour more blanks into their muzzles, await the next order to fire together, pull their triggers in a puffing crackle, and then reload, proving Civil War gunplay was a laborious process that provided ample opportunities to fumble a bullet or chicken out. Now and then, one of the players would abruptly lie possum like on the ground for a moment, indicating their extinction, before propping themselves into a lounging position to enjoy the sight of the cannons and rifles rage on without them. They looked like they were picking buttercups. Needless to say, this is not what happens to the human body when it is riddled with bullets at close range. Blood looks good in the movies, but in real life, it stings with sickly sweet iron, and its rotting stink haunts survivors until the end of their days. Yet the crowd cheered each order to fire as if every volley was a three-pointer at the buzzer.

If the afternoon's intent was to agonize over one of America's darkest days, you wouldn't know it. The announcer was heatedly aroused as he delivered play-by-plays over the loudspeakers. "There's the third United States Infantry Regiment," he chirped, in the same tone of voice as Ryan Seacrest announcing the arrival of Taylor Swift by limousine. "There you see General Thomas 'Stonewall' Jackson through the smoke!" His explanations were about officers, flags, and positions, but the subtext was always death, death, death, and how everyone on the battlefield was trying to better align themselves to better inflict it. This did not seem to inhibit the crowd's eagerness to ingest sno-cones and pretzels.

"Upon them will be the Hinge of Fate!" the announcer cried. I don't know what that could possibly mean, but it snapped me back to reality, which under the circumstances was the surrealism of a phony battle. Instead of spent powder casings and body parts, the area was strewn with a rain of tens of thousands of empty water bottles—except for on the battlefield, where participants were asked to rely on hydration delivered to them in approved canvas buckets. Channel 7's cameras zeroed in on the go-getters who most confirmed the reenactor stereotype—the prettiest girls in Southern belle petticoats and the most grizzled beardy men—and avoided capturing the lemonade drinkers in Walmart fashions who made up a larger portion of the attendees. The largest contingent, though, was that of Middle-Aged Men Loudly Explaining Things. Their voices rose above each other in an endless report of unrequested trivia. Their gossip attached itself to anything that came within their range of attention, from the authenticity of coat buttons to the next antici-pated steps in the choreographed carnage taking place in center field. As someone who doesn't know my hardtack from my haversack, I could only admire them in the way I admire anyone who finds rapture in immersing them-selves in something they love. If Stonewall could have harnessed the fastidiousness and passion of the reenact-ment circuit, he would have won the war.

The announcer knew that ultimately, the day was all about us, not the dead. He compared us to those real-life day tourists, like silly Congressman Ely, who skipped out here to watch things unfold in 1861: "You are also performing your own living history today," the voice told us. It was true. This was one battle with an authentic role for gawkers like me. Near the end of the battle, which was about eight hours shorter than the original one, the announcer summed everything up. "Ladies and gentle-men, as we leave today's living history theatre, when we see the feud between the blue and the grey, we ask ourselves, 'How did they do it?' What we're really asking ourselves is: 'Could *I* have done it?'" He was hoarse from exertion.

The crowd burst into howling cheers. A middle-aged woman turned to her husband. "*I* don't know how they did things without air-conditioning," she agreed.

"Or bottled water," he said.

At the last moment, long after most people had gotten up and left their sweaty, wet spots behind on the grandstand, the narrator dedicated the preceding battle to the United States military, linking the fun to our ongoing foreign wars, and concluded with the playing of "Taps," which only a few people stopped to observe, and pretty much no one removed their hats for.

We all tried to be time travelers to July 1861, to stand in the shoes of those luckless guys (or at least sit in bleachers and eat fried dough while someone else stood in them). When the dust settled, we had 148 evaluations for heat exposure, and eleven people had been taken to the hospital. And our battle didn't even have bullets.

Before I left, I approached one of the event organizers. I asked him whether the debacle of 1961 had directed their planning this time around. He said, "The event fifty years ago turned into a battle over civil rights. We wanted to make sure that wasn't going to happen. I think the fact there wasn't even a hint of that is an indication of how far the county has come, but especially how far our country has come." He concluded by flatly calling the 1961 event a "fiasco." That's when the head of the local Convention and Visitors Bureau clocked me as a journalist and leaped into our discussion to refocus the topic onto her office's organizational prowess, extolling her staff's heroic rental of ample portable toilets.

Politicians mounted few other major events to officially commemorate the war's 150th. President Obama gently issued a nonbinding proclamation requesting Americans to commemorate the war somehow, please, maybe, if they happened to think of it. Weeks before the official start of the anniversary, two Democratic legislators, Jim Webb in the Senate and Jesse Jackson in the House, introduced proposals for a federal sesquicentennial commission, but neither made it past the Republican-controlled Congress. The lack of federal recognition this time around meant anniversary programs were again left to local municipalities, which meant most events would have to earn a profit if they were going to happen at all. Republican Kentucky Senator Mitch McConnell, the Senate Majority Leader, was able to slip in a resolution honoring the Battle of Mill Springs in his home state.

Making it harder, some politicians were still editing the topic. In April 2010, Virginia Governor Bob McDonnell proclaimed a Confederate History Month to coincide with the anniversary of the start of the war—with a proclamation that made zero mention of slavery. When his omission hit the news cycle, the *Washington Post* asked the governor to explain himself, and he stuck the other foot in: "There were any number of aspects to that conflict between the states," he said. "Obviously, it involved slavery. It involved other issues. But I focused on the ones I thought were most significant for Virginia." (When the Civil War began, 30 percent of Virginians were enslaved.) A day later, a media-bruised McDonnell publicly ate Jim Crow and declared slavery an "evil, vicious, and inhumane abomination" and retroactively added, "it is important for all Virginians to understand that the institution of slavery led to this war" to the fourth paragraph of a seven-paragraph proclamation. Five months after that, he canceled Confederate History Month outright and announced a new, big-tent "Civil War in Virginia" month. Modern-day Rebels declared it the latest insult to their honorable heritage. "Nobody's ever been able to reason with me and tell me why we're honoring Yankees in Virginia," grumbled the commander of the Virginia division of the Sons of Confederate Veterans to the *Post*. "The only northerners in Virginia were the ones that came to Virginia and killed thousands of Virginia citizens when they invaded."

Maybe there's something mystical about the land in Manassas. Not that it's sanctified with the blood of thousands of lives snuffed out short—lots of places are. But that time and again, this pocket of rural Virginia keeps demonstrating, century after century, that no one agrees on the right way to observe a sacrifice. Successive generations try to shape Bull Run into something that speaks only to them, but no matter which name or costume they give it, this land has flummoxed tourists since 1861.

It's weird to cheer a cannon anyway. It's an implement of mass murder. Cheering a cannon demonstration is, if you stop and think about, as bizarre as clapping for Zyklon B or doing the wave for the Plague. The Romans cheered the lions, but only because they hated the Christians. Yet in lavishing efforts on the mechanisms of troops and weapons, that's what we do. At most battlefields, there is nothing much to jar a sense of empathy. The janitorial services of the long passage of time have swept all sensory evidence away. The remnants now exist in the confines of the imagination only; we read about the final judgment on museum placards, heavy on tactical descriptions like stage directions in a script, but the viscera of actual horror remain permanently offstage. *Civil War soldiers exit, pursued by a bear.* You'll just have to guess about how it all felt at the time.

There are many reasons American death tourism often seems like it's sponsored by *Guns & Ammo* rather than *Smithsonian*. One is about tangibility: firearms endure while smoke does not. World War II was the first American war to have the technology to record and distribute oral histories in quantity. Prior wars have only machinery to speak for them. The permanence of weapons is the only way for many visitors to gain even a lateral understanding of something as complex and unaccountable as our Civil War. For other Americans it's simpler: They just love guns. They love them a lot. They look in every display case not to wonder, "How many broken hearts did that rifle leave behind?" but to ask, "Hey, where can I get me one of those?" It's historic engagement on a peculiarly American level.

The curators at the museum at Manassas' visitor center seem to subtly undercut that excitement by prominently displaying a quote attributed to a soldier after the First Battle: "I had a dim notion about the 'romance' of a soldier's life. I have bravely got over it since." Nonetheless, no one seems to heed it. Guns, and the firing of guns, are by necessity a crucial part of National Battlefield interpretation, and the admiration of them makes the sites money. Gun gossip is why Petersburg National Battlefield Park adopted as its souvenir logo the thirteen-inch mortar known as the Dictator, a 17,000-pound iron behemoth that fired 225-pound shells intended to pummel the Confederacy into supplication. It's a powerful symbol for the park. There's even a sign beside it that implies this impassive hunk of metal needs donations: "Your Entrance Fees Funded the Rehabilitation of the 'Dictator,'" it reads—but beware any museum sign that couches facts with quote marks. They often gloss over a deception. In this case, that mortar displayed as the Dictator is not the Dictator. It's an imposter that arrived from somewhere else when Petersburg was first being prepped for tourism, and the park curators know it. No one is sure what happened to the real Dictator after the war. It probably got melted down and made into something innocuous, like coffin nails for civilians killed by the Dictator. So Petersburg's logo is of a cannon that was likely never in Petersburg before. Like its namesake, its infamy is the point.

There's also an institutional reason for the American fixation with *Guns & Ammo* tourism, and it has to do with the way Americans were conditioned to visit battlefields from the very start. In our first century, neither national parks nor national cemeteries existed. All our big tourism sites remained in private hands. In fact, there was an active streak of disdain for the king-making qualities of memorials. When Congress debated the construction of a mausoleum pyramid to George Washington in 1800, North Carolina representative Nathaniel Macon, no fan of federalism or kings alike, told his colleagues that history books, not marble, should do the job of instructing a people. "Can stones show gratitude? Since the invention of types, monuments are good for nothing," he said to the House committee, calling tombs "pernicious acts of ostentation." (He was no longer alive to complain when he got his own monument in the form of types: Macon, Georgia, was later named for him.)

After the Civil War, though, the military got into the history business. At the close of the first war that belonged solely to the nation, the United States government and veterans moved to preserve a few crucial battlefields, including Antietam, Gettysburg, and Chickamauga, as "military parks," but they were primarily used as object lessons for soldiers-in-training, not strictly for pilgrimage.

The commission that established the memorialization of Chickamauga was headed by Adolph S. Ochs, publisher of the Northern *New York Times*, and its vision for how the park was stern and didactic: "There will be no place here for the gaudy display of rich equipages and show of wealth; no place for lovers to bide tryst; no place for pleasure seekers or loungers. The hosts that in the future come to the grand park will come rather with feelings of awe or reverence. Here their better natures will be aroused; here they will become imbued with grand and lofty ideas; with courage and patriotism; with devotion to duty and love of country." (He missed on his prediction about gaudy displays; Chickamauga has 705 monuments. In places, they resemble giant chessboards halted midgame.)

Military parks were, at least at first, about streamlining military prowess. The first one, Chickamauga, was established in 1890, and, by the end of the decade, the place where 34,000 had been killed or wounded within living memory of most people was being used to teach boys how to slaughter Spaniards better, as if nothing had been learned. At Antietam in Maryland, the infamous Bloody Lane, a gully where 5,500 men were cornered and mowed down for three hours, the War Department built a sixty-foot limestone observation tower where officers could scrutinize the landscape more effectively than the Confederate commander had. Now the officers' lookout tower is a perch for perfect vacation snapshots of the rolling Maryland countryside. True to Och's vision, Chickamauga attracts more than a million people a year, but in defiance of his strict wishes, most of them are biking and hiking its fifty miles of trails, not mourning.

Toward its goal of instruction, the War Department also covered military parks with thousands of awful metal plaques, thick as battleship cladding with even thicker prose scrutinizing minutiae about maneuvers. Antietam installed 350 of these roadside cast-iron plaques in the 1890s, and although many have been lost to vandalism and weekend joyrides gone awry, there are more than enough left to defeat the spirits of countless young children on school outings. Their legacy has sent many a family station wagon right back onto the highway toward Hersheypark instead. Those leaden turn-of-the-century War Department plaques are why reasonable people find most battlefields deadly dull. Here's an electrifying snippet of the one at Turner's Pass at Antietam:

> On the 13th Pleasonton's Union Cavalry, moving from Frederick on the National Road, forced the passage of Catoctin Mountain, Stuart's Calvary retired to Catoctin Creek and then to the east foot of this Pass. Cox's Division moved to Middletown. Willcox's and Sturgis' Division bivouacked at the west base of the Catoctin, and Rodman's at Frederick. The First (Hooker's) Corps bivouacked on the south side of the Monocacy near the crossing of the National Road, the Sixth (Franklin's) Corps at Buckeystown and Couch's Division between that place and the Potomac.

If you're still conscious after reading that, then congratulations, you're suited to the military. Historic signs, though, aren't. The first placards at our most important battlefields were devoid of humanity or sensation, but they were the only official telling we had, so they set the narcoleptic tone for how generations of Americans still frame our most suicidal moments. Just once I want to pull over and read a rusting sign that says, "Boy, we really fucked this whole thing up. We'd all have been so much better off as friends." But America doesn't do regret.

Once the United States owned the most important Civil War settings, to head off accusations of federal dominance or bias, the commission in charge of developing the first military parks invited state legislatures to fund, design, and build monuments. In most cases it gave them free rein in locating them because the federal government now lived in terror of renewed arguments between states. The outcome at Chickamauga was predictably uneven. Between 1893 and 1910, there was a flood of hundreds of markers—grove of trees, grove of memorials, grove of more tree-like memorials. At the time, there were only a few battlefields the public had the legal right to walk on. The Civil War took place in farmers' fields, through the windows of old widows' barns, in people's backyards, and down city streets, and not every landowner cared to remember what happened to defile their homes. The National Park System wasn't established in 1916, a half century later, so state memorial societies only had a handful of military parks into which to pour the symbols of their admiration. Or, more often, of their continued superiority—poor states often couldn't afford to buy any monuments at all. At first, Alabama and Mississippi were shut out at Chickamauga, which was hardly fair given the losses they had contributed. Meanwhile, Ohio rubbed it in, erecting more than fifty, mostly so it could outnumber Illinois. In the light of such inequity, the tension between North and South simmered on, but in the form of tablets and obelisks.

Monuments mostly sanctify the acceptable dead; they are popularity contests in stone. A tourist at Antietam Battlefield will take in ninety-six memorials, but it's a sobering reminder at how polarized America has always been that only one of them, Maryland's, is dedicated to men who fought on *both* sides, so it is the only marker that overlooks ideology to, you know, actually honor wasted souls. In National Park land, every soldier was "brave." No memorial acknowledges that thousands of the men were dragged to those battles kicking and screaming, some met their deaths with abject, but understandable cowardice, a fair number might have been awful people who beat black citizens in the shameful Draft Riots—the multitude of personalities and motivations is painted with a single brush: valor. By making every death noble, we erase the pain. In that way, every death site is like Disneyland: a perfection, a sojourn in a tale with an ultimately uplifting moral, each ragged soul canonized to rhyme with an agreed-upon spirit.

Nor are the biggest monuments always indicative of

the biggest loss. One of Antietam's grandest structures, a thirty-foot weeper down by the deadly Burnside's Bridge, celebrates William McKinley, who at age nineteen—and this is a direct quote from the inscription—"personally and without orders served hot coffee" to his fellow soldiers. Despite its grandiose size, which would seem to bemoan great loss, it's probably the world's only known memorial to a barista.

It should go without saying that it went up in 1903, not right after the battle, but soon after President McKinley, the heroic beverage pourer, was assassinated by a man who wanted to end wealth inequality. McKinley was, at the time, the martyr of the rich, so the monument makes sure the hyper-imperialist forever plays the role of humble servant. So although the inscription purports to honor a coffee break, the installation was actually there as a suck-up. As it seemed to always be, I was finding.

THE REVISIONIST PICKLE

Andersonville

JUST ABOUT THE ONLY THING THAT'S UNDYING about mankind may be its tendency to hover near self-destruction. The human urge to rubberneck is primal. Jesus himself depended on attracting an audience at his execution to germinate his message. We don't bother to hang out where Lincoln wrote the Emancipation Proclamation, no matter its importance. We go where he got shot in the head.

It may be ill-mannered to have a favorite mass murder site, but it's even more impolite to have created one, so I feel liberated to say there's one in particular I like to visit. What I like most about it, and there are so many things to cherish, is that few people care it exists. Located irretrievably in middle Georgia, forty minutes off the interstate, is a place called Andersonville. This was America's concentration camp. It killed 13,000 people in just fourteen months, most of whom are buried out back. Yet this extraordinary place welcomes a paltry 132,000 visitors a year. It's also the official national museum dedicated to all prisoners of war, only it's civilians who remain missing. No one seems to care. What if you threw a warning of the brutality lurking within everyone, but nobody came?

During the final act of the Civil War, the place we now call Andersonville was the dreaded Camp Sumter, a twenty-acre open-air stockade for Union prisoners. At times, its population hit 25,000, or 1,200 soldiers per acre, which, had it been an actual town and not a field of mud trenches, would have qualified it as the fifth-largest in the Confederacy. Owing partly to supply blockade of the South, plus the fact that in the 1860s people acted like rank savages, the death rate was a ghastly 29 percent. More than 13,000 bodies are buried there now.

Many of the guards at Camp Sumter were good old boys from Georgia. I say this without specific blame, because Georgia good old boys made me. Many of my forebears were from Greene County, a place not too far from Andersonville, but a little closer to the home of Honey Boo Boo Child. My people were too poor to own much, but it's also true that a few of my people owned people, and a few others wore grey in the war. I'm not particularly ashamed nor proud of it, because I didn't do any of these things myself. Still, I cannot deny that at least genealogically speaking, I am linked to Andersonville.

The prison opened in 1864, nearly three years into the war, and by that time most of the able-bodied Georgia boys were off fighting, home broken, or dead. The only men available to run the fort were the elderly or kids, none of whom had been considered fit to fight, and most of whom had never had the educational benefit of traveling more than a dozen miles from their beds. All of them were coping with poisoned feelings about an enemy they had never seen before. Wars may start out as ideological, but once blows start landing, they turn personal. Let one man kill another and events tumble into a pile-up of recriminations. This is how a war becomes about itself and metastasizes into an interminable slaughter. Georgia boys had everything to avenge when captured Yankees came limping into their neighborhood.

Before my first trip there, I dimly recalled having seen a low-budget 1996 TNT movie advertised on the sides of bus shelters nationwide. *Andersonville* the TV movie starred a lantern-jawed young actor named Jarrod Emick, recently off his leading role as a crooning Vietnam soldier in the national tour of *Miss Saigon*, as a Camp Sumter prisoner named Josiah. Josiah's fortitude is tested by Colonel Klink villains, harsh klieg lighting, and inspirational monologues bellowed as if everyone is auditioning for a remake of *Hoosiers*. In the end, he weathers starvation and dysentery without sacrificing Soloflex muscle tone. However, despite the magnanimous efforts of TNT to educate America about one of our greatest atrocities using the twin arts of beefcake and corn syrup blood, Andersonville faded into an occasion that even Nielsen's ratings forgot.

Every visitor's introduction to Andersonville's horrors begins with the gift shop that dominates the lobby. When I went, the shelves were filled with candy (Andersonville National Historic Site milk chocolate drops, $7.95), frivolous books like *The Confederate Cookbook: Family Favorites from the Sons of the of Confederate Veterans*, and toys (a plastic Andersonville prison fence, complete with guard towers, that snaps together for hours of concentration camp amusement, "for children over three years"). In the middle of the wares was a metal bramble, roughly in the shape of a tree, that was, bizarrely, festooned with glass pickles. Each one was tagged with a green slip of paper entitled "The Legend of the Pickle Ornament." They offered, as a sales pitch, the tale of Bavarian-born John Lower, a Pennsylvania infantryman who was imprisoned at Andersonville and was near death. "On Christmas Eve, in poor health and starving, he begged a guard for just one pickle before he died." Okay, right off, the scene was a little strange, but go on. "The guard took pity on him and found a pickle for Private Lower." This pity pickle, "by the grace of God, gave him the mental and physical strength to live on." I would rather the story have ended there. It was already fantastic. But this was a prison camp pickle miracle, and that warranted a big finish. It wrapped up by saying that after he survived Andersonville, Lower hid a pickle under his Christmas tree every year for luck. The slip of paper conveniently omitted the fact that miraculous Christmas Pickles actually have a centuries-long tradition in Germany, nor did it mention the average pickle contains fewer than 10 calories, so the ignorant souvenir purchaser would come away with grossly inflated ideas of both the nutritional value of pickles and of this horrid place's proven track record for actual esteem in the merciful eyes of God, but so be it.

"Do people actually buy these?" I asked the girl behind the counter incredulously.

"Oh, yeah, they're one of our most popular sellers," she said brightly. "It's the Christmas Pickle!"

I turned one of the pickles over in my hand. It was iridescent green and pocked with wart-like bumps. People hang these on dead trees to worship Jesus. It was not the first time that I felt like a foreigner in my own land.

People in my own neighborhood might believe this revisionist pickle magically turned mass execution into proof of God's benevolence. That pickle glossed over proof of America's capacity for unaccountable barbarism, clouded the inevitability of death, extracted cash from vacationers, and gave torture the warm and fuzzies. That was some pickle. And it was only $7.95. Naturally I bought one.

Out back, I passed through a Memorial Courtyard dedicated to prisoners of war—in the Georgia heat, the modernist sculptures of detainees appeared to be melting into their ornamental fountain—into a long clearing where the stockade once stood, but was now mostly empty. It could have been any football field except for two additions: a tiny recreated swatch of wooden fencing and, over to one side, a cluster of elephantine turn-of-the-century monuments, each erected by various states to honor their dead. A no-nonsense volunteer ranger, Jimmy Crump,* convened a walking tour for a dozen visitors at the base of the largest one, buttressed and huge as a beached ship. "You might want to get comfortable while we're here for a few minutes," he told us. A few of the visitors seized the invitation to squat on the Wisconsin memorial—toll: 378 men, maybe more.

Crump's stony demeanor was suited to delivering ugly truths. He said when slave labor built Camp Sumter— named for the Georgia county, not the Charleston fort, as I had assumed—it was just a timber-walled enclosure in this field. Picture it. Captured Northerners were trans-

---

* Of course I don't use their real names. I'm not trying to get anyone in trouble.

ported deep behind enemy lines and dumped into this pen to fend for themselves. For as long as they were held captive, they were exposed to the elements between the cement-hard Georgia clay and the brutal Georgia sun. "It was like walking into a jungle with only the clothes on your back," said Crump. An elderly woman among us clucked her tongue in solidarity. Crump nodded in acknowledgment before continuing. Only a third of the men—many of whom were just boys, really—managed to cobble together flimsy shelters using scavenged belongings, and many of the rest, shoeless, in rags, had to dig holes to hide in. They also tried to tunnel out, and if they weren't done in by snitches who betrayed them to the guards, they were liable to be entombed by the slippery red soil.

"Buried alive!" Crump emphasized, I thought a little too lustily. A woman issued another tongue cluck, her way of signaling both rapt attention and disapproval. She clucked whenever Crump said something distressing or remarkable, but given the setting, I suppose I preferred it to applause. Crump pointed to the base of a nearby tree, whose roots had exposed one such long-forgotten tube to nowhere. "We didn't find anyone in that one," he assured the group, but we all craned our necks to look anyway. It was nearly impossible to imagine a man being in a space that small, yet someone had been, long ago, because there was the evidence.

Next, Crump pointed to a line of pickets marking out a long narrow aisle, and that kicked off a monologue that solicited a hail of disapproving clucks. If a prisoner put so much as a filthy pinky toe outside their ascribed zone, he said, they were instantly shot. The boundary was the "dead line," which gives us the word *deadline* today. Now and then, meager rations were tossed into the pen, like slop to hogs. Despite the starvation, disease was the worst killer. The Georgians built the stockade near a marshy stream, but by the time water flowed into the stockade, it was foul and sluggish. In short order, the filthy runoff from 45,000 excreting, dying bodies oozed into the supply, incubating dysentery and hookworm that doomed anyone who touched it, no matter how thirsty they were. "In those conditions, even a mosquito bite could result in gangrene," said Crump. The average life expectancy of a man in Andersonville was ninety-five days. Right about this time, I thought a Christmas Pickle sounded real nice.

Someone asked why the North didn't exchange prisoners. Crump said they were more or less given up for dead because the Union didn't want freed Southerners returning to the front lines. Another person asked if there were still artifacts buried in the field.

"They have a contraption that looks like a baby carriage with a red light on it," he told us. "If they did the whole section over here, they'd probably find some bodies." We glanced anxiously in that direction. Someone gestured to a stone chapel-like building down the incline, by some snake warning signs. "What's that?"

"Well," said Crump, moistening his lips for another

enlivening anecdote. "There's an old newspaper saying: 'When the legend goes beyond the fact you print the legend.' So I'll tell you the legend."

That memorial, he told us, was Providence Spring, from the early twentieth century, and the constant fountain inside it commemorates the spot (more or less) where (so the story went), a bolt of lightning (so they say) hit the earth one day (maybe). Or as the building's plaque prefers to phrase it, "God heard and with His thunder cleft the earth," issuing "His sweetest waters" that enabled prisoners to endure creeping death a little longer. Between pickles and smote earth, God's generosity was all over Georgia's interpretation of Andersonville, contrary to the evidence presented by 13,500 corpses massed a few hundred yards away. The gift shop sells ninety-five-cent glass bottles, small enough to get past the TSA, that true believers may fill at the spring's constantly flowing spigot.

"But don't drink it," warned Crump.

Turns out God's miracle gift will give you the shits. "That water's no good."

Back inside the center, we visited the second component of Andersonville: the National Prisoner of War Museum. In truth, it's as much a museum as a military-themed haunted house. As I set foot in the first darkened exhibition room, sensors triggered a sweeping searchlight to the sounds of rapid gunfire. A military drumbeat cued up. The lights readjusted, and I found myself standing by what looked like smashed rebar concrete with a bouquet of thirty-four guns pointed directly at me.

It achieved the intended effect: to make a visitor feel ambushed and captured. Once I was good and harrowed, I was bombarded with artifacts from the incarceration of generations of Americans across the world. Scavenged bits from Camp Sumter (the lock to the southern gate, a few centimeters of the dead line, a canteen) shared space with coffee mugs from Stalag 17-B and sandals from a prisoner in the Philippines in World War II—sundries as mundane as the knickknacks in the gift shop. They were tragic precisely because they were so ordinary.

Real survivors told their stories on tape. Watching them, seeing the flicker of remembered brutality in their eyes, was enough to stoke a panic attack. Imagining 1864 and Civil War soldiers trapped under a field is abstract, but hearing the quaver in a man's voice as he revisits Vietnam makes you realize that terrible events don't end just because they're over. They affect lives until *those* lives are over, and then they become haunted ideas. Standing by a video wall of moving oral histories by family members, I contemplated the pointless cruelty of mankind when two boys, probably about eight or nine, walked in and glanced around.

"Scary!" said one of them.

"It's not as cool as I thought it would be," said the other. He stalked back out, and the first kid followed him.

Andersonville wasn't the only Civil War prison camp. It just killed the most people. Not by much: Elmira, which housed Confederates in New York, had a death rate of 25 percent, something modern-day Rebels are rightfully quick to point out. In the end, the nationwide prison scorecard was 25,796 killed by the North and 30,218 killed by the South. Most sites were quickly repurposed—Chicago's notorious Camp Douglas (estimated Southern dead: about 4,500, including Will O'Neal's uncle, James Augustus) is now a windswept terrain of modern apartment towers near Lake Meadows Park—but because some swift-thinking partisans put a rope around Camp Sumter and their kids envisioned earnings potential, Andersonville survives to represent them all, fair or not.

Andersonville almost wasn't preserved. In the years after the war, the site of Camp Sumter took on the name of the nearest hamlet, Andersonville, and Northern charity groups swooped in to purchase the land so it couldn't be developed and whitewashed by bitter Southerners. Soon enough, the old camp became the setting of a rousing annual Memorial Day celebration by African-Americans. Only about one hundred blacks had been imprisoned there, but freed men were understandably grateful for the sacrifices made by the soldiers on their behalf. (The first stirrings of Memorial Day festivities in America, in fact, were held by grateful freedmen in May 1865.) In time, locals grew cranky about the annual party for reasons I shouldn't have to elucidate ("the ground was covered with negroes," lamented one local paper's report), and in 1894 the event nearly instigated a race riot. That was when white businessmen finally embraced the potential of organizing visitation with for-profit death tourism. They built fancy hotels like the Windsor in Americus (still standing) and marketed package tours by train, which of course were segregated and excluded black visitors, who started the whole thing. That helped detach emancipationist meaning from Andersonville, whitewashing it after all. For a century more, Andersonville occupied an uncomfortable niche in Southern memory: it wasn't a proud episode, but it filled pocketbooks. It was one of our first major dark tourism sights because it was so thoroughly American made.

Amazingly, it took until the mid-'90s for this type of tourist site to acquire a term: *dark tourism*. Ironically, the name was popularized by a British professor named John Lennon—whose namesake's murder inspired an unofficial dark tourism pit stop of his own at Central Park West and 72nd Street in New York City, but never mind. Scholars like Lennon are still observing and gathering data. They will be for a while, too, because the field is governed by so many shifting factors that anyone who hopes to grasp its appeal will have to marshal a range of disciplines—psychology, sociology, history, politics, economics, media analysis, philosophy, and the hospitality industry—to understand how sites are selected, preserved, interpreted, commoditized, visited, and remembered. It's messy. And it all depends on a concerted collaboration of specialties conducted in an interdisciplinary symphony. Lennon and fellow lecturer Malcolm Foley mulled a topline version of these implications in their 2000 book *Dark Tourism: The Attraction of Death and Disaster*. "Our argument is that 'dark tourism' is an intimation of post-modernity," they wrote. "Objects of dark tourism themselves appear to introduce anxiety and doubt about the project of modernity," adding that "the educative elements of sites are accompanied by elements of commodification and a commercial ethic which (whether explicit or implicit) accepts that visitation (whether purposive or incidental) is an opportunity to develop a tourism project." A translation for the nontenured is that dark tourism sites make us anxious about all the ways life can go terribly wrong, and exploiting that anxiety is a peachy way to make money, because it purchases comfort. Whatever the impetus for dark tourism, Lennon and Foley seem to agree that mulling the departed is all about assuaging our self-centered anxieties. I would like to submit that dark tourism has been a thing for as long as there have been religious shrines. *The Canterbury Tales*, from 1400, is about a bunch of common folk making a pilgrimage to a murder site. Needless to say, the complicated psychology of the dark tourism urge may never be fully understood.

By the turn of the century, with Civil War tourism

gathering steam among the curious children and grand-children of its participants, groups from both sides of the Mason-Dixon raised funds for the most persuasive expressions of their losses. Northern states deposited twenty-three monuments on the grounds—arches, obe-lisks, friezes, pylons topped by spheres, and the pricey Wisconsin Monument, which from a distance looks like a ship's prow cutting across the sacred clay, and is now used to support the overburdened bones of elderly and physically ample tourists.

This angered locals, who felt the North was making them look mean. In rebuke, Southerners gathered donations for a memorial to the camp's commander, the Swiss-born Captain Henry Wirz. Scumbag or saint, people still argue, but Wirz still gets more sympathy from some Georgians than enslaved Africans ever did. In an unintended exercise of liberal thinking, his defenders protested that Captain Wirz was only following orders and was working against a stacked deck without supplies (both true). Many Southerners, as my kindred are wont to do with our tarnished saints, seized the ambiguity to argue he was a martyr. In 1865, when it became clear just what had happened at Andersonville, Wirz was so reviled that in November, he was executed for war crimes.

One of the notable outcomes of our American Civil War was that, unlike civil wars in other parts of the world, our victors did not blindfold the losers, line them up over a ditch, and sock them full of lead. Many Confederates fled to Europe to escape the anticipated wrath of the North, but the feared mass execution of the Rebel elite simply never materialized. Most went back home to resume normal lives. Except for Wirz. His neglect was deemed so extraordinary, the allegations of gleeful cruelty so pernicious, that he was railroaded through an overly hasty war crimes trial and hanged before a cheering crowd beside the US Capitol. (It probably didn't help that he wasn't American-born.) Wirz's was the sole scalp the North claimed in recrimination for the war. The speedy trials and executions of abolitionist John Brown and Captain Wirz, Northerner and Southerner, were twin bookends of the war, the required bloodlettings during the conflict's first inhale and its final exhale. At the dawn of the war, the South ushered Brown into martyrdom after his failed slave insurrection at Harpers Ferry, and at the war's dusk, the North made a legend out of Wirz by doing the same thing. Today, the location of Wirz' public execution is where the US Supreme Court dispenses its own form of justice.

"There was never a trial more unjust in profane history," opines a sixty-four-page defense of Wirz written in 1921 by one Miss Mildred Lewis Rutherford and on sale in the gift shop as a curiosity. "Had Wirz been really guilty, all officials connected with this prison would have been hanged also for permitting the atrocities of which he was accused—but not one was ever called to trial." (Rutherford, you may recall, was the writer who profiled Atlanta poet Orelia Key Bell in a "textbook" I Googled at her grave.) Southerners funded a Wirz obelisk, but Camp Sumter's owners banished it from its soil. Backers squabbled for years about what to do with the solemn column. Atlanta refused it. They could send it to Richmond, Macon, Savannah, or the nearby town of Americus, but they finally settled on the teeny square of Andersonville town, a short distance away from the stockade site, where it now sulks, hemmed in by a tight traffic circle and cracked by vandalism. Its plaintive inscription laments he was "at last the victim of a misdirected popular clamor" and this stone sought "to rescue his name from the stigma attached to it by embittered prejudice."

Time passed, and it passed Andersonville by especially. Charles Lindbergh bought his first airplane and embarked on his first solo flight eight miles away. The next year, Jimmy Carter was born on a nearby farm. The War Department acquired the Camp Sumter land. But the North still bemoaned the events while the South still insisted they got railroaded. Interpretive tensions persisted until 1970, when finally, Georgia lawmakers were talked into accepting federal curation of Andersonville on the condition that a new national prisoner of war museum would also be established on the grounds. Jimmy Carter, then a state senator, promised his reticent neighbors that the intent was not "to reconstruct a one-sided version of what took place at Andersonville." The POW exhibition is a consequence of a compromise agreement distract from straight talk about Andersonville as a Southern failing. Instead, subhuman treatment is presented as one of those things that just kinda happens in war, whoopsie.

The scheme diluted Southern responsibility and pointed out similar Northern sins. The fearsome truth, though, is that at Andersonville, Americans murdered other Americans, dumped them in mass graves, and got away with it. It's a political pickle indeed.

Behind a copse of trees is the most challenging component of Andersonville: the still-active national cemetery where rows of identical tablet gravestones mark the resting places of some 20,000 bodies, 13,000 of whom died at Camp Sumter, but none of whom got pickles of their own, I guess. It's a dignified setting, but six of the graves lie set apart from the others. These were the nefarious Raiders, a roving gang of brutal thugs who took control by slitting throats and stealing the pitiful scraps of cloth from their fellow prisoners. Wirz, who preferred to observe from the perimeter of the camp, responded like a WWE ringmaster: He issued heavy clubs so that the prisoners could defend themselves. A rival group, the Regulators, retook control, tried the Raiders in a kangaroo court, and after an approving nod from Wirz like Tina Turner at Thunderdome, hanged them to the jubilation of their fellow prisoners. The Raiders were not buried with dignity. They're facedown. When I drove up, a middle-aged couple of hobby motorcyclists was standing next to the stones, grinning and pointing down and taking photos of each other on top of their plots. Even in death, the Raiders suffer ignobly.

That accounts for six marked graves. But how did the thousands of other discarded bodies go from ditch burials to luxuriantly marked military commemoration? The skin-crawling answer: Every corpse, some 13,000 of them, was painstakingly identified, and all thanks to the courage of a nerdy Connecticut teenager named Dorence Atwater, who paid a devastating price for it, and whose stroke of derring-do made memorialization into a federal crime.

Dorence Atwater was a sickly kid, not the sort of character you'd think could impact a room, let alone American history. He had trouble doing much well. He found minor redemption in signing up as a Federal boy, but very soon, his humiliating capture by Southern troops played out like a Tom and Jerry cartoon: While he was traveling through some woods, a few Confederates dressed up as Union soldiers, tricked him into approaching, and nabbed him. Dorr was one of the first prisoners to show up at Camp Sumter, and as was his way, he arrived ill. As he recovered, someone noticed his beautiful penmanship and, as luck would have it, he was impressed into office duty rather than a work detail that would have killed him quickly. When a Union man died, one hundred a day sometimes, it was Dorr's job to record the dead man's name on two lists: one for the Confederates, and one to be furnished to the Federals when the war was over. Atwater, a bookish type, saw the conditions of the prison and knew that the Southerners weren't likely to preserve either list. So, at the risk of execution, he kept a third, secret one of his own in the lining of his coat, because as the nerds in your own life are always telling you, you should always keep a backup. When Andersonville was liberated, he walked straight out with it, undetected.

Sure enough, when peace came, the main two lists were smeary, incomplete, and useless for identifying the dead. After overcoming a bout of diphtheria, Dorr altruistically informed the authorities in Washington that he possessed his own priceless list. But he presented his news clumsily and got tricked again, this time by the bureaucrats on his own side. They offered him $300 for it, but Dorr refused, telling them he'd rather see it published. When that went nowhere, Dorr came around to saying the government could rent his information as long as they paid him the $300, gave him a desk job that would enable him to keep an eye on the list, and returned the list to him as soon as it was copied. It sounded a little like extortion, but they went along with it.

Months went by and no copies were made, and all the while, Dorr shuffled paper in an office alongside his bullies (in my mind, they all look like William Zabka in *The Karate Kid*), one eye on the cabinet, while thousands of families grieved in limbo over their missing boys and their bodies became more unidentifiable by the day. To make matters worse, his father died, orphaning him. For a while there, it looked as if Dorr might as well give up and vanish into a lifetime of anonymity as a sniffling governmental lackey. Other traumatized veterans were descending into far worse.

Finally, disconsolate that this was going nowhere, Dorr resorted to responding to a poster he'd seen on the wall of the post office, the postwar equivalent of Craigslist. The ad was put up by a nurse who wanted to identify the dead at Andersonville, but needed a way to start. The nurse was Clara Barton, another long-suffering government lackey who had earned wartime celebrity (and lifted gender equality to a new, high water mark) by valiantly tending to brutalized bodies on the battlefield. Dorr nervously paid a call to the famous Barton, who was something of an outsider herself, and told her he knew where she could find the list she needed. Barton became Dorr's Miyagi. Within weeks, she hatched a cloak-and-dagger plan. She got Dorr to snatch his list back—in a cloak-and-dagger operation that later got him thrown back into prison—and together with the second, sloppy Confederate list, the unlikely duo embarked on a mission back to Andersonville.

It must have been horrifying for poor, sensitive Dorr to return to the scene of so many tortures, but Barton was an iron-stomached broad and worthy company. The stockade stood abandoned, strewn with rotting refuse, and nearly 13,000 corpses were piled nearby in their recent trench graves. When local blacks heard rumors that a famous Yankee lady had arrived, they walked up to twenty miles after their day's work to meet her. "I discovered they were in a state of ignorance, generally, at that time of their own condition as freedmen," Barton told Congress the next spring. "[They asked] me their little questions in their own way, which was to the effect, if they were free, and if Abraham Lincoln was really dead. They had been told that he was dead; that he had been killed; but at the same time they had been informed that, now that he was dead, they were no longer free, but would all be slaves again." Their former masters were lying to them to keep them in bondage. Barton firmly assured the bewildered slaves that they were no longer slaves, "that they were free as I was." One of the women she met, named Rosa, would become her chief paid domestic assistant.

Then she set about using Dorr's third Death List for the purpose he had so bravely created it. Soon, only 440 men were left unnamed. One day, a War Department goon showed up in the camp demanding the Death List back. The government wanted it to prosecute Captain Wirz. By now, though, Dorr had learned how to trick the tricksters: he handed over the crummy Confederate copy. The goon didn't realize he'd been suckered until he got back to Washington. In a fury, his bosses had Dorr court-martialed for larceny. Soon, they were also accusing Dorr of extorting $300 from families desperate to know their sons' fates. It wasn't exactly true, but tell that to a nation whipped into a judgmental fury. Dorr was clapped in chains and marched in shame through the streets of Washington.

"My offense consists in an attempt to make known the relatives and friends the fate of the unfortunate men who died in Andersonville," Dorr wrote in a sublimely bitter public statement, "and if this be a crime I am guilty to the fullest extent of the law, for to accomplish it I have risked my life among my enemies and my liberty among my friends." Barton wrote Secretary of War Edwin Stanton for mercy: "Young Atwater, honest and simple hearted, both loving and trusting you, has more need of your protection than your censure." To no avail: Once they're in government, Americans never admit when they're wrong. Dorr was tossed into another prison—this time the Union's worst. "I forgot that the soldier who sacrificed his comfort and risked his life to maintain these liberties was the only man in the country who would not be allowed to claim their protection," he wrote acidly.

Things were bleak. Dorr's health collapsed. Barton, whom history deifies as indefatigable, was defatigated, if not devastated. That winter, she wrote in her diary, "I could hardly find it in me to rise and dress, and did not for some time, it seemed to me that the whole horizon was overcast and the clouds shut down all around." She hassled anyone who would listen about Dorr's good intentions, not that anyone listened.

Finally, dumb luck. President Andrew Johnson issued an unrelated general pardon and the Death List, at long last, was published on Valentine's Day 1866, by newspaperman Horace Greeley. America was riveted. In its preface, Dorr publicly shamed, by name, every War

Department bureaucrat who had persecuted him. "I regret that you have waited so long for information of so much interest to you," he told the parents of America. Barton wrote a second preface that concluded: "For the record of your dead, you are indebted to the forethought, courage, and perseverance of Dorence Atwater, a young man not yet twenty-one years of age; an orphan; four years a soldier; one tenth part of his whole life a prisoner, with broken health and ruined hopes, he seeks to present to your acceptance the sad gift he has in store for you."

So many struggles, even after death, are about the basic human desire to be recognized. Dorr's valor finally was, but only after people actually saw the list. The *New York Citizen* hailed him as "one of the unquestionable heroes of our recent war." Mothers sobbed his name in prayerful praise. But it came too late. He was shattered and diminished, disillusioned by the patriotism to which he had given everything. The sight of a man in uniform made him blind with rage. Dorr, who entered the war bright and eager was now rendered dark and desolate, and by his own side. A sheepish government awarded him a consulship in the tropics—a consul-ation prize— where the climate would agree with him and he could be far from the country that had done nothing for him but betray him.

He remained one of Barton's lifelong best friends, married a Tahitian princess, and lived most of his days in redolent luxury in the South Pacific, growing vanilla, coffee, and pearls, and working with lepers. His descendants maintain he brought the first carousel and the first tandem bike to the islands, a blissfully mild legacy concerning the gruesome horrors that led him there.

Years later, having finally served its noble purpose, the much-chased Death List, Dorr's secretarial dybbuk, met its own spectacular destruction worthy of the MacGuffin in an *Indiana Jones* picture. He kept it locked in the mostly unused townhouse he kept on Market Street in San Francisco, far from his new haven in the South Pacific. And there the list slept on the early morning of April 18, 1906—the date of the great San Francisco earthquake. Miraculously, it survived the jolts just fine, although much of the city surrounding it instantly crumpled. But as hours passed, gas fires in nearby blocks gathered into a conflagration, and firefighters determined they had to establish a firebreak. As the firestorm raged around them, they rigged Dorr's house with low explosives, and with a single lighted match, the government blew it, and the so-called Atwater List, into dust. Just like Dorr, his list of the mass murders in Andersonville was a final casualty claimed by the team tasked to protect it. Born of one cataclysm and destroyed in another, it joined the anonymous ashes of the rest of the city as they floated up into the San Francisco sky. American history is always taking things back.

Dorr died four years later.

How did his hometown tribute him? With a gun.

It put a cannon in a park.

PR AND PROFIT

Gettysburg

THERE ARE TWO GETTYSBURGS. THE FIRST ONE was the setting for one of America's most brutal slaughters. The other, which rose a few months later, was the town that made a mint off it.

Gettysburg, as elementary school teachers used to tell American children, was one of the deadliest battles in their history. It was a real bloodbath—as many as 51,000 people snuffed out or mutilated in a surprisingly small area—and a scalding reckoning that we as a society are still not able to fully forget. Today, few things in Gettysburg stand taller as a testament to grievous national dissipation than the menu of the Blue & Gray Bar & Grill. The menu features chicken wings named for various death traps and units made infamous in the battle: Devil's Den wings are spicy like the rocky slaughter pen they honor, the hobbled Irish Brigade features raspberry jalapeno sauce, the Peach Orchard sasses things up with a peach habanero, and the 1st Minnesota offers a foolish combo of honey and horseradish. The menu's most dangerous tribute flavor, Gettysburg Ghost (spice rating: five cannons), comes with a warning: "**Must sign waiver to consume.**"

I chose a General James Longstreet "Little Round Top" burger with bacon, caramelized onions, and creamy peanut butter—a combination I found peripheral enough to be an apt recognition of the guy who tried to warn Robert E. Lee his battle plans stank—and pored over tourist brochures to get a bead on my sightseeing options. The cover of Gettysburg's Official Visitor Guide depicted a young white family of four strolling through the grass on the battlefield with the domed Pennsylvania Battle Monument behind them. I noticed they carried no cameras and the mother had no purse. Instead, the father held his son's hand and the mother had one consoling arm around her daughter's shoulder. Inside, by the table of contents, the same family skipped, laughing, through the grass, merrily a-frolic, as if the photographer had captured them in a game of tag in the clover and not on a killing field. The brochure had plenty of suggestions for how to pass my time here. "The story of Gettysburg is larger than three days [sic] in July 1863," read the copy. "It is a story of our nation."

By that, they mean a story of unleashed commercialism. Gettysburg took the Chickamauga-style, turn-of-the-century craze for melancholy pillars and intentionally metastasized it into a tourist cash mill, an economy the town still depends upon today. In addition to bus and Segway tours and nine outfits offering walking tours for ghost stories and paranormal detection, I could visit the Wendy Allen Lincoln Into Art gallery where Abe is the sole subject. I could dawdle in the Gettysburg Museum of History, a homegrown kitchen-sink reliquary that claimed to own such sinister relics such as the upholstered stool where Adolf Hitler has rested his *tuches*, the shell casing from the bullet Jack Ruby killed Lee Harvey Oswald with, and the Ruger Blackhawk.44 Magnum Elvis used to murder his TV. I could shop at The Union Drummer Boy, or Ronn Palm's Museum of Civil

War Images, or the Colonel's Lady Civil War Attire, or the Horse Soldier, which promised an "extensive inventory ranging from artillery to battlefield relics." Although I couldn't imagine a circumstance in which I could require nineteenth-century artillery in my home, I could imagine engaging in some tactical maneuvers of my own at the large dessert table at General Pickett's Buffet ("Southern hospitality just north of the Mason-Dixon Line!").

There's no polite way to describe the putrefying carnage that overtook Gettysburg in 1863, but it must be understood if you're going to understand why hallowed ground had such a pungent need to be hallowed. At first, Gettysburg was notorious, not hallowed. A conservative guess would say the three-day July calamity killed 7,000 men, plus their animals, and another 21,000 soldiers required medical attention. All those bodily humors swamped a hamlet of only 2,400. There wasn't much of a clean-up crew. It was the war, and the government was occupied. Townspeople gave up trying to bury corpses—not enough manpower, not enough places—and had to abandon many to rot in the open air. "We could not open our windows for weeks because of the horrible stench," remembered one Gettysburgian, Nellie Aughenbaugh. The sickly sweet funk of death was so wretched the luckless townspeople walked around with peppermint oil smeared on their lips. This went on for months, well into the autumn.

Their lovely Pennsylvania town, Gettysburg, was suddenly synonymous around the globe with bloodletting and bloated carcasses, but burying that problem only required savvy public relations. It needed redemption. Antietam was stained, too, but Sharpsburg was a teeny hick burg that would just have to get over it. Gettysburg benefitted from the key ingredients for a more polished future: a train station and hungry entrepreneurs. Greed is the ugly stepmother of invention, and mass martyrdom made all the difference.

Four months after the fight, with both sides of a fractured nation united in its disgust of allowing the dead across the nation to fester without Christian graves, Lincoln came to town to deal with the backlash. That was when he delivered his famous Gettysburg Address—to christen the National Cemetery that gave the corpses, or at least the ones that could be scooped up by that point, a little respect. Presciently, the Address said to remember the dead in a way that would motivate the living, a theme that partisans have run with ever since: the dead are dead, Lincoln told the crowd, but "it is for us the living, rather, to be dedicated here to the unfinished work which they who fought here have thus far so nobly advanced." Even as Lincoln spoke the eloquent words that are now carved above his likeness in the Lincoln Memorial, the four-and-a-half-month-old corpses of lost Southern lads were decomposing, unconsecrated and defiled, in the fields surrounding him. The wooden planks marking them were being plucked out and burned for firewood. It took as late as 1873—nine years after the conciliatory nice-nice of the Gettysburg Address—for anyone to actually grow a heart and move those 2,935 Confederates from their cursory ditches, which qualifies the Gettysburg Address, for all its subsequent adoration, as a dubious motivational failure in its own time. Even during Lincoln's appearance, townspeople approached spectators to sell them debris right off the battlefield, and when that ran out, they hacked down trees to sell walking sticks. Self-destruction for profit was now Gettysburg's survival technique.

From the moment of Gettysburg's rebirth, memorials and commerce were interlaced. Amid the bonanza, an opportunistic local attorney named David McConaughy scrambled to create the Gettysburg Battlefield Memorial Association (GBMA). He sold shares to a cluster of powerful businessmen for $10 each, and in 1864, secured government backing that gave him authority to control seventy acres of the battlefield, including the right to groom it as he saw fit and build monuments, which he hoped would attract even more visitors. Now there are more than 1,300 of them, doing their job daily as some of the best long-term investments in tourism history.

By 1866, McConaughy was a state senator, and he used his seat to legitimize his next pet project: a resort built around natural springs that, what a coincidence, had just been discovered near the battlefield. He and his board of directors (including David Wills, the man in whose home Lincoln wrote the Gettysburg Address) pressured politicians and journalists alike to publicize the so-called miraculous powers of the springs. *The New York Herald* oozed about "the remarkable cures that this water has made on chronic diseases" including, the bottlers claimed, "chronic diarrhea, torpid liver, gout, chronic rheumatism, nodosities of the joints...gravel, albuminuria...hematuria, abdominal dropsy, cholera infantum" and stones. The spring was named the Katalysine Springs, a made-up word said to derive from the Greek for "loosening below," which was also an etymological euphemism for the waters' purported effect. For nearly half a century, tourists trekked in by train to have their bowels liquefied while they pondered the brutality of battle.

The GBMA was sneaky about stoking rivalry among monument builders. One of its directors would trick tourists by erecting crappy signboards to indicate where their states' regiments had fought. As related by 1897's *A History of the Gettysburg Battlefield Memorial Association*, "the placing of these cheap boards had the desired effect." Visitors would see the inferior signage, "inquire with indignation," and pen testy letters to their state governments demanding money for respectable stones. Gettysburg was soon flush with tourist draws funded by other states; there is a grossly immoderate 1,328 monuments there now. Outside the battlefields' boundaries, schlocky tourist traps sprouted, such as waxworks based on the life of Christ, train displays, a golf course, and a Fantasyland storybook village. Every inch of non-sanctified soil catered to hand-wringers and air-takers alike and set up a never-ending tug-of-war between preservationists and capitalists. The pendulum swung from piety to avarice and back again, as in 1893 when someone started plowing an electric railway across the fields to the battle area known as Little Round Top, which made the veterans howl for the Supreme Court, which in turn, reversed the destruction for a little while. Then the opportunists would aim their schemes at a different part of the battlefield, business versus beatification, on and on.

Although Gettysburg lost the war, it won the PR battle. New attractions came and went, each supplying visitors with a way to pay cold cash while they paid their less profitable respects. Park-peepers in 1913 saw the arrival of the cyclorama that's now the jewel of the modern visitor center. Cycloramas, huge canvas rings painted with lurid panoramas that spectators would view from all angles, were a truly gaudy trend in post-battle tourism, like a Victorian forerunner to virtual reality. Four copies were made of the Gettysburg cyclorama to accommodate blockbuster crowds around the country, but only one survived to reach us, saved from dereliction in Boston. Meanwhile, control of the battlefield passed from the GBMA, to the War Department in 1895, to the National Park Service in 1933. The government never had as much of the land as it wanted (though it had enough to imprison German POWs on the battlefield during World War II), which allowed developers to vomit up junky motels at a disheartening rate. The hundredth anniversary in 1963 finally prompted locals to take a hard look at the eyesore they had wrought. They realized they were edgy even by Pennsylvania standards, and those would produce Rick Santorum.

The visitor center in Gettysburg, by Viennese-born modernist architect Richard Neutra and Robert Alexander, was plopped in the middle of the battlefield, over where countless boys perished during Pickett's Charge. The official Park reasoning for destroying the land it purported to honor was that visitors would be most likely to find the center there. That's what you call government logic. "A department store does not prepare a prospective customer for a display of dress shirts in a building two blocks away from the store," said one NPS curator helpfully at the time. Neutra and Alexander tried to mitigate the lousy idea by claiming that their "forward-looking" design also respected the land, but that's the kind of nonsense architects blurt out to keep a gig. Their design was so flawed that hairline fractures in the concrete damaged the cyclorama painting it was designed to house. ("This building will last forever!" Neutra blustered to the press in 1959. In 2013, it was demolished within ten days.) Nevertheless, the investment spurred annual visitation to the national battlefield to a record high of 6.88 million by 1970.

Tourist traps became Gettysburg's new rotting stench, the noxious thing the town needed to rise above. In 1989, when Ken Burns finally got Americans reenergized about the Civil War with his PBS series, Gettysburg's citizens finally agreed they were mortified about what they had allowed to happen. They resolved to restore the battlefield properly and they petitioned the Department of the Interior, which controls the National Park Service, to get on board and bury ugly telephone wires so visitors could see the battlefield as it was supposed to look. But in the United States, preservation is considered an optional expense, and the government, cash strapped and gun shy, said no. That's when the most influential citizens banded together to form the nonprofit Friends of the National Parks at Gettysburg. The Park might have been too broke to roll back the clock, but the Friends knew how to get their hands on cash (for one, they got Ted Turner to donate $50,000), and they weren't afraid to lobby for more. Soon, the management of Gettysburg's battlefield was two-pronged: Park rangers had interpretive control, but it was the Friends who got their hands dirty filling the purse and cutting red tape. Soon, nothing got done without the Friends' backing, and its ambitions grew. It acquired more land, secured grants, rectified past planning mistakes, and even created educational programs that it essentially gave to the Park Service as marching orders.

Emboldened in its quest, the Friends redoubled efforts to enforce its version of acceptable visitation through careful restoration. Thanks to the private sector, Gettysburg underwent the largest, most careful restoration of any historic site in the history of the United States. It uprooted midcentury motels, spruced up memorials, dismantled unsightly modern barns, paid $15 million for the largest painting restoration in US history to repair the cyclorama, and arrayed itself against anything on the battlefield that it thought carried the whiff of tourist trappery.

The watershed moment, in 2000, was the demolition of a 307-foot-tall observational tower that had literally overshadowed National Cemetery and the site of Pickett's Charge for twenty-six years. To the Friends, the Gettysburg National Battlefield Tower represented the heedless hucksterism they were fighting to counteract—Niagara Falls-styled honky-tonk on hallowed ground—and it cheered the federal government's controversial decision to use eminent domain to clear the private land it stood on. The eyesore was detonated live on CNN at the snidely symbolic time of 5:03 p.m. on July 3—the very minute Union soldiers repulsed Pickett, which turned the tide of the war; open capitalism being the stand-in for the Confederacy here.

The moment was also confirmation that an identity shift had transformed the American death tourism market, of which Gettysburg was a natural leader. Major development has frozen in the 1860s, making it impossible to fully disconnect from the calamity. According to the Friends, the ideal death tourism site should appear to be time stunned, with an authentic appearance intended to stir contemplation and to encourage the consumerism it deemed complementary—an idealism shared by the National Park Service. The irony is that having eliminated so much crass commodification, the Friends now must wallow in it to stay afloat.

Gettysburg's National Military Park Visitor Center is a powerhouse pastiche of homespun architecture dressed up in red siding, LEED-certified stone facing, and a silo roof like a circus big top. As I drove up to the field from the Blue & Gray, I found it squatting on sacred land like the mother ship that spawned every red barn in Pennsylvania.

Shuttles to the battlefield and the nearby Eisenhower National Historic Site, Ike's country house, departed at regular intervals from a lunar plain of a parking lot. Inside the 139,000-square-foot building, a long ticket counter offered a roster of diversions as varied as the one at my local multiplex. I proffered my National Parks annual pass, but a fat gruff man at the counter waved it away.

"That don't work here," he said.

"Why not?" I asked. "Isn't it a national park?"

"Because the National Parks don't own it," he answered.

Control of Gettysburg's official exhibition center was wrestled from the federal government. By 2008, the Friends, with its brother group the Gettysburg Foundation, splurged on a $103 million visitor's center where the actual federal park rangers are mere tenants, confined to an unobtrusive kiosk in the rear while guests are plied with jars of apple butter and Abe Lincoln tees. It operates with the efficiency of a factory, but the numbers of paid visitors to the battlefield have gone down: 1.65 million in 2007 to 1.08 million by 2015, a far cry from the seven million who flooded town in the so-called dark days of 1970. Now, battlefield tours cost $35, and adult tickets to the center's attractions cost $15 (in 2017, the National Park Service had to hike entrance fees by 20 percent to keep the lights on), which buys admission to a twelve-room multimedia "artifact gallery." Instead of a dinky little middle school theatre, Gettysburg is equipped with the state-of-the-art Anne and Robert Kinsley Theater, a plush hall named for the CEO of the construction firm that built the center, among other big government contracts. It screens *A New Birth of Freedom*, a twenty-five-minute documentary narrated by Oscar winner Morgan Freeman and featuring the voice talents of Sam Waterston and Marcia Gay Harden. When the lights come up from the screening, two gleaming escalators, reaching out like mandibles, whisk visitors upstairs into the crown of the false silo to view the neatly restored, 360-degree cyclorama. It's 370-feet long and forty feet tall and was created in 1884 by an entrepreneurial Frenchman named Paul Dominique Philippoteaux, who also titillated customers with gargantuan paintings of Niagara Falls and Egypt. Periodically, the entire building trembles from the vibration of cannon fire that roars every time a new audience relives the rigors of battle before the tableaux.

The "artifact gallery" is among the best at any death tourism site in America. It's not some greenish tube-lit room full of guns and fading pea coats. This was assembled with a flair for theater. Screens show movie-quality tidbits "sponsored by History Channel"—most guests prefer to watch these rather than read signs—and overhead rods of focused can lights pick out a collection selected to draw out personal stories. As the narrative moves forward in time, it refocuses Gettysburg not as a series of troop movements, but as something bad that happened to people with feelings like you and me. You can see Jacob Sheads' case clock, which caught a stray bullet that whizzed into his home, and the metal sign that hung in front of William King's tailor shop, also perforated. There's the bullet-pierced table behind which a Confederate sharpshooter tried to hide, but died. There are the requisite relics to arouse the Lee acolytes (his gauntlets, coat button, insignia star), and you'll also see William Tecumseh Sherman's hat, which is odd because he was 1,000 miles away at the time, but I guess Gettysburg needs to keep drawing audiences with the best stuff, so it serves as America's attic. There's 50,000 more square feet of storage space in the center's basement hiding more good stuff waiting to be un-forgotten.

I was especially touched by the ambrotype of three children found in the lifeless hand of a Union man. He was probably staring at the image of his kids as he died. No one had discovered his body for days. Newspapers across the North published a detailed description of the picture—they couldn't yet reproduce images—in the hopes someone could identify him. His wife finally figured it out, and the country learned their adopted mystery man was Sgt. Amos Humiston of New York. His three kids, Frank, Freddie, and Alice, aged eight, six, and four, became known as "Children of the Battlefield," celebrities so beloved they inspired a popular song by a singer named James Gowdy Clark. Americans, eternally susceptible to momentary pop culture causes, donated enough funds to open an orphanage in Gettysburg where they moved with their widowed mother. It goes against the grain of our idealism to admit the story wasn't entirely pure: the man who spearheaded both the campaign to identify the kids and the fundraising drive to house them was accused of embezzling the money. Still, it's inspiring to think that although Amos died like an animal in a Gettysburg street, he would come to mean much more. He, much like Anne Frank, could almost trick you into believing death is never in vain. In fact, Amos became so symbolic that he became the only enlisted man to merit his own monument on the battlefield today. (And, small world: little Alice ended up in Glendale, California, where she died in 1933 at age seventy-six. She lived a few miles away from Orelia Key Bell and Ida Ash, those closet Atlanta lesbians. They might have even known each other.)

The actual National Park rangers are consigned to a little desk, barely noticeable beyond the phalanx of credit card-swiping ticket sellers. I ask one of the younger rangers if he missed the demolished Neutra buildings this facility replaced, particularly the old "Electric Map," a full-room diorama theatre studded with little lights that showed how troops advanced. It was a much-beloved and much-missed attraction among old-timers.

"That place was a firetrap if you ask me," he said, waving it away with a flick of his hand. Apparently millions of American tourists had unwittingly been on the cusp of fiery and cartological deaths.

I ask if the Gettysburg Foundation is nonpartisan.

"'Nonprofit' is a better way to put it," he said pointedly.

At least now you could get more for your money here. But before I could get another question in, he sidled away from me without a farewell, letting an older ranger take over our conversation.

"You won't see a visitor center like this anywhere in America!" the replacement ranger crowed. "I'll say even Yosemite doesn't have one like this!"

I didn't have the spine to tell him that with four times the visitors, perhaps Yosemite should. But I did ask why only the artifacts a guest can see at Gettysburg without shelling out money are a few minor cases of antiques in the lobby. They contain nothing but crap: weapons, brass musical instruments, and uniforms. The high ticket price means that even though citizens' taxes subsidize this National Military Park, they can't learn to connect with the faces of the past if they don't have the cash.

He considered this. "Well, there's a Resource Room," he volunteered. "People just come to go in there and do...all kinds of things." He was referring to an ancestry research nook where, I had noticed, only four of the ten terminals actually worked. It was desolate. A sign propped up beside one of the terminals encouraged people to visit the Adams County Historical Society instead.

But the gift shop, where all bus tourists were deposited after their rounds of the historic areas, was big enough to host two simultaneous basketball games. "Hello, sir!" a woman called as I entered. "Would you like to try some apple butter?" She held up a Club® Mini cracker she'd spooned with some. When I declined, she offered fudge. The nonedible selection was just as in your face. I wavered between American flag flip-flops, a printed bib that makes infants look like sword-wielding infantrymen, rubber bracelets reading YANKEE and REBEL, and Gettysburg golf balls.

One lime green kids' T-shirt had caricatures of Lee, Grant, and Lincoln pulling faces: "Making Funny Looks from the History Books!" it read. Maybe I can brook the impropriety of Lee delivering a raspberry to the town where he left 51,000 crushed lives behind, but I stand my ground in saying that Grant was nowhere near Gettysburg in early July 1863. He was 1,000 miles away in Vicksburg, Mississippi, but that didn't stop this gift shop from selling his image low and high. I finally selected for the most inappropriate souvenir, a shot glass fused to a little cannon. If I wanted to get smashed, I couldn't go wrong with the corresponding instrument of mass murder, and if I knocked back enough shots, I could approximate the numb sensation of annihilation. I took that one home.

When Steven Spielberg's *Lincoln* came out, the center pushed the Lincoln stuff to the front tables, but the swag didn't sell. For a long while, that serious stuff was marked down as overstock. But you can still have your choice of plush dolls, snow globes, paper dolls, shot glasses, T-shirts (Abe in a polka-dot bow tie, Abe grooving to an iPod), and USB thumb drives with little top hats.

"Lincoln! Number Sixteen!"

I jumped back from the table.

A shop clerk was greeting me with a smile a mile wide. "Lincoln! Number Sixteen!" he said again, thumbs up like the Fonz.

"He sure was," I replied.

"You like bobbleheads?" he asked me.

How could that be anything but a trick question?

He pressed on, grinning conspiratorially. "We had John Wilkes Booth, but Harold Holzer got upset so it got pulled," said the clerk, who wore a shirt stitched with "Frankie." "Katie Couric talked about it."

He was referring to the uproar that flared up when a local newspaper reporter spotted the Booth bobblehead souvenir and, for reasons of his own, raised a stink. That journalist tracked down Lincoln scholar Holzer to have him weigh in on the propriety of turning an assassin into a toy, and Holzer, who has presidential medals to defend, was quoted saying the bobbleheads were the creation of "a sick marketing person." The visitor center yanked them the next day. It made news worldwide because, you know, go USA.

"They don't seem to mind the toy rifles," I noted. "Or the Abe Lincoln USB thumb drive wearing a top hat."

"I know. It's crazy," Frankie agreed. "Thirty dollars for that USB. America!"

I told him I also noticed that bottled Coke in the "Refreshment Saloon" cost twice the going rate outside the center, but no one seemed to complain about that. "It's like the airport in here!" I said. Frankie chuckled knowingly.

Frankie's sweetheart cheer was irrepressible, and fortunately for me, he was as bored as he was garrulous. Visitors were down again this year, he confided. I sometimes find that I have a face built for confession. So he was eager to make time to chat.

His job was the product of privatization. His employer was not the National Park Service or even the Gettysburg Foundation. He worked for Event Network, a contracted operator of gift shops for nearly eight dozen tourist attractions, from zoos to science museums. It takes the stress of running souvenir stands off rangers and then makes the contract worth the hassle by upping prices. To give an idea of the fortune to be made in souvenirs, in 2009, the year after it joined forces with the Gettysburg Industrial Complex, Event Network was doing more than $100 million in sales nationwide. The outfit had cut its teeth cashing in on the *Titanic* merchandising craze in Boston in 1998, and today it takes care of sales at attractions ranging from Chicago's Willis Tower to the Mob Museum to the La Brea Tar Pits. Its website enthusiastically promises to "work on furthering the missions of our partners and spreading the spirit of GUSTO!" because "people spend more when they are engaged and treated well."

Frankie said he applied for the job not because he cared anything about history. He thought it would be steady work. So it was tricky for him to suggest the best Lincoln book, although it didn't stop him from offering unschooled opinions. On the battlefield, guides have to take a qualification test, but because he wore a name badge at the visitor center, Frankie said, people asked him factual questions all the time. He'd try to answer them, if he could remember the facts. If he got stumped, he'd stop pretending to be a docent and give them directions to the ranger desk. Frankie admitted he was envious of the rangers.

"They only work April to October. And they still make thirty Gs—on the low end!"

ILLUMINATED

Antietam

GETTYSBURG AND ANTIETAM ARE SISTERS, EXCEPT one became the homecoming queen of the Civil War and one stayed behind in the farmhouse and never married. If you're one of the millions of Americans who can name the first winner of *Survivor*, but not the victor of a single Civil War battle, here's all you need to know about Gettysburg's and Antietam's strategic roles: They were the Confederacy's two major attempts to gain ground in the North, and neither worked. They happened ten months apart: Antietam in September 1862 and Gettysburg in July 1863. Antietam still holds the record as the bloodiest one-day toll in American history—23,000 killed, wounded, or missing—while Gettysburg, which took three days, holds the record as the bloodiest overall battle—51,000 killed, wounded, or missing. Both were pivot points. After Antietam, Confederates abandoned hope of getting significant assistance from European governments, and once Americans saw photographic evidence of the carnage, Abraham Lincoln felt confident enough to play his trump card of the Emancipation Proclamation. After Gettysburg, the wobbly South retreated to its own turf and spent the rest of the war playing defense until it lost.

The two places are only an hour apart by car, so it's easy to combine them on the same trip. Except most people don't. In 2017, the silent fields of Antietam attracted 366,000 people while the flash and dazzle of touristy Gettysburg drew over a million. Gettysburg is Marcia and Antietam, Jan.

My first visit to Antietam was in the spring, and on

that day I began my tour, as I tend to do, at the visitor center, which is yet another National Parks ranch-style box doing an impression of a midcentury Palm Springs vacation rental. There was a cannon out front, as if you doubted they might forget.

Whenever you walk into an American battlefield visitor center, the exchange invariably goes like this:

Ranger: "Hello, and welcome to [Place of Death]."

You: "Hello. Thanks!"

Ranger: "Just so you know, there's a movie about to start right through those doors. Gives you a little background about [Place of Death]."

You: "Thanks! I'll go right in."

Do *not* go right in. Bone up in advance and skip the movie. The documentary is a time-honored crowd management technique. It keeps you from clogging the museum as well as progressing past a third-grade comprehension level so that your questions won't be too hard to answer. The movie is usually on sale in the gift shop anyway. When I first went to Antietam, there were two films. One was called *Antietam*, an hour-long, spare-no-expense production of painstaking veracity and sensitivity which the rangers proudly boast is "award-winning" and "narrated by James Earl Jones." I saw the other one. Mine, trenchantly titled *Antietam Visit*, is a stew of 1970s folk music and Playskool-red stage blood produced by the government, an entity not renowned for its film work unless it concerns beating back the Hun or avoiding venereal disease.

Antietam Visit is the most unintentionally homoerotic
Civil War documentaries an ironist could dream of discovering at a military site. It stars a slouchy group of soldier
misfits credited as "Warren's Brigade"—very plainly, area
townies shootin' a movie with their hobby guns on their
days off. Their acting abilities can only be described as
"porn caliber." While the narrator invokes the names of
commanders and lustily bemoans the "human holocaust"
that was upon them, the visuals stroke tension into a
fetish. The battle approached like a courtship between
two men: Lincoln was nervous, McClellan wouldn't
submit, but Lincoln had to get his way, something had
to give! Finally, to a climax of orgasmic, high-pitched
Rebel yells, amateur performers brandished their guns,
tumbled with each other in a cornfield, and clutched at
themselves while barely concealed blood packets popped.
As the men played dead in a pile, we were treated to long,
lingering hand-held shots of their still-breathing bodies,
entangled, wet, spent. "The blasted landscape around
Sharpsburg smoldered and smoked," said the narrator
with satisfaction, "chilled with the pitiful cries of thousands of wounded men."

The lights came up, and I saw we were in a concrete
room with a US flag standing limply to one side, like a
middle school cafetorium. I didn't know whether to
salute or smoke. After that, in another room overlooking the expanse of the battlefield, a ranger oriented new
arrivals in instructive detail. He obsessed over military
tactics for a half hour, pointing to every ridge and gully

in view and naming every pertinent commander of rank. The gun people and war buffs lapped it up. It took until the last sixty seconds of his talk, almost a footnote, to tack on what I thought should have been the lead: "We must make sure we never lose sight of the simple fact that each one of the 23,000 was a person, just like you and I. They had families, they had homes, they had jobs, and they left it all to go and fight. And for much, much too high a number of those men, their last days came out on this sacred ground."

Afterward, I chatted some more with Ranger Alan, and off script, he admits the losses were on top of his mind. "I don't think we would have an understanding of what it was like on September 17 when there were 24,000 people maimed or killed in 3,000 acres of land," he said. "I don't think any of us can visualize that." The nearest we can come, he said, was the Illumination held each winter. I asked him what that was. I hoped it was like a Renaissance festival.

The Memorial Illumination is the only day Antietam pulls huge numbers, and it's always on the first Saturday of December. On that night, the Hagerstown-Washington Convention and Visitors Bureau, with the help of a battalion of Boy Scouts, spreads 23,110 "luminaries"—candles in bags—around the vast expanse of the battlefield. Each light represents one person killed or wounded there on September 17, 1862. A few other parks, including Petersburg, Virginia, mount their own versions, but as America's bloodiest day, Antietam's is the most significant. "It's an abstract figure, but when you drive through and look at those candles and try to imagine what it must have looked like, what it sounded like," Ranger Alan said. "Some of these guys laid out here two or three days. The smells, the odors—there also were 2,200 horses killed. I don't think we can rationally get ahold of that. And these guys went home and wanted to forget all that."

When we're children, we don't think about death being an actual end. When someone dies, it's as if they've just become unavailable for a while. It's not until we're older that we realize what can't be gotten back. Something about the mealy language and grainy photos at these National Parks kindles our childish perception of death as something inconvenient, but not necessarily permanent. At death tourism sites, the deceased are still doing things—looking thuggish in ambrotypes, retreating or advancing, and being permanently gallant because engravings describe them that way. Come back tomorrow, and you can revisit them again. We even take our children to these National Park sites, which are purportedly all about death, and yet they don't usually come away disturbed in the least because there's so little to truly clue them in to the might of the darkness that descended there. They never see the bodies, and no one shows them the silent screams of bereaved parents.

I decided to come back in December for the Illumination. So far, none of the death tourism attractions I'd visited had made me feel very much—and there were so many left to go in more states. It was as if everything I had seen had been designed to distract me from the true cost of what had happened. I learned about the Hollywood-style fantasy of the afterlife, about generals and tactics, about competition between state memorial makers, and about the harsh realities of saving an economy by attracting pilgrims. But I still needed to feel what so far no place could lead me to feel.

The day I returned, I arrived at 4:00 p.m., and although it wouldn't be open for another three hours, cars were already pulled over on the side of the highway, lined up around bends and over hills into the countryside. This was the History Nerd's version of the ticket line for the new *Star Wars* movie. I had half expected a party atmosphere, with carhops selling hot cocoa and singing battle ballads at barbecue tailgaters. But everyone remained sealed in their vehicles, many of them left running. I waited two tedious hours behind the noxious emissions of a Chevy Suburban, reminding myself I still had it better than soldiers who once marched through the same Maryland farmland.

The wait was worth it. As soon as I coasted into the park, moonless and dark except for a constellation of orange lights on the grass, the enormity of the day's cost became tangible. Row after row, column upon column of candles stretched into the invisible distance like runway landing beacons, undulating with unseen farmland on either side of our slowly advancing parade of onlookers. When the road curved, another vista of pinpricks added to the galaxy, and another group fell behind and out of sight forever. I would have felt bewildered in an array of hurt except for the glow of taillights in front of me. I could stare at a single bag near the road and imagine it represented a kid with a name, and a mom and a dad, and opinions and fears, or I could fix my eyes on the middle distance where a thousand lights watched me pass, hinting at a thousand silent personalities in a wilderness of lost souls. On and on this went, mile after mile like a funeral train through the dark, as my mind numbed to the accumulated individualization.

Anyone who lived through Antietam was changed for life, but when we see it, we are not. The Antietam Illumination gave me a mathematical understanding, but the emotional heft was still too big to process. Soon, I could only absorb the generality of beauty. It was emblematic of the frustration I was encountering at every death site I visited—any clear visions of the blood-gushing horrors that happened here were once again obscured by the regal beauty of the art that was unveiled to symbolize it. At the last mile, a huge orange orb caught my eye through my window. I turned to see a sumptuously full moon had just risen, the precise same color as the candles, hanging mournfully over the fields. I tried to get a photograph, but some pictures are only for the soul to capture.

It took me about an hour to finish the five-mile route, and it would take well past midnight for everyone to get through. The CVB reported approximately 20,000 spectators rolled past the lights that night—as big as this event is, it's still not equal to the people killed and wounded at the actual battle.

I noticed Antietam's rangers referred to death with the phrase "heavy losses." It's a common one at places like these. It's a military term, a perspective of taking inventory. It is the language of business, not of bereaved mothers. When we talk about battle, we talk about "casualties," but we rarely say "destruction of human life," and we never say "murdered." We will never know the real number anyway. Men who appeared to walk away from the battle often died of infection a week later, or they curled up to rest in a forest miles away and were never found. And for what? The hope they were creating a perfect country that in fact would never arrive.

One of my favorite paintings hangs in the Tate Britain gallery on the banks of the Thames in London. Painting going in London can be tedious stuff—on many of its salon walls, a long procession of peacocky uniformed men, puffed and preening for their portraits, a glossy military procession of vainglory and public school legacies. But then you get to J.M.W. Turner's *The Field of Waterloo*. He visited the battlefield in 1817, mere months after the bloodbath that signaled the end of the Napoleonic Wars. As many as 50,000 lives ended at Waterloo, making it the deadliest man-made event in Europe, at least until then, so like Gettysburg and Antietam, the terrain became an instant tourist attraction. But Turner's painting isn't like the others. It doesn't celebrate a diorama of rearing cavalry and brave officers in fearless advance, or banners proclaiming nations to the heavens, as were the usual traditions of the day. At six feet by nine feet, it was the same size as the monumental military paintings that were being produced for large civic buildings, but its structure was all wrong: mostly dark, strewn under a light-weeping crack in a thunderous sky. Rather than the glory of battle, Turner focused on the ruinous decay it causes. Through the shadows, you see not brocaded valiance, but a heaped pile of mangled corpses, mounds of blank faces and limbs packed together with slaughtered horses and receding formlessly into the blackness, bleeding red. Instead of being bathed in a triumphant glow of victory, the dead are harshly lit by a torch carried by their own grieving wives and as they search uncertainly for the corpses of their young men. Turner makes no distinction between French boys and the allies except for their soiled uniforms. They are entangled together as like brothers, an imponderable vista of destroyed bodies and stillness. It's a haunted-house version of war's result, but Turner seemed to understand that glory is a fabrication that exists mostly in the retelling, and the reality is something much balder and more scarring. To shift a nation's border is a king's prize, but to drag a crushed son from a thicket of stiffening bodies is the price the participants pay. Turner had visited Waterloo as a death tourist, and that's evident. Once he laid eyes on the actual soil, he was unable to deliver a canvas equivalent of toy soldier heroics. War is nothing glorious. It's a mass grave for all.

The artist can share what governments will not.

We should let women write the signs at war museums instead. Our present mercenary overtones strike me as depressingly macho. And for Antietam's Illumination, it would be more accurate for Boy Scouts to strew the battlefield with vivisected pig meat as a Halloween-themed event to drive home the horror of what Americans did to themselves. But humans seem genetically programmed to believe that if you want to survive something wrenching, don't tell the truth about it. Pretty it up. This was proven by the hostile reception to *The Field of Waterloo*— ironically, the *Annals of the Fine Arts* dished, "we really thought this was the representation of drunken hubbub on illumination night." As overly twenty-first-century people, we seem to find observing other people's grief to be profane. The Antietam Illumination works because it acts as its own version of twinkly fabulousness designed to burden the beholder subtly, comfortably secured in their private car bubble, with the impact of human stupidity. I wish it happened every night. Maybe then we'd all get it. "War would end if the dead could return," wrote Stanley Baldwin.

A CHILD'S BOX
OF LETTERS

HERE LIE THE USES OF
REMEMBERING

"Commercial republics, like ours, will never be disposed to waste themselves in ruinous contentions with each other. They will be governed by mutual interest, and will cultivate a spirit of mutual amity and concord."

—ALEXANDER HAMILTON, *FEDERALIST NO. 6*

"Control of the presentation of history is so often the control of the future of a people."

—CHARLES H. WESLEY

"We perpetuate war by exalting its sacrifices."

—PADDY CHAYEFSKY, *THE AMERICANIZATION OF EMILY*

PATRIOTISM MISFIRE

Fort Sumter

IT WAS BARELY PAST 9:30 A.M. ON THE FERRY AND my fellow Americans were breakfasting on hot dogs and potato chips. I should have taken that as a warning.

As we disembarked from the ferry, a voice on loudspeakers reminded us to dump trash in the proper receptacles before participating in our heritage. The sign in front mixed up Os with zeros in a ransom note announcement: WELCOME FORT NATIoNAL SUMTER MoNUMENT.

Fort Sumter isn't a place you can just drive by, pull over, and check out, which is probably why my parents never brought me as a kid. It's an island—the last thing you pass as you leave Charleston, South Carolina, as you head toward the Bermuda Triangle. It takes effort to reach. For years, I wanted to see it, and finally, while I was in the South, I was able to carve out a few days' detour to indulge. I got to Charleston a day early just to reserve my spot, checked into a hotel—the Francis Marion Hotel—and went to bed nice and early. (As so often will happen in my tour of death tourism sites, something was making a reappearance in the story: the Francis Marion was the same hotel that refused to host the African-American legislator from New Jersey in 1961, dooming the Civil War centennial plans before they began.)

There's no point in pretending I'm not a nerd. You've figured that out already, and because you're reading this book, you might be as well. Being a nerd, I left the Francis Marion just after dawn so I could be one of the first people at the dock, and when I saw the brown platter of its nineteenth-century battlements rise from the sea on our approach, Old Glory blazing high over it, I felt like I did the first time I walked into Tomorrowland on the day I was tall enough to ride Space Mountain. Everyone in school read about the place where the first shots of the Civil War were fired, or at least they did when schools still taught American history. As a flash card refresher, Fort Sumter's importance goes like this: When Abraham Lincoln was elected in November 1860, some Southerners realized things weren't going their way for at least four years, and that would be long enough for him to tip the balance of power in the country. By Christmas, South Carolina became the first state to secede from a nation that, at that time, was younger than some people's grandmothers. By January, Southern states were seizing federal weapons from government warehouses, an act of war that wouldn't go unpunished for twenty-five seconds today, but back then, was permitted because no one seemed to think things would get too serious. That changed on April 12, 1861, when 3,700 South Carolinians began firing cannonballs at a Federal island garrison in Charleston's harbor. In retrospect, the white flag of the hastily surrendering US government was the checkered flag that sent the Civil War racing.

The thing is, no one died that day. Government being government, the miserable place had been under construction for about a half-century. Of the 128 guys toodling around Sumter that April morning, only a shade over half were actual soldiers. Instead, forty-three of them were just construction workers and eight were merely musicians, which meant that valorous South Carolina was actually declaring independence from some bricklayers and a house band. Because medleys do not make for effective defensive maneuvers, the Northerners had no game. The assault was over in thirty-four hours, and the handover was as cordial as the dedication of a city park. The Southerners strolled into the smoldering fort and stood by politely as the musical troupe finally got to do something and played some songs. So pleasant was the moment that the Southerners even let their defeated enemies pick up some loaded weapons for a hundred-gun salute. Given what Fort Sumter came to represent in hindsight—the merest mention of it motivated Americans to bray for the blood of strangers—it's almost unbelievable to imagine the jolly flag-lowering celebration the boys of both sides put on. It was quite the stirring kumbaya that, had you been there for it, might make you think the war would never happen.

Stirring, that was, up until the forty-seventh gun, when a spark ignited a pile of ammunition, mortally wounding two Union privates, Edward Galloway and Daniel Hough (who wasn't even born in America—he was Irish). The salute was respectfully called off three guns later and the injured Federal men fruitlessly rushed back in Charleston, a city with which they were supposedly now at war. It was particularly generous of the Southerners since up to then, the Union men had been known to occasionally lob shells at the city. So the first two official deaths of the Civil War, a slaughter that would eventually claim some 750,000 lives and radicalize the contours of the nation, were the result of a party foul. Worse, half the casualties were Irish, not American. None of these small facts stopped many in the South who wanted a war and needed symbols to power it. "The eagles of victory have perched upon the Southern standard in the first great battle of the 'Irrepressible Conflict,'" cheered the *Memphis Daily Appeal* just hours after the brotherly handover ceremony. The Northerners did their share of fibbing for politics' sake, too. One of the Union guys inside was Abner Doubleday, who forevermore went around calling himself "the hero of Sumter" despite his hasty defeat. Later on, he also bragged that he invented baseball, and most people think he didn't do that, either.

Sumter tore America apart—or, more accurately, angry people seized it as a symbol so they could tear it apart—and from the look of things, the National Park Service was worried about it happening again. Perhaps recalling the fort's résumé for mishaps, rangers had plastered the entry with photocopies warning us, as unaware of irony as only government can be, that it was forbidden to keep firearms in this garrison. A ranger issued additional verbal advice that hinted at dark consequences to careless explorations of the old brick ramparts: "Placing a child inside the cannons is prohibited as they tend to get stuck and removing them by the Circus Method is quite dangerous." This made me wish that instead of attending a reenactment of the Battle of Manassas, I could watch a recreation of whatever happened to necessitate that warning.

A young ranger named Brent addressed our incoming group with heavy import that suggested that his ranger-approved backgrounder script was actually laden with metaphorical warnings. "This is the spark that lights the powder keg that had been packed since the Constitutional Convention of 1787. Don't be mistaken. Eighty years and four generations of Americans failed to compromise over the issues of slavery and led us to this point," he said. "We the American people," he said firmly. "Let me repeat this: *We* the American people have elevated this place to the level of Yellowstone and even the Statue of Liberty in New York Harbor." Here he looked some of us directly in the eye. "She stands paramount in the hearts and minds of visitors to say that those who cannot remember the past are doomed to repeat it." With that stern admonition, he dismissed us to go have fun in the war zone.

There were enough sights to fill an hour before the ferry left for its scheduled return to Charleston. One of the most popular things to see was a huge bullet-shaped shell, the size of a loaf of bread, that was fired from a mile away and got permanently lodged in the mortar. The museum made a fuss over guns, and bombs, and cannons, like the Swamp Angel, and the Columbiad, and the "15-Inch Rodman" (which apparently will give you quite the pounding). Two wandering ladies ignored the guns, instead contributing to the story of our national suicide pact by loudly talking about someone they knew who had just spent $700 at a T.J. Maxx. It was that kind of place. Sumter's past was past. Now its role was no more fraught than to bask dully in ocean breezes day after eventless day, a lump of brick and cannonballs suited to unchallenging family outings and grudging field trips. The past has forgotten itself. Still, it was hard to fathom the blood that boiled because of this windblown sandbar.

Before I knew it, the ferry back to Charleston—run by a private-sector vendor, not the present-day Union—was loading to go. As I headed toward the gate, I flitted between inscriptions I had ignored on the way in, all of which were put there years after the fact. One lily-white marble tablet, installed by a group named the United Daughters of the Confederacy, praised the "Reverential Memory of the Confederate Garrison" who "Defended This Harbor Without Knowing Defeat or Sustaining Surrender." (They did get a lot of slaves killed, actually, although no one's sure how many because Confederates didn't count those as losses with quite as much Reverential Memory.) There were installments for the North, too: A metal slab listed eighty-three names of the Union defenders, including the band—a funny bunch to cherish, really, since these are the guys who fled from Charleston Harbor and let the war happen. Just whose symbol was Sumter—North or South? They can't both claim the same place as a victory, can they?

I was lining up a photo of that one, looking at names through my viewfinder, when my breath choked with a surprise blast of sharp smoke. I look up to see a man, maybe seventy, in a baseball cap and hunting vest. He was blowing cigarette smoke into my face. He locks eyes with me, but he calls out to someone else.

"Does this name look familiar to you?" he asks—in a languid Southern accent. Annoyed, I look back through my viewfinder—and through it, I see him pointing at a name on the Union list with his middle finger. He's not looking at the name. He's staring into my eyes, smirking, extending his middle finger in my photo.

I look up at him again, glare back hard with all the defiance anyone can muster while carrying a guide map. It must have been enough, because his eyes finally darted away—but his Southern middle finger remained extended into my shot of the plaque to the Northern defenders.

"What is that?" I say. "Why are you giving the middle finger to me?"

The old man shrugs, grinning with smug satisfaction, but now another guy, a younger one, pipes up from nearby. "What?" he shouts at me, striding over, as if he had been lying in wait to start something.

"He's sticking his middle finger out in my picture," I tell him, and as the words cross my lips, I feel like a tattling Yankee, the consummate dandy.

"Don't give me that," the younger man, probably his son, barks at me. He's instantly enraged, itching for a scrap. "He's talking to *me*."

Rather than be provoked into another North-South rumble at a National Monument, I head toward the boat dock. This is my country. I must behave even if it means behaving like a coward.

The old man, vindicated, half-sneers, half-chuckles.

"Fuck him."

Brokenness lies beneath the feet of all Americans. It is the foundation of everything. Abuse is in the national bones—it came by ship, grew our crops, and built our castles. Most of our poor white ancestors left their European homes to chop wood and fry rabbit meat in the dark of the Blue Ridge Mountains because of abuse back home. Why should we be surprised, in our era, to see brokenness surface now? The proof of rupture has been around us all the time, embedded in tributes and epitaphs, infused in the tears that are commanded of us wherever crying is called for.

But I have crossed over the fracture, although I look like my ancestors. I belong to the South, yet for some reason my Southern brothers think their definition of our shared heritage means something and mine does not.

The next civil war will essentially be about the first civil war, and there will always be people who try to seize a Sumter as a symbol to wage it. When death attractions become symbols for everlasting hereditary rage, as my next few stops proved to me, the aftereffects can make one's very self-image begin to blur.

THE MEN WHO CARVED THE MOUNTAIN

Stone Mountain, Atlanta

Photo: Tracy O'Neal Photographic Collection, Georgia State University Library

BY 1939, WILL O'NEAL'S SON, THE EIGHT-YEAR-OLD who looked down on the burned body of his father as it cooled in a makeshift casket in north Georgia, had grown into a man. His name was Tracy. He was now a photographer in Atlanta, working for the *Journal*, the very newspaper that gushed about his father's death and "the message of disaster" that prostrated his mother, Rosa. It's probably no accident that the boy who watched his father expire after being burned alive would ultimately choose to make his living taking pictures of hotel fires and the aftermath of car wrecks. He kept a darkroom at home, and he never allowed his granddaughter, my mother, to wander inside it, just in case she found herself idly repeating the sort of trauma that made him a man at the age of eight. Tracy also took pictures of things that seemed boring at the time, like company meetings and Oldsmobile dealerships—things now distantly mundane enough to feel adorable for the first time. His collection is kept at Georgia State University, alongside the papers of Georgia songwriter Johnny Mercer; thumbing through the photos is a romantic tour through moments and minutiae of midcentury America that would otherwise be as utterly forgotten as the ancestors we share. At least, most of the time.

Tracy freelanced, and one of his regular photography clients was a gentleman's club. It occasionally met about fifteen miles east of Atlanta at a place called Stone Mountain, which looks less like a mountain than like a massive grey loaf that God pinched out over the Georgia countryside. Tourist brochures name it "the world's largest exposed granite monolith," whatever that means. Indeed, Stone Mountain is a destination that is only enjoyed with a lot of dodgy qualifiers, and that's largely to do with its inextricable history with the gentleman's club my great-grandfather was paid to photograph.

This funny little club Tracy photographed was founded on top of the mountain on Thanksgiving night, 1915. Its rituals started quietly, not keen to make a public show of the proceedings. But by the 1930s through the 1950s, when Tracy was hired, it grew confident enough in its stature to commission publicity for recruitment purposes. Members even felt emboldened enough to distribute informational leaflets in downtown Atlanta. I have photographs of the members of this strange-looking group in full regalia, atop Stone Mountain during one of their peculiar little meetings, during which they'd build knee-high altars out of rocks, beat drums, hail with their left hands, and wave the American flag. As my great-grandfather's photographs attest, members did not always burn crosses and wear hoods. Sometimes they wore mitres, and as time went on, sometimes the crosses were electrified. Let no one claim that the Ku Klux Klan was not progressive.

Today, Stone Mountain, the one-time meeting place of the KKK, is essentially a theme park to all things antebellum. It's run by Herschend Family Entertainment, the managers of Dollywood in Tennessee and Silver Dollar City near Branson, Missouri. People come to hike, boat, golf, ride a tourist train, listen to a 732-bell carillon from the 1964 World's Fair that was donated by Coca-Cola, and tour an "Antebellum Plantation & Farmyard" that celebrates how dandy life was when cotton was king. If you were to receive your complete knowledge of that era from Stone Mountain (and don't fool yourself—many Georgia kids do), you'd think that prewar Southerners dressed solely in sherbet-colored hoop skirts and enjoyed a lifestyle rich in jam and petting zoos. At dusk, visitors gather round the side of the mountain, where a three-acre carved trio of Robert E. Lee, Jefferson Davis, and Stonewall Jackson is bathed with a laser light show "in Mountainvision." My grandmother took me when I was a kid. As the sun set, we spread a summer picnic before the holy trinity of Confederate commanders. Lee's horse, Traveler, was made to "gallop" off the side of the mountain via electric green squiggles. I can't decide if this constitutes a consummation for the Rebels or resounding proof they are forever consigned to the B list.

On a good day, a half kilometer up on Stone Mountain's rounded top, you can see all the way to the Appalachians, sixty miles north, leading KKK members to believe God had gifted them with an ideal vantage point from which to light crosses and warn Negroes. Which is what they would do: light fires on the mountain to warn all black people to stay in their place. Stone Mountain became the lodestone of Georgia hate, a beacon of segregation, and the fact that it happened to be in the middle of General Sherman's destruction zone imbued this innocent rock with a special subtext of Northern resistance. A hundred years ago, the owner of the land, Samuel Hoyt Venable, was a high-ranking KKK member sympathetic to neo-Confederates. In 1915, right around when *Birth of a Nation* got Southern tails wagging, he again invited the newly revived Klan to throw little barbecues on his mountain. At the same time, he deeded the north-facing side of the outcropping to a Civil War-commemorating women's group called the United Daughters of the Confederacy for a twenty-foot sculpture of Lee. Both schemes were in full swing by the end of that year. After all, the mountain didn't seem good for much else. Runaway quarrying left it too ugly to merit preservationist resistance.

The Daughters created a spin-off group, the Stone Mountain Memorial Association (SMMA), run by ladies who would manage the project. *New York Times* publisher Adolph Ochs—he who had helped consecrate the Southern battlefield of Chickamauga—kicked in $1,000. The SMMA elevated its endeavor by purchasing talent. It hired an Idaho-born sculptor by the name of Gutzon Borglum. Borglum, a man of no small ego, required a canvas no smaller than a mountain. He convinced the ladies that a twenty-foot carving of Lee "would look like a postage stamp on a barn door," and greedily went about revising their concept into a gargantuan neo-Confederate memora-complex that could be seen from space. His magnum opus would rival the works of Wren, Jefferson, and the Egyptians combined. His carved men, and there would be a militia's worth, would march in full figure across the side, and at their vanguard Lee, from hat to hooves, would be taller than a seventeen-story office building. There would be a giant Memorial Hall, a repository of priceless Confederate relics, a reflective pool, and sanctifying smoke wafting eternally from a shrine. "It will be bigger than anything of the sort ever before attempted," Borglum said. The ladies were predictably seduced by such a narcissistic vision, and to seal the commission, Borglum joined the Klan.

Anyway, before much could happen, World War I intervened, and by the time Borglum got back to work, the SMMA had lost fundraising steam. So even though the memorial exalted a bloody anti-Federal insurrection, the ladies enlisted the US Treasury to issue fifty-cent pieces cast with Borglum's design, which the SMMA then sold at a 100 percent markup. Ultimately, the blueprints were too lunatic. The SMMA soon discovered it could no longer control both the budget and Borglum. Chafing at what he perceived as meddling by his employers, he smashed his working models and then in true *Dukes of Hazzard* style, skipped town with the sheriff hot on his tail. The next sculptor, Augustus Lukeman, literally blasted Borglum's carving off the face of the earth and started over with a white supremacist paean more appropriate to a modest budget. He banged out Lee and Traveler in time for the sixty-third anniversary of Appomattox, which the SMMA hoped would jostle some donations out of Southern patriots. It didn't, and eventually Lukeman died. Even as the KKK frolicked in the lens of my great-grandfather's camera, the white supremacist megasculpture languished unfinished beneath their boots. To validate and perpetuate their flagging cause, they required the memorializing power of the camera that Will O'Neal's son carried and was not afraid to focus on them.

I'm hesitating here.

I want to think that my great-grandfather didn't know what he was doing when he photographed those white men. I don't know if he was actually a member of their club. Maybe being their photographer was just a gig, one of thousands of gigs he did, like taking passport photos and recording company picnics for corporate newsletters. Or maybe you don't get a gig like shooting the KKK without being one of them. Maybe calling it a gig was just plausible cover.

Or maybe Tracy was overjoyed by the verdict of *Brown v. Board of Education*. After all, among the family keepsakes we found a browning copy of the *Atlanta Journal*'s front page announcing it, saved for sixty years. That, and a campaign yard sign for Lester Maddox, who rose to the Georgia governorship by chasing black customers away from his Atlanta restaurant with an axe handle. Perhaps Tracy preserved those things as a warning to future generations, like me, of the cancer of racism—except he never warned me about racism or warned me it's a cancer. One of the only photos I have of my great-grandfather Tracy, who died when I was six, is of him sitting with me on a porch swing, reading a book—so I know he cared that I learned at least some things. When he identified his own father's corpse, he was only a little older than me in our photo. This old man who loved me—had he quietly been a part of that Klub atop Stone Mountain, taking photos to boost its mission? Would he have told me if he was? Would he have told any of us? We can only be sure of what people record, and then again, not even that, for the artifacts that survive are usually as posed as one of Tracy's company picnic photos, or a gravestone.

In 1996, fully aware of Stone Mountain's tortured history with symbolic fire, the organizers of the Summer Games bullheadedly chose to dispatch the Olympic Torch Relay to the summit on its way to the official cauldron in downtown Atlanta. The torch actually spent the night on top, so the flame that Muhammed Ali used in the Opening Ceremonies was the very one that burned over the footsteps of all those cross burners. A few days after that, the tennis, cycling, and archery competitions were held at venues around the mountain. I traced the route the torch took in 1996—aboard the rock's cable car. I took the Summit Skyride to the top and began a search for any sign that the KKK was ever there. It only takes a glance to realize that the top of Stone Mountain is no unspoiled wilderness peak. It's well used, almost as if a small town had been erected and pulled down. It's pocked with old asphalt, chain link barriers, and patched cracks, but on my visit, it was unmarred by context. Whereas every visitor to Uluru in Australia is warned the area is sacred to Aboriginal people, Stone Mountain, from which the Creek Nation was evicted in 1821, is merely a tall place. Aside from a few dull signs naming the moss and lichen, there were no historical markers of any sort. Stone Mountain as a modern tourist attraction was born out of hatred, so to me, the decision to not talk about it at every step is a missed opportunity to hang the racists, as it were, by their own nooses. The KKK is as much a part of Stone Mountain as Lee, Jackson, and Davis, but it's excused from the record since this is a family pleasure park. Lee, Jackson, and Davis, who inarguably killed more people than the KKK and more Americans than Hitler, are celebrated with the fancy light show.

I was rambling around the top of the mountain when a smiley guy in his upper thirties zeroed in on me and strode over, fearless of personal boundaries and radiating a zone of contentment that all of us envy. He introduced himself as Thierry. He announced he was taking a long period off work to travel across the nation.

"I noticed you down by the bottom," he said.

I asked him if he knew about the KKK and the cross burnings and the true origin of the carving below us.

"Huh," said Thierry. He might have heard something vaguely about it, he said, but he wasn't sure. He was staying with friends in Atlanta and he just wanted to go hiking somewhere, and they suggested he come here. To be honest, that seemed to be the main reason most people come to Stone Mountain these days.

"How about I take your picture?" Thierry said. "Would you like that?"

I said yes, that would be very nice of him, and he took a few. Then I offered to take a few of him.

"I noticed you at the bottom," he said again.

Now, I'm keyed into the nuances of museum signage, but when it comes to the signposts of courtship, I can be clueless. However, my own head would have to be made of carved granite to miss the fact that I was being hit on. I found deep symbolic satisfaction in the fact a man was trying to pick up another man in the very spot where the KKK burned crosses as a terrorist warning to all living souls for miles. There was a rich, rebellious closure to the reality of Tracy O'Neal's great-grandson casually declining homosexual advances in the same place where he took yearbook shots for the grand wizards, and it was a sign, I hope, that the bigots had altogether failed to win over America to their societal views. I did not take Thierry up on his invitation to dinner, because the irony was satisfying enough, but I did take his photograph for him.

The exchange, right there atop the South's great symbol lasting grudges against victims, made me realize how unlike my ancestors I had become. And I recalled, more than a little uncomfortably, something my grandfather, Tracy's son, had said to me once. I was probably fourteen or fifteen, a product of a society that had changed too rapidly for him to fully grasp. My grandfather was raised by the son of a man born during slavery.

"Jason," my grandfather told me. "You can do whatever you want to in this life as long as you don't marry a nigger and you're not gay."

What a legacy. I should have taken Thierry's number. If he'd been black, maybe I'd have blown him right there on Stone Mountain just for the total victory of it.

As Thierry hiked back down, I bought water at the little gift shop in the upper station. Betty, an elderly African-American woman with that lovely lilting Southern accent that reminded me of home, was behind the register.

I wanted to ask her thoughts about the KKK as a Southern woman of a certain age, but I couldn't spit out the letters. It felt woefully disrespectful, like asking her which episode of *Amos and Andy* was the funniest. I settled on, "What do you think about the awful things people used to do up here?"

"Oh!" cried Betty. "When I saw that program on TV, I got sick."

Was she telling me she only learned about the KKK and Stone Mountain on television? There was no way anyone, black or white, could grow up in Atlanta and mistake the symbolism of giant carved Confederate leaders. So I tried saying that I noticed there were no informational signs about that past, and although I had looked, I couldn't find any other evidence of things that might have been left behind up here. I meant altars, but again, I couldn't say it to this woman who only wanted to ring up my water without ripping open psychic scars.

Betty pointed out the window. "See over there, between that tree and the Skyride?" she asked. "There used to be something over there."

"Is there anything left?

"No, nuh-uh. They got rid of that there," she said.

"Now why would they want to do that?" I said. "This is history."

"Oh, that's because people come up here sometimes in normal clothes and then they take clothes out of their bags and want to do stuff. They do it over there on that side." She pointed to a place directly above the Confederate carving, where a chain link fence ran the length of the mountain. "They would burn stuff."

"They *do*?" I said. I was amused by the mental image of good ol' boys trying to smuggle fifteen-foot wooden crosses and jugs of kerosene through the gift shop, past the refrigerator magnets and the plastic sparkle mugs.

Something about my curiosity in the subject (or perhaps because maybe, to her, my surprise made it seem as if I was distressed that the Klan wasn't allowed), I just can't imagine what, abruptly made her decide to steer the topic about something else, and my genuine attempt to learn more was halted.

Back at the base, in Stone Mountain's main museum, the KKK is dispensed with quickly via a short sign labeled "A Dark Side of Our History: For forty years, Stone Mountain had the dubious honor of being the Klan's 'sacred soil,'" it admits. "The marches of hooded men and cross burnings continued until the state of Georgia purchased the property in 1958." That's when, in the wake of the *Brown v. Board of Education* verdict, the state of Georgia decided to turn the racist totem Stone Mountain into a pleasure park—and gather it around the military sculpture. They ran the KKK off the property, at least formally. Informally, white supremacists still rule it.

The museum neatly avoids celebrating the three Confederate figures on the mountain by discussing the sculptors instead. *The Men Who Carved the Mountain*, an eleven-minute movie screened at the museum, also dances around Borglum's spat. "He and his sponsors fell into a bitter dispute," it says cryptically. "What stands before you now," the narrator says importantly, is "a tribute to Borglum's ability to dream." It's the same word Disneyland uses to silence reality and invoke Walt. Just what that dream was, and what exactly he was doing to black people in that dream, is left unsaid.

As the public relations team of *Avatar* knew, praising the designers of anything is a sure way to deflect close inspection of its subject. "This distinct work has become a monument to the men who actually carved it," intones the film as if it was genuinely true. The nearby written exhibits introduce us to a wacky parade of Borglum's successors, all white, including Charles J. Tucker, the studly dynamite man; Cohen Ludwig, who was hired despite a mordant fear of heights; and the valiant Walter Hancock, who noticed amidst the confusion that Davis had been carved wearing the wrong hat and the horse, Traveler, had been given a mule's ear. He ordered them returned to accuracy, but no one possessed the budget or the will to carve anything lower than midhorse. Rather than calling him cheap for skimping on the legs, the film dauntlessly claims that the unfinished limbs gave "the whole work a greater sense of majesty and focused attention on the heads and faces of the heroes."

The Men Who Carved the Mountain skips the juicy truth: Georgians knew this was a KKK symbol. Even as Martin Luther King, Jr. invoked Stone Mountain by name along with his figurative mountaintop in his "I Have a Dream" speech, the enshrinement work persisted. The largest Confederate memorial in history was dedicated shockingly recently, on May 9, 1970.

A tiny sign in the museum mentions that President Richard Nixon was invited to cut the ribbon, but he canceled at the last minute and sent his vice president instead. This tidbit intrigued me. Why? The exhibition at Stone Mountain doesn't say, but the answer is in fact one of the more bizarre episodes in presidential history, present company excluded. Instead of taking an hour's flight to Georgia that morning, Nixon got out of bed at 4:40

a.m. and instructed his driver to take him and his butler to the Lincoln Memorial—the very spot (you'll remember, but he probably didn't) where King had cannily invoked Stone Mountain in his rebuke to the CWCC seven years earlier. What tantrum or penance he planned there is anyone's guess, but when he arrived, he found a group of students who had traveled to Washington to protest the outrages of Vietnam and the murder of anti-war demonstrators at Kent State University five days before. Insanely, Nixon got out of his limousine without protection and walked directly into the protesters' camp.

At first, astonishment eclipsed the tension as the addled president attempted to engage them with rambling cocktail party chatter. He dictated their exchange to his infamous tapes later that morning: "I said, 'I know you, probably most of you think I'm an S.O.B. but, ah, I want you to know that I understand just how you feel." Nixon blithely suggested the kids might enjoy vacationing in Prague and Warsaw because there they could appreciate beautiful architecture. "We're not interested in what Prague looks like," snapped one of the protesters. "We're interested in what kind of life we can build in the United States!" Nixon, with the same stubborn cluelessness that would eventually cost him everything, pressed on.

> I pointed out that I knew that on their campus, their campuses, a major subject of concern was the Negro problem. I said this was altogether as it should be, because the degradation of slavery had been imposed upon the Negroes,

and it was, it would be impossible for us to do everything that we should do to right that wrong. But I pointed out that what we had done to the American Indians was in its way just as bad. We had taken a proud and independent race and virtually destroyed them. And that we had to find ways to bring them back into, into decent lives in this country.

All this, mind, when he was supposed to be getting ready to dedicate Stone Mountain in a few hours. As the agitated crowd grew more confrontational, the Secret Service swooped in and whisked him away before he was torn limb from limb. ("I am concerned about his condition," Chief of Staff H. R. Haldeman wrote in his own journal. "There's a long way to go, and he's in no condition to weather it." He called it "the weirdest day so far.")

Because Nixon mentally disintegrated on the steps of the Lincoln Memorial, the emancipationist symbol where MLK inspired a generation with his invocation of Stone Mountain, Vice President and virulent anti-Semite Spiro Agnew was summoned to go to Georgia instead. It was he who officiated the ribbon cutting of a neo-Confederate icon dreamed up by white supremacists. Once again in my journey, history came so full circle that it's as tight as a noose.

Then there is this. The mention of Martin Luther King requires I tell it.

The year Engineer Will O'Neal's son turned thirty-nine, thirty years after the train derailed the family's male lineage, all of Atlanta society turned out for the gala premiere of *Gone with the Wind*. This MGM picture was tailored to the tastes of Atlanta: an epic about people who couldn't relinquish the supposed glory days of the Old South, and Atlanta was ecstatic that the rest of the country was apparently enamored with the Confederate point of view. Hollywood, which had sunk a ton into production costs and needed to whip up some publicity, shipped all its stars from Culver City to Georgia to make a big event out of the debut. The pinnacle of the week's festivities, other than the screening at the Loew's Grand Theatre, was a gala ball mounted by the Junior League. Hollywood's party was a huge validation for a city that burned to rubble at a key point in the plot, so being selected to entertain at the Junior League bash was a lot like being simultaneously resurrected and elected to the Homecoming Court. On December 14, 1939, an all-white audience gathered to fete the visiting Hollywood cabal. Movietone's newsreel was breathless about the night: "Grand march! Governors of neighboring states and notables from all the nation see Atlanta's elite and Hollywood's elect revive the grace and gallantry of the Old South!"

Black people were not invited unless they were the help or the entertainment. One of the community groups chosen for the gala was the "negro boys choir" of Ebenezer Baptist Church, the church run by Martin Luther King, Sr. on the east side of town. As it happens, Will O'Neal and the Kings were neighbors, if only in the geographic sense. Ebenezer was less than a mile from where Will lived, and where crazy Rosa O'Neal had accepted that dawn phone call announcing her husband's mortal injuries, but by 1939 it was somewhat on the "wrong" side of town, as Atlanta's elites might say.

A painted facade of a plantation house was placed center stage. And in front of it, ten-year-old Martin Luther King, Jr. wearing a slave costume, stood with his choir and sang spirituals to amuse rich white people.

Will O'Neal's son, Tracy, was there, too, photographing on assignment. He ignored all the African-Americans even though they were the ones on the stage. It's true that Tracy couldn't have guessed that one of those "negro boys choir" kids from the wrong part of town (near the grave of his daddy, the Engineer) would bloom into one of the most crucial figures in American history. To him, the black people were not participants, but pieces of décor. The boy was there only to gratify the white daughters of Atlanta in their pretty frocks, who wished they were, but never would be, as coquettish and as desired as Scarlett O'Hara. As a result, all you'll find in his photo archive today are a pile of shots of white girls' debutante dresses—awkward, all teeth, at the zenith of what would be anonymous lives—but little Martin Luther King, Jr., forced into a Bojangles routine in a ratty slave outfit, is recorded as no more than a smudge in the background of a few spare frames. I pored through Tracy O'Neal's photograph archive at Georgia State, but there were no clear images of young Martin to be found. Either the camera had been focused on the beaming girls or time had buckled the cellulose acetate negatives into rippled, mottled cards with no clear image. (The decay process is called *channeling*, and it's common among antique images. Americans simply don't invest enough to preserve their past. Many of Tracy O'Neal's shots are self-destructing this way, shrinking and smelling of vinegar, vanishing our origins a little more each day. In a city undergoing dramatic racial rebalancing like Atlanta, his subject of choice—prosperous white people the middle twentieth century—is, for the first time since photography began, not considered a priority for preservation.) And what a shame that is. If Tracy had been sensitive enough to record the black people, he would have captured an image so jarring that most people in our generation would know it as an iconic illustration of the urgency of King's struggle to rise above degradation and into dignity. It would be the only photo Tracy took that would still matter.

And then there is this.

Did what happened to his father cause him to direct his lens away from the black boys? When I tried to Google more articles about the accident, I didn't find any. But I did find notice of a nearly identical crash, seven years earlier, on the exact same stretch of railway, that sent my research in a new direction: "Three switches near the scene of the wreck were found to be tampered with, intentionally, it is believed. An attempt is being made to discover and capture the wreckers." That's why Will's last recorded words were "It was set." He wanted everyone to know the wreck wasn't his fault.

In his last breath, Will wanted everyone to know the truth of what had happened. Yet despite his dying act, his descendants still had no idea who was behind the sabotage.

So I traveled to the little library of Walhalla, South Carolina, to find more. Secreted away deep on a roll of rarely used microfiche, one of the local papers picked up the story of the train wreck a month later, in March 1909.

CHARGED WITH TRAIN WRECK

State Holds Evidence Against Two Negro Men

John Terrell, colored, was arrested last Wednesday morning by Sheriff Kay and Special Agent James Altom, of the Southern Railway, on a warrant charging him with wrecking passenger train No. 35 near Harbin's, on the morning of February 22. Sheriff Kay later arrested Jim Lewis, also colored, on a warrant charging the same offense.

John Terrell was eighteen years old. Lewis was even younger. They were just kids.

When I read this, I sat at the microfilm reader and welled up with anger.

It was the first time this information had made it to my generation.

No one, not my mother, not my grandparents, and not even Tracy O'Neal himself when he was alive, had said anything about two black kids being arrested for the murder of our patriarch. The death of Will O'Neal was always discussed as an accident, not a martyrhood.

All I could think about was how angry I was at my family for that. I wasn't angry that my ancestor had been murdered. I wasn't even angry at the two accused kids— that part was thrillingly potboiler. I hated the century of omissions—no one had ever told any of us that they caught two kids accused of deliberately killing Will. I was angry I had never been told. If my family hadn't known, which is hardly likely, I was angry they hadn't learned. When people unearth the ugly truth of their ancestry, especially African-American people, they're are often angered by the injustice they find. I was angered by the injustice of what was never told.

Another clip. The arraignment report. "A bolt which had been removed from the switch and which caused a freight train which preceded No. 35 to break a rail, was the cause of the wreck." Apparently the wreckers hadn't intended to endanger an entire passenger train. Whatever the motive, the official version of events was that they wanted to derail the cargo train that ran before it, but the first freight train simply loosened the unbolted rails instead. It was Will's locomotive, the one that came speeding after, that bore the brunt of the sabotage.

The "two negroes," as the *Koewee Courier* called Terrell and Lewis, were sure to "swing," since they had respectively been fired from the railway or had a family member who was. A conviction was a foregone conclusion.

To prove it, the newspaper brought up "the negro, Arthur Agnew, who wrecked a passenger train near Duncan's last fall...As he appeared to be half-witted, the jury recommended him to the mercy of the court, thus saving his neck." It closed the story by suggesting Terrell and Lewis wouldn't be so lucky since evidence was mounting every day.

Did the next generation carry out revenge in its poisonously polite, Southern way, by embedding it in their habits? If the people accused of murdering his dad had been white, would Tracy O'Neal have then turned his camera in the other direction and captured a world-famous photograph of the brilliant Martin Luther King, Jr. suffering the formative humiliation of performing as a pickaninny?

Because here we have a photographer traumatized by staring at his dad's scalded body as it cooled on a slab in a strange town. While he raged in torment and grief, police caught two black kids. In time, though without a father to guide him there, Tracy ended up a valued member of elite Atlanta society, not as wealthy as they and not as powerful, but embraced by the post-plantation aristocracy as an ever-reliable observer. And once in his social station, he picked up the best tool he could wield to remain secure among them, his camera, and he used it to turn the spotlight on the KKK, consecrate his white neighbors, and omit black citizens—in one case specifically, black kids—from the record of recognition.

How to add all that up? There are too many unknowns. Even my family, which is supposed to carve our own memorials, didn't leave any clues. Like Tracy's disintegrating photos, the picture of what shaped my family's attitudes and its course has been channeled beyond restoration. This is the essence of systemic racism in white America, where you can argue about the crime but, in the end, it doesn't really matter because you can plainly see a body lying there with a bullet in it. The only things my family's crumbs leave behind as evidence are doting images of that smug men's club on Stone Mountain and smeary blots that might be MLK in a despicable Sambo costume. Here is a sprinkling of dots, my origin tells me, and now I challenge you to connect the prettiest picture you can out of them. It's very likely you can't.

Not even when the dots are as pretty as the pristine tablets of the nation's most exceptional cemetery: Arlington.

"NOT THE LIE, BUT THE MYTH"

Arlington

ARLINGTON NATIONAL CEMETERY, THE ULTIMATE
American amalgam of myth and memorial, is one of the
only cemeteries on the planet with its own subway stop,
and that sets the tone: its enormity is a destination, and
I mean that spiritually, too. As I struggled up the wide
ornamental drive that rolled up from the Potomac River,
I eased into a sense of calm reflection despite the fact
the humidity was so extreme I was panting like a Saint
Bernard in a SoulCycle class. As I wheezed past, children
clutched their parents in concern. Yet so respectfully
reflective was I that I could not keep the impropriety of my
sweat-sodden figure from joining the more human-look-
ing tourists in the air-conditioned visitor center.

Unless we witness a death for ourselves, everything
about it must be conveyed to us. The method of it, the circumstances of it, the purpose of it, the valor or cowardice
therein—all of it gets filtered through someone else, be
it coroner, stonemason, or historian. That may be why
Arlington strains to appear neutral. Arlington's stones are
simple enough that they elicit whatever you want them
to, and arranged in such symmetry as to imply duty, not
personality. Here, it would be rude to hang a painting like
Turner's *The Field of Waterloo* and remind the bereaved
how they got bereft. Here, anonymity is respect.

About four million people come to Arlington each
year, and I must say that overall, it does an admirable
job of balancing tourism with decorum. In summer, the
visitor center is busy, but not in a carnival way—more
like an avoiding heatstroke way. I noticed the gift shop

reined in the tchotchkes and restricted itself to the usual souvenir spoons and books about dead presidents, and unlike so many death tourism sights, it wisely steered away from profiting on selling toy versions of the weapons that created its victims. There was no snack bar, and not even so much as a soft drink vending machine. The Department of the Army, which runs Arlington, rolls in cash, so it can operate differently from the historic sites run by the National Park Service, which is always under pressure to earn its keep. The Army has no need to license its vending to Coke or Pepsi, or at least until Congress decides the military needs to turn a profit. In fact, the only kiosk of note was not for pressed souvenir coins or candy, which you'd find at any battlefield. It was purely for the honorable purpose of looking up a name in the famous gardens of stone.

The Yelp reviews of Arlington National Cemetery may not prepare the tourist for the experience within. "The constant whine of the leaf blowers was a nice touch; really added to the serenity of the cemetery," whines Edward A. of Bryn Mawr, Pennsylvania, in his scorchingly sarcastic two-star pan. "My advice would be to...just wait until whoever makes the landscaping decisions gets canned... (really, has anyone heard of a rake? They're quite effective...Jesus H. America, we're so much better than this.)" In his one-star review, Jett P. of Durham complains there's "not a lot to do here," while M.S. of Barstow, California (three stars), suggests a more rigorous door policy: "Why are we charging Americans to park at Arlington? I came to pay my respects to some friends who died in Iraq, not to support your parking lot fund. Seriously, charge the tourists for parking, let the mourners in for free." You quickly realize that when it comes to online reviews, we mostly value places that stir the right emotions. Conditioned by a lifetime of entertainment, Americans appraise milestones of national pain as if they were consumer items. A memorial has to fulfill expectations to be worthy. Zagat, better known for restaurant ratings, once judged Arlington's "Appeal" as a twenty-six, but its "Service" only rated a nineteen. It also assured readers that Arlington is a "historically rich," "emotional experience" that "takes your breath away," which may not be the correct choice of phrase for a place for dead people.

Outside the visitor center, there was a stop for the kind of trams normally used in the parking lot at Six Flags or Wally World. A new "Tourmobile" pulled up at regular intervals to roll visitors past the major tombs. The Army contracts them to a company called Martz Gray Line, which collects $13.50 from every adult rider. Its website invited guests to "step into our nation's history," forgetting the entire point of the tram is that they won't have to take any steps at all. Trudging up the hill in one-hundred-degree heat would be nothing compared to the terrible things endured by the people buried all around me, so I walked. Boo-hoo, I was sweaty. It was the least I could do.

We bestill ourselves at military cemeteries. None of us wants to be the asshole caught yawning or farting. The solemnity, any solemnity, makes us feel connected to something stronger and more enduring than ourselves. As Abraham Lincoln implored in his First Inaugural, "The mystic chords of memory, stretching from every battlefield and patriot grave to every living heart and hearthstone all over this broad land, will yet swell the chorus of the Union, when again touched, as surely they will be, by the better angels of our nature." Angels conducting choruses must be why Arlington had to post signs on graves shouting in all caps like a forwarded email, "Please DO NOT TOSS COINS."

Arlington has three blockbusters. One is Arlington House, a colonnaded manse atop the hill, and the second, just below it with the same stirring view down the National Mall of Washington, is the eternal flame marking the gravesite of President John F. Kennedy and his wife, Jackie-before-the-O. The third is the Tomb of the Unknowns, where a few unidentified soldiers have been entombed since 1921. It's fairly unusual for a resting place in that you are required to arrive on time for it. The Tomb of the Unknowns operates on a schedule, like Old Faithful or Shamu. Every half hour, the guards change.

I wasn't expecting much out of Arlington's Unknowns ceremony as I took my place in the stone grandstand with hundreds of other people. My first reaction was pity. If I was slippery with sweat in my T-shirt and shorts, and believe me I was, the guards' discomfort in their white gloves, hats, and tailored military coats must have been extreme. Just as it had at the Fake Battle of Manassas, it took my misery to find my sympathy, and I was finally able to put myself in their shoes, their shiny leather shoes with a tap dancer's click. I felt awe, too and, I'll admit it, mild jealousy. Not one of them gave a hint of the slightest distress, no matter how much sweat leaked into their eyes or how the searing rays of July sunshine pried into their collars. I wanted some Gatorade so badly I would have sucked it off a football field after a game, but these guys, all of them volunteers, endured much worse solely to honor someone they had never met. The military is so peculiar about arcane symbolism it would make even a Mason roll his eyes—changing guards walk twenty-one steps, pause twenty-one seconds, and walk at precisely ninety steps per minute. Don't ask me to explain why, but weird dedication is inspiring.

This is what the review was going on about. You really do hold your breath while it's going on. The pageantry is stirring—the young soldiers perfectly put together, not a thread out of place, respect made manifest through tidy ritual. But if I can be meta for a moment, it was also impossible not to be moved by the fact we were moved. Everyone present knew there is no logical need to guard these tombs, that they are under siege by no enemy, and because we all agree on the symbolism of such an unstrategic act, the virtues become heartbreakingly profound. Both the soldiers and the tourists are unshakably absorbed in watching an impractical mania repeated to absolute perfection. The fact that the honorees, lying anonymously behind them, lived their lives without any knowledge they would be the focus of such trouble—it's moving the way it's moving that Anne Frank and Amos Humiston had no idea, deep in their suffering, that what they thought was pointless was actually destined to transform the world after they were gone. We can agree that many who lie in Arlington sacrificed more than most of us will, but seeing a few of the unluckier ones singled out inspires people to live to higher aspirations.

But as with so many myths, it's better not to inspect too closely. The United States has actually given up adding soldiers to the Unknowns. The last one was a calamity. Vietnam's Unknown Soldier was enshrined by President Reagan in 1984 despite the fact activists kept telling the government they thought they could figure out who it was. But it was an election year, and Reagan wanted his ceremony, so the Army was pressured to schedule the interment—horse-drawn caisson, 250,000 observers, TV cameras. The official who signed off on the order even took the items originally found with the remains and sealed them in the casket so that no one would be able to connect them to him and blame him. "We write no last chapters," Reagan said at the event. "We close no books. We put away no final memories." He was sadly correct. As insiders continued to raise the alarm, the ruse unraveled. In 1998, the government admitted its fault and 1st Lt. Michael Blassie, the twenty-four-year-old from Missouri who was essentially kidnapped after death by the US government and passed off as the Vietnam Unknown, was finally allowed to depart Arlington and go home. The Vietnam Unknown crypt was never reconsecrated. Instead, it stands in symbolism of all those missing in action. There have also been no American Unknowns ascribed to Kuwait, Afghanistan, or Iraq, and there won't ever be now that DNA identification is standard technology.

It pleases the soul to imagine that, thanks to science, those who make the ultimate sacrifice will never suffer the indignity of an anonymous burial again. But it's not so. Arlington's haphazard rate of identification error hasn't improved much. The culprit isn't technology—it's us. In 2011, an Army report confessed that 64,230 headstones in Arlington are possibly mismarked. That's no little figure—shockingly, that equals about one in four of its 320,000 graves. Thanks to inadequate equipment, corrupt contractors, the usual bureaucratic laxness, and an impatient zeal to venerate lives with the imprimatur of an Arlington internment, burial mix-ups are everyday occurrences. Getting your name spelled wrong by the nation you died for is disgustingly commonplace. Fully 25 percent of veterans did not even lie where their stones said they did—or their graves appeared to get their names wrong.

The year 2011 was a nadir for military burials in the United States, if there can be said to be a high point. That March, the cremated remains of eight unidentified people were found in a single mass grave in Arlington, summoning the FBI and raising calls for forensic testing. Then the news got worse. The Army admitted that 976 body parts from at least 274 people who died in Iraq and Afghanistan were not buried with honor at a military cemetery, which was unquestionably earned, but were tossed in a municipal dump in Virginia. The US Army responded to Arlington's mismanagement like the military-industrial complex does: by quadrupling its budget to $174 million.

We are attracted to Arlington because of its sanctity, for the brand-name value of being associated with it. Its mythic power is something we cling to, and that untold numbers of soldiers have died clinging to, knowing they had earned their place there. But the unforgivable truth is that its concept of sanctity is more theatrical than we allow ourselves to admit.

Still, only a sociopath would dream of desecrating the holiness of Arlington National Cemetery. With one notable exception: the man who started it by an act of desecration.

It was one of the nastiest, dirty tricks in American history.

Take yourself back to the early 1800s. When you look at Arlington from the Mall, the first thing you notice is its most central landmark: the Custis-Lee Mansion, the house near the top of its hill that rises like an invocation over the Lincoln Memorial far below. Like many Washington landmarks, including Lincoln's, it's colonnaded in the Greek style, but it actually predates most of its imitators by some one hundred years. It comes from the first, rough-draft generation of this upstart country. Martha Washington's grandson, George Washington Parke Custis, built it (or, to be more precise, his slaves built it, since it was a slave estate) with money he inherited. G.W.P. was lousy at business, but he threw a fabulous party, which kept the cream of Virginia society good and jealous about who his stepdaddy was. G.W.P. wanted to call his place Mount Washington, just to remind them a little more, but his family talked him into cribbing some Old World classiness by naming it after the Earl of Arlington, a blue blood from England. None of them had actually met the Earl given that he'd been dead since 1685, but he was responsible for the Washingtons' original land grant on the Potomac, gifted from afar. Who cared if the columns on G.W.P's showpiece estate were only made of wood and or that the *trompe l'oeil* merely give the appearance of marble? It *looked* rich. Arlington House had a borrowed pedigree in a ragtag new country—even its style, Greek Revival, is fake—but if you were connected enough to be invited to one of G.W.P.'s retreats, you came away with the mixed impression that Arlington House was a little bit royalist, a little bit classical, and a whole lot cool. It was, in short, exactly how the Southern gentry preferred to picture itself. This was the family Robert E. Lee decided he wanted to join.

On a June day in 1831, G.W.P.'s daughter Mary wed the bright young Lee right there at Arlington House. Lee was hot stuff, militarily speaking. He graduated second in his class at West Point. From the start, he got plum assignments. When he was thirty, one of them was to head out to the Mississippi River and figure out how to make it easier to navigate. His assistant for that assignment was a younger man, also a West Point graduate, named Montgomery C. Meigs. North of St. Louis. The two of them found a half-sunken steamboat, staked out quarters in the dry cabins upstairs, and spent their days living like a Huck Finn buddy fantasy or a montage from a romantic comedy: exploring, mapping, sitting by the fire on shore, and catching and eating catfish and pike together. "He was one with whom nobody ever wished or ventured to take a liberty, though kind and generous to his subordinates, admired by all women, and respected by all men," Meigs swooned in his writings. "He was the model of a soldier and the beau ideal of a Christian man." When the Mexican War arrived, Lee had matured into a formidable soldier and became the golden child of the War Department. He was securely on the presidential track, which naturally made him the number one pick for the Army when the Civil War broke out. Both the South and the North offered him the quarterback spot on their teams.

Jonathan, a young National Park ranger who helps look after the Arlington House grounds explained it, saying, "Back then, you would say, 'I'm a New Yorker' or 'I'm a Virginian,' *perhaps*, before you would say, 'I'm an American.'" (I noticed this ranger had the sensitivity to insert the word *perhaps* into sentences that might carry even the slightest tremor of controversy.) "A vast majority of people who lived back then, *perhaps*, would not even leave their communities or towns, let alone their states, at all, in their lifetimes." In other words, back then, Virginians were ridiculously puffed-up about their home state, always bragging about being God's favorite and forever prattling on about their ponies. Virginians believed everyone else in America was inadequate in comparison, when in reality, everyone else was rolling their eyes behind the Virginians' backs. This seems foreign to us today until we remember Texas.

When the Civil War broke out, Lee the Virginian wrote the government a perfectly genial, if evasive, resignation letter, praising the "uniform kindness and consideration" and "most cordial friendship" of his Army buddies, saying essentially, so sorry, but I'm going to be a Rebel and to kill you all now. At the last minute before mailing it, he scrawled an apologia in between the lines: "Save in the defense of my native State, I never desire again to draw my sword." That defense was more than enough to brand Robert E. Lee a traitor as soon as the postmark was stamped. Lincoln was particularly disappointed, as you can imagine, because he was counting on him to murder tons of people for the North instead. Once he made his choice, Lee and his wife, Mary Custis Lee, the spoiled offspring of G.W.P., packed up their stuff (mostly his wife's George Washington memorabilia)— well, their 196 slaves did—and ran for cover deeper into Virginia. Mary was much aggrieved to abandon her pretty flower garden, which stood beside her ancestral home, not to mention her populous slave cabins, which would be so hard to replace.

In 1864, the North coolly informed Ms. Lee that she could easily have her land back as long as she paid the outstanding tax of $92.07. That might have been the end of it, because they could afford it, but the government, as it always does, upheld the highest standards of inconvenience. It demanded she pay in person. The wife of the Confederate poo-bah couldn't simply stroll past enemy lines into Washington and expect to emerge again with a receipt, so she blamed her arthritis and declined. So naturally she didn't show up, the tax didn't get paid, her land was seized, and the Union army moved into Arlington House. It's a disillusioning truth that the boldest strokes of history are often clerical.

The new boss of Arlington House and its land was none other than Montgomery Cunningham Meigs, now US Quartermaster General, the very same man who once shared a wistful Mississippi steamship bromance with Lee. But Meigs was another Southerner, and he didn't care for the way he had manned up and stuck with the United States while Lee took his considerable manly talents to the Confederacy. In fact, like the petulant Messala in *Ben-Hur*, Meigs was frenzied over the breakup with his *beau ideal*. So on Friday the Thirteenth in May, 1864, he marched his men into his fishin' buddy Lee's yard and deposited a corpse there, with no clergy or bugle tribute to send him off and just a pine plank to mark him.

It was a dick move for the ages. Meigs used a dead soldier to vandalize Robert E. Lee's garden so that, from that point on, if he and Mrs. Lee should ever return, they would be forever reminded of what they did by dint of the fact there was now a body in view. You can see the grave for yourself today, upgraded to stone. His name was William Christman, a Pennsylvanian no more than twenty-one years old, and although he died of the measles and not of battle wounds—disease did much of the killing work during that war—the interment was unquestionably meant to defile Lee and his precious Virginia farm.

Time did not record how the Christman family felt about their son becoming the latest lawn ornament of some rich Confederate's yard, but the statement was made and Meigs was on a roll. A few minutes later, he buried young William H. McKinney, a Pennsylvania cavalryman, next to him. The next week, Meigs upped his game. On May 15, he marched his men straight into Mrs. Lee's rose garden, then in its spring bloom, and buried Captain Albert H. Packard, who suffered the disgrace of being shot in the head at Wilderness and now had the honor of being the first officer to fertilize Ms. Lee's flowers. A month later, Meigs declared their entire property a permanent cemetery. In all, 16,000 Federal men would be dumped at Lee's place, including Meigs' own son, John Rogers, and in due course, Meigs himself. It was like the most ghoulish prank in American history. And it worked: the Lees never moved back. In fact, Lee was radicalized by this turn of events.

And the sacrificed kids kept on pouring in, spilling out

of Mrs. Lee's garden, down the slope, into the abandoned slave quarters, and eventually constituting Arlington, the National Cemetery built on a slave farm, named for English nobility that never cared, and established less out of honor than out of spite.

The gravestones old and new undulate in speckled rows, placed without regard to the 1,100-acre estate that used to be. They ramble down the hill all the way to the Pentagon, the direction Ranger Jonathan indicated now. When they look out their windows, the people who send many a soul into war are confronted by the fruit of their work in precisely the way Lee never was, because he never came home again.

Ranger Jonathan led me around a tall hedge, where to my surprise a giant above-ground granite chest was discreetly hiding. Aside from the crimson brilliance of a patch of well-tended flowers, it was solitary and undiscovered feeling. The four benches surrounding it attracted no well-wishers. The tomb's side read:

BENEATH THIS STONE

REPOSE THE BONES OF TWO THOUSAND ONE
HUNDRED AND ELEVEN UNKNOWN SOLDIERS

GATHERED AFTER THE WAR

FROM THE FIELDS OF BULL RUN, AND THE
ROUTE TO THE RAPPAHANNOCK.

"Two *thousand*?" I said.

"And one-hundred-eleven," added Jonathan, out of fairness.

Just down the hill, the more fabulous Tomb of the Unknowns held a mere ten soldiers, was guarded around the clock, and attracted hundreds of people to its marbled patio every thirty minutes. It was like a country club down there. Up here, there were 211 times more unknowns crammed together in a single tub. Further proof that Americans have no taste for tragedy if it isn't seasoned with theater.

One of the reasons Americans dropped these unknowns out of memory might have been outright shame. Jonathan explained, "One of the most horrid examples, perhaps, of the difficulty identifying people: After the Battle of Gettysburg, 1863, July, in Pennsylvania, the battlefield was littered with not only people, but horses that had been shot and killed. And if a body was lying there for days in the heat, it would become bloated from the gases, and often when a soldier would throw a body into the ditch, it would burst on contact. In that situation, how do you know who's whom?"

To add to the mess, no Civil War soldier was issued identification. American soldiers wouldn't have that until 1906, when they were outfitted with tags, and serial numbers weren't added until 1918. Regular battlefield ambulances also didn't exist. Neither did government cemeteries that tended veteran graves. Neither, for that matter, did *any* system of scooping bodies from where they fell. As the foolish tourist party of the First Battle of Manassas had proved, we had zero concept of what large-scale artillery war would entail. Most of us organize our garages better. If you got hit, you would just lie there, dying and eventually rotting, while everyone else walked all the way home. Maybe someone tossed a few inches of dirt over you to mask your stench. If you were lucky, your buddies pinned a note to your coat, something along the lines of, "If found, please return to Vermont."

How bad was it? Farmers near Shiloh refused to eat the local pigs for years because the animals had been living off corpses. In other places, people commonly made a few bucks selling bones as souvenirs. Facts like that will certainly make you readjust your perception of what war is—as well as the depths you thought your fellow Americans were capable of sinking to.

After Meigs had found a way to legally legitimize the desecration of the Lee estate, he moved to legitimize the graves of all his missing Union soldiers. There were a lot. Most of the war had been fought on Southern farm-land—remember, they weren't considered battlefields until after the battle; in reality, people just collided in people's yards and went at it—and many of those North-ern bodies had to be left behind to collect in safer times. Soldiers would jot little notes about where they remem-bered their friends going down, and if they were shot next, someone would have to rifle through his pockets for those notes next and then jot down one more note. After the war, Meigs lobbied for an exploratory group to fan deep into the South and dig up the hundreds of thousands of corpses that could possibly be found, no matter how intermingled beyond recognition, no matter how looted by sore losers, and no matter if scavenging animals had run off with portions of them.

As Drew Gilpin Faust chronicles in her stomach-churning *This Republic of Suffering*, the United States government spent years recovering whatever body parts it could—but it did next to nothing for the Southerners who were similarly abandoned up north. For all of General Grant's jibber-jabber about, "Let us have peace," that compassion didn't extend to helping Southerners rest in it. You can imagine how furious all these stray sons made Southerners who couldn't afford to be reunited with the boys they loved. As late as 1924, some Confederate graves in Elmwood Cemetery in Columbia, South Carolina were still marked like paupers, with nothing but rotting wooden planks.

It's estimated that half of the Civil War's dead lost their identity this way. That was no easy number to calculate. Given our current estimates of 750,000 dead, that's 325,000 Americans, or roughly the entire male population of Fort Worth, Texas, or Charlotte, North Carolina, decaying nameless in ditches while their families wondered forever what their fates had been. The Civil War manufactured anonymity in volume. "When one person dies, it's a tragedy," said Joseph Stalin. "But when a million people die, it's a statistic." At Arlington, we are all Stalinists.

America fixed its honor problem by turning Arlington into the ultimate stage for the perpetual drama of sanctification. Requirements for an Arlington burial are rigorous. On paper, the only four ways to be granted a plot are if you die on active duty, serve at least twenty years for the armed forces, are an elected official or a high-level federal appointee who once served on active duty, or you earn one of the elite medals such as a Purple Heart. Your spouse can be buried with you, and so can your minor children, and as of 2013, your same-sex partner.

But as with all things American, you can also know the right palms to grease. You can blag your way past Arlington's black velvet rope if you have the right connections. Boxer Joe Lewis never saw combat, but Reagan waived the military requirement for his burial because they appeared together in 1943's *This Is the Army*. Jack Valenti was the guy who invented parental ratings for Hollywood movies and then spent thirty-eight cushy years in a screening room, doling out Rs and Gs as head of the Motion Picture Association of America. Valenti didn't qualify for a full-sized plot since he had only served as a former bomber pilot and a special assistant to President Lyndon Johnson, but he had one thing going for him: he was on Air Force One on November 22, 1963. That's him in the famous photograph, behind a dazed Johnson as he swears in, squeezed against the side of the fuselage. (He's right above Judge Sarah T. Hughes' head as she administers the oath of office. She couldn't find a real Bible, so she's using a Roman Missal she found by JFK's cot on the plane, which means one American president was sworn in like a Catholic, and—surprise—it wasn't Kennedy.) In Valenti's twilight years, he booked a few strategic lunches with George W. Bush's defense head, Donald Rumsfeld, whom he charmed into bending the rules for an Arlington burial. Thus the Hollywood big shot parlayed his photobomb of an American milestone into an eternity as a background player. He's buried near Kennedy's well-visited Eternal Flame. So are Robert F. Kennedy, Edward Kennedy, and Jackie O., who found herself in the enviable position of helping design her own world-class resting place years before her own death.

Before 1963, about two million people visited Arlington a year. In 1964, after JFK's arrival, it drew an incredible seven million, all of whom were drawn like moths to his Eternal Flame. That, set in a ring of Cape Cod fieldstone, was lit in 1967 and took a while to get right. In the first days, stewards jerry-rigged it out of a luau torch attached to tubing that carried gas from a tank hidden in the bushes outside Arlington House. When my parents brought me to see it as a kid, I remember turning to them and asking if they were sure the fire never went out. My father promised it never did. My child's brain found that reassuring, and I guess lots of presumably mature adults feel the same, because there's always a crowd. It's a dirty secret that the Kennedy's Eternal Flame is always going out, and we're always rushing to light it again as if nothing happened. My favorite story from the '60s comes from Robert M. Poole's *On Hallowed Ground*: "One woman brought a bottle of holy water, shook it over the eternal flame, and watched in horror as the cap flew off and doused the fire. A solider from the Old Guard, standing nearby, whipped out his Zippo, restarted the flame, and reassured the visitor, 'There, ma'am,' he said. 'And I won't tell if you won't tell.'" Today there are built-in systems that monitor the flame and spark reignition should it die.

That flame, even more than the Unknowns, has become the icon of the cemetery. It flickers on a terrace below Arlington House that commands a breathtaking vista of the National Mall, subtly informing visitors by its perch that it's more important than just about everything else on the grounds, which fortunately no one seems to interpret as an insult to all the surrounding servicemen who died in war. The touristic obsession with John F. Kennedy's flame, and the nonsensical implication that it's as undying as his patriotism makes me think of one of my favorite quotes by him. He said it at Yale University's commencement the year before he died:

> The great enemy of the truth is very often not the lie—deliberate, contrived, and dishonest—but the myth—persistent, persuasive, and unrealistic...[Belief in myths] allows the comfort of opinion without the discomfort of thought.

Needless to say, that is not one of the quotes carved into his elliptical terrace. It would be bad for souvenir sales.

It was hard for me not to think about his message as I

observed the ever-changing scene at his flame at Arlington. Now and then, a fresh salvo of tourists burst into the plaza from a newly arrived tram, spent three or four minutes scrambling and jockeying to take photos with the best view, and then hustled back to be driven away to the next stop. None of them paused for so much as a minute's reflection. They didn't seem to be paying respects as much as snatching proof for a scavenger hunt.

For me, there's no grander political structure in Arlington than the Confederate Memorial. I know because it tells me it is. Most tourists don't even reach it, partly because they're doubled over with cramps by the time they locate JFK. It takes sleuthing to find the Confederates. I found the South assigned to a spot hidden by the quiet back wall. Technically, by its own aspiration, the Confederate States of America was another country and its men, my ancestors among them, died for the right to be foreigners. In doing so, the Confederates seized federal courts, guns, and military installations, which are not activities that typically earn you red carpet treatment in Arlington. Still, every May, the sitting president usually sends a wreath to their graves, which I call good sportsmanship.

Arlington's Confederate Memorial stands like a wedding cake in metal, nearly thirty-three feet tall, ringed with busy friezes and topped with a robed female figure bearing a laurel wreath of peace. Its ostentatious flourishes brazenly flout the decorum of the rest of the monuments in the park, like a drag queen crashing a Shriner's meeting, which makes me like it even more. But it plays to an empty house. The grass around it is poorly tended and patchy, the graves encircling it freckled, and no one else except me was anywhere nearby, though occasionally a tram scooted by in the distance. The sense of abandonment made me feel a little sorry for it.

But when I looked closely, I saw a lot that surprised me. A foundry mark revealed it was made in Berlin. That seemed odd, but in truth it mostly seems sinister in retrospect since many turn-of-the-century statues and parlor knickknacks were forged in Berlin, which had the equipment that was later turned against us. The life-size bronze friezes encircling the column are as idealized as an Uncle Remus version of my old Georgia home; in one panel, a soldier heading off to war pauses midmarch to kiss the baby reaching from the arms of his Mammy. In another, a black man marches alongside the white Rebels. The modern Rebel will doggedly repeat his learned catechism that claims African-Americans fought for the South, but in fact, scholars still have found no evidence of a single enlisted black man in the Confederate army. We can partly blame images like the memorial in Arlington for helping perpetuate the increasingly fuzzy memory of where black men were actually commanded to serve. *The*

Confederate and Neo-Confederate Reader, a companion tract published for the Memorial's dedication (which was at the time termed a "Monument"), admits both images deliberately correct our perception of race relations: "The astonishing fidelity of the slaves everywhere during the war to the wives and children of those who were absent in the army was convincing proof of the kindly relations between the master and slave in the old South," it said. Barely concealing a lust for agitprop, it called that fidelity "a story that cannot be too often repeated to generations in which *Uncle Tom's Cabin* survives and is still manufacturing false ideas as to the South and slavery." As for the black marcher among troops, he is explained as "a faithful negro body-servant following his young master." The sculptor, the esteemed Moses Ezekiel, a Jewish Confederate veteran, is heralded as "writing history in bronze." That's what the Memorial's backers said when they introduced their work to the public. It was designed to be a rebuke.

So the Confederate Memorial permanently enshrines the image of the faithful Negro on the sacred ground of Arlington National Cemetery, a place that was consecrated during a war waged to correct such racial manipulation. This was erected in 1914, a full half-century after emancipation, by which time you'd hope cooler heads would prevail. All of the graves around it were plucked from soil elsewhere and moved here some two generations after the war's conclusion. Three American presidents had a hand in bringing this to Arlington:

President William McKinley, hero barista who authorized the reburial of Confederates "in a spirit of fraternity"; President William Howard Taft, who authorized the memorial itself; and President Woodrow Wilson, who attended the final ribbon cutting.

For political reasons, none of the three had a desire to edit the visual rhetoric of the South, least of all Wilson, who was perhaps America's most gleefully racist president. Even as he presided over the opening ceremony of this monument, he was working behind the scenes to segregate the federal government. Wilson grew up in Augusta, Georgia from 1858 to 1870, the roughest years of the war and Reconstruction. His father, a pastor, became a chaplain for the Confederate Army, and after the family church was seized by the CSA for a hospital, his mother attended to the solemn influx of mangled soldiers. From age four to fourteen, young Wilson helplessly witnessed a daily parade of suffering, grief, privation, and despair. That kind of upbringing tends to leave a mark. At the Monument's dedication, at which Wilson began the long tradition of the presidential wreath laying, he declared himself "proud that I should represent such a people." Less than a year later, he attended a special White House screening of the epic picture *The Birth of a Nation*, in which the heroic Ku Klux Klan rescues the South from those wicked, uppity Negroes—so much for the "faithful negro" depicted on the side of the memorial. Afterward, Wilson was said to have rendered the most infamous review in filmdom, which helped it become a blockbuster and fire up black rights movements: "It is like writing history with lightning, and my only regret is that it is all so terribly true." Whether written in bronze or lightning, Wilson's two approved depictions of Southern history settled personal scores from his ruined childhood.

Wilson's upbringing also fed into his work in brokering an armistice at the end of World War I. He won the Nobel Peace Prize despite the fact that the United States' plan was, at the last minute, swapped for a peace deal that caused Germany so much suffering, grief, privation, and despair that it led it to World War II. The Treaty of Versailles to a German was a lot like Reconstruction for a Southerner, and it fomented the same lingering resentments. So, in a manner of speaking, the fallout from the American Civil War mirrors the spark of World War II, and Wilson's praise of the Confederate Memorial in Arlington could be seen as a bridge between the two catastrophes. The fact it was sculpted by a Jew and cast in Berlin just makes the knotted-up irony even richer and sadder.

The Memorial also sticks out because the graves around it have pointed tops, out of sync with the thousands of other Arlington stones that are gently rounded. An old myth claims Confederate headstones were pointed to keep elderly Yankee veterans from sitting on them, but that's a stretch because the angle is so slight. The design was adopted Congressionally in 1906, so in all honesty they could just as easily be said to point up like Klan hoods; squint and it looks like a rally. But more noticeably, the stones don't align in regimented rows consistent with the rest of the grounds. They rebuff Arlington by closing ranks in a circle, henge style, as if the Confederate sculpture is an altar to which they bow. There are only 267 graves, a token really, dug up and relocated some forty years on, but even in death, these Rebels refuse to lie in symmetry and harmony with the Federals, mourning once again transformed permanently into a political act. Gravestones, no matter where they are, are already little statements of indignation. When people we love die, we don't just leave the corpse behind and get on with things, the way animals do. We mark them with something that will tell the world that our person mattered and we'd rather they were still here.

Even though America's Civil War had ended in 1865, the memorial boom took decades to gestate. Tourists visit battlefields by the millions, but few look closely at what they actually see there. They assume the monuments went up by mourning families in the few years after peace was declared. But if they took the time to inspect the dates that are actually carved on them, they'd be shocked to see that nearly none of them went up in the 1870s and 1880s. Construction didn't gather speed until the second generation following the bloodshed, thirty years after the last bullet, by which time the war had calcified into a legend. Arlington's Confederate cemetery wasn't dedicated until three weeks before the assassination of Franz Ferdinand and the stirrings of World War I.

The turn-of-the-century memorial boom is usually explained away, even by park rangers who ought to know better: Americans wanted to honor veterans while there were still some left to tribute. This is partly true, but it's a drastic oversimplification of complicated and strategic political movements. In the 1890s, as American concerns turned imperial and international, domestic tensions between the North and the South were at low ebb, providing an ideal opening for activists to slip some revisionism onto our battlefields (and into Arlington) using the Trojan horse of "honor." The American system depends on uneasy coalitions of rivals, so if you want things to function, how else can you assert your enemy is unrighteous without openly saying so?

The last detail on the Confederate Memorial is easily missed because it reads like something we've seen before on a hundred other sculptures:

TO

OUR DEAD HEROES

BY

THE UNITED DAUGHTERS

OF THE CONFEDERACY

VICTRIX CAUSA DIIS PLACUIT

SED VICTA CATONI

What appears to be standard statue fine print is, when translated, some pretty nippy stuff: "The winning cause pleased the Gods, but the conquered cause pleased Cato."

To decipher this one, you have to know something about ancient history, which is doubtful if you grew up American, but once you do, you realize they're giving the middle finger in Latin. Cato was a Roman politician from a noble era of the Empire who was noted for his stubbornness and his hatred for corruption. He represents the South, vanquished, but still superior to the pagan North. So the South might have lost, it says, but it's still nobler than the North. *You are not forgiven.* Which is why the gravestones refuse to line up with the rest of Arlington's. The section was dedicated on what would have been the birthday of Confederate president Jefferson Davis.

The sculpture was a veiled threat of an insurrection that was merely dormant, a romance poem carved with venom, a time bomb placed on the Union's holiest altar. Who are these United Daughters of the Confederacy, or UDC, who managed to get protest art this insolent enshrined in Arlington, the most sacred resting place of their enemy?

"SOUTHERN TRUTH"

The Confederate Monuments

HISTORY, IT IS SAID, IS WRITTEN BY THE WINNERS.

This actually isn't true.

History is written by the people most eager to write it.

We're also told that mankind's story has always been essentially patriarchal. But women have done more—far, far more—to shape the landscape of American death tourism than any other group. Put simply, the women of the South—allegedly on the losing side, allegedly powerless—directed the most powerful public relations movement that America has known.

The United Daughters of the Confederacy sounds like a quaint circle of tea socials and quilting bees. But this was no quixotic Red Hat Society. It was a memory industry. Its turn-of-the-century handiwork was so effectively installed in American landscapes, textbooks, debates, even Arlington, that most of the time we no longer even notice it. The fact you've probably never heard of the UDC only testifies to these women's brilliance. Under the cover of a docile-sounding ladies' club, the UDC imposed the Memorial Age at death tourism sites. It redefined us. Most insidiously, the UDC managed to omit the Negro (their preferred term) from the story of a war that had ultimately been fought over them. Whatever fleeting victories of reinvention African-Americans had seen during Reconstruction were concertedly reversed, remaking them into passengers on the white man's journey of righteous redemption, or, like the black marcher on Arlington's Confederate Memorial, faithful allies of their beloved owners. Whereas black Americans were suddenly being educated and elected to office nation-wide, Southern memorials often put them back into service, silent and supportive.

It takes protracted and focused effort to turn something horrific into something glorious. So the ladies started small. In the years after the war, the surviving women of the South formed Ladies Memorial Associations. The LMAs tidied up their broken land under the watchful eye of the Reconstruction government, doing work that most people agreed was necessary. They retrieved far-flung corpses, gave them Christian burials, and planted a few inoffensive cenotaphs and obelisks, usually using uncontroversial iconography such as eagles, which they solemnly decorated each year. The first one is thought to have gone up in the spring of 1867 in a cemetery in Cheraw, South Carolina. As a UDC historian portrayed it nearly forty years later: "The faint-hearted (and the most of them were men) decried the undertaking, saying the United States would never allow such honor to be conferred on Confederate dead." But no one did stop them, victim complex notwithstanding, and in fact, the column is still there. When it became clear that Southern resentment could be successfully channeled into monument building in scale, the Confederacy, which had essentially gone underground in 1865, reemerged as a kind of shadow organization dedicated to orchestrating installations by the thousand.

Cowed by Reconstruction's watchful regulations, the first projects set a tone by pushing boundaries with subtle messages; the Cheraw memorial's east side pictures a falling tree with the darkly promissory legend "Fallen, but not dead." Usually, though, the LMAs dabbled in nothing more controversial than veterans' aid. On the surface, their deeds were nonpolitical stuff, and it gave ladies something to do. Underneath, a resistance movement bubbled, developing verbiage that federal overlords would find palatable and perfecting unassailable schemes to accomplish their work. It's such a perfect metaphor for the character of the United States, isn't it? We pretend like we're calm and righteous even as under the table, we frantically knife each other in hatred.

Northerners had no interest in slowing the UDC's efforts—the country had seen enough conflict, the reasoning went, so let them mourn their defeat as long as they accept it. This was the state of the re-United States, limping along in awkward détente like when you dump a guy but pretend you'll still be friends. In that way, the South was like a bad roommate that the North couldn't get off the lease. During Reconstruction, the great slave uprising that haunted Southerners with centuries of sleepless nights had finally happened, and now their property wore suits, read books, and passed laws.

After atrocities in any nation, a crucial part of a society's survival is a forgiveness of the oppressors—many political scientists say, for example, that South Africa's insistence on holding and publishing its Truth and Reconciliation Commission in the months after the end of apartheid was a keystone in holding back revolutionary bloodshed. In America, though, true reconciliation was never achieved—only the pretense of it. Other nations slap the disagreements out of each other for decades, but the American system, depending on mutual compromise, discouraged ongoing violent recriminations—even the most high-ranking Rebels resumed respectable lives—so people quickly learned to embed hatreds within gamesmanship as they quietly nursed resentment of thwarted ideals among their own kind. Reconstruction drove all confessions underground, and both sides only pretended to be over the Civil War as a way to placate the other side and prevent future flare-ups. The mutual false appearances the North and South presented to each other were ancestors of the now-familiar bubbles that America's two camps occupy today—one side feeling wronged and oppressed but refusing to show weakness, the other incredulous that their opponents won't rejoin them in full diversity.

Taking full advantage of that climate, the women's groups became ingenious. The South required its own information ecosystem for processing its defeated condition, and the women's groups cultivated it. By the 1890s, Reconstruction, the grand effort to enforce a "New South" had fallen apart, and federal policing of Southern self-expression had been retracted. But because the economy remained in shambles, the ghost of better times loomed large. The people most traumatized by the war began to die off, leaving behind children who were embittered by the ongoing denigration of a lifestyle that, thirty years on, was still a shadow of its former vitality. The United Daughters of the Confederacy was founded in 1894 by a new generation of motivated Southern socialites bent on rehabilitating the reputation of their despondent parents who raised them in privation. The UDC women were too young to remember much of life before the war, but they could glimpse its idealized sweetness in their families' lore and taste the sourness of the wreckage in the broken lives of the people they loved. They grew up in ashes and hated the people they blamed for lighting the fire.

To call these women merely determined would be patronizing to both their breeding and their brains. Their war was as total as Sherman's. The essence of their message went like this:

> Southerners once lived in a harmonious and functional society of whites and blacks working together, and they believed in the Constitution as the Founding Fathers wrote it.

> They died for those principles when the North tried to force them to do things that weren't in that Constitution.

> The battle was not directly about slavery, but a battle to maintain a state's rights to preserve its own economic system.

> The phrase "New South" means nothing, because there was nothing wrong with the old one.

If you've heard this capsule ideology before, it's because the UDC, and a few lesser groups, so brilliantly fused it to the national narrative that even astute historians gave it berth. It was a textbook rationale; the children of the South declared themselves correct, because if they weren't, by God they'd be wrong, and the slaughter of 750,000 would be on their heads. Instead of focusing on the cruel reality of the situation before and during the war, they focused on the pure idealism of principles—a common disconnect still prevalent in a country that was founded on pure idealism. The Daughters' principles are now known as "the Lost Cause," and it was so effective that only now are people questioning it openly.

By 1896, when the *Plessy v. Ferguson* verdict threw its Supreme Court blessings over the art of segregation, the UDC was supercharged with boldness. The women's groups' most salient work was in partisan memorials. Its postcard-ready monuments converted many a lonely field into a shrine of pious pilgrimage. Although UDC chapters often rose from some of the country's most impoverished districts, they made sure the Lost Cause counterpoint was articulated in the biggest, if not several of the biggest, monuments on the landscape at the nation's most important death tourism sites. Gettysburg, Antietam, Shiloh, the Confederate capital of Richmond, and Petersburg were given close attention because of their fame, but just name a Civil War site and you will find, if you read the plaques, that the UDC canvassed its premium locations for top prominence. Soon, they existed without question, like end tables or garden gnomes—and people forgot they were the product of a concerted misinformation campaign. Only in our times, as a new generation of diverse young Americans protests their presence in their public spaces, has the UDC's triumph started to crack.

The war's killing fields were just the tip of the spear. UDC propaganda—or, to use its motivating term, "Southern truth"—was installed in nearly every town throughout the South and much of the Midwest. Every modern road-tripper through Mayberry has passed through countless central town squares with old brick courthouses and city halls. Out front of most of them sits the prototypical stone column with the lonely soldier standing vigil on top. Today we take them for granted as evidence of some bygone antique grief, but they got there by the UDC's tireless campaign. If high society in one county erected a shaft, their sisters in the next county demanded to follow. The women of the UDC charmed or cajoled funds out of neighbors and politicians alike, and if they found resistance at any level, they would shame their opponents in the local press. "Surely the finger of scorn will not be pointed at Oconee [County] anymore," scolded Marye R. Shelor in her appeal for donations in one South Carolina paper. "It is the only county where the women have not banded together to preserve the history and care for the soldiers...Ask her to do as your father did—offer yourself to your country." Having a UDC chapter in your town was like living next door to Patty Simcox from *Grease*.

The highest-ranking members were the high-born

wives and daughters of the South's most established men—in typical society style, they referred to each other by their husbands' names, a not-so-subtle reminder of each member's relative wealth and power. Lacking the ability to vote themselves, and often not interested in winning the right to do it so as not to appear revolutionary, the women threw their weight into influence and lobbying. There was nothing unseemly in it. Honoring soldiers fell within the bounds of their paternally ascribed role as caretakers of men and children, and venerating them to excess was a perfect expression the filiopietistic fantasies of nearly every white Southerner appalled at how low losing the war had brought them. You will search long and hard to find any black people who lobbied alongside the UDC to erect these landmarks. In towns that had freed slaves on the city council, such as Richmond's John Mitchell, Jr., they were always outvoted by the white members when it was time to place the newest one. Over the objections of Mitchell and two other black councilmen, Monument Avenue was created and named expressly to showcase all the incoming Civil War monuments, several by the UDC.

Because they so intensely desired their catechism to be true, the UDC brandished wistfulness as a weapon. The ladies held essay contests, fiddling contests, bake sales, concerts, barbecues, rummage sales, and penny drives. The group funded scholarship homes for the Confederate aged, too, but the heart of its mandate was what psychologists now call *generativity*, to inculcate the next generation with the glories of the previous ones. That's why they targeted kids as their most important standard carriers. Through local chapters and neighbor-on-neighbor pressure, it convinced teachers to read only from UDC-approved textbooks that published "true history" (its phrase), and it persuaded or blackmailed school boards to ban any book that implied Confederates had erred. They hung portraits of Robert E. Lee to lord over classrooms from Florida to New England, for their success was not limited to the former Confederacy, and they understood that beliefs are asserted through whatever sentiment is dominant.

The Daughters always orchestrated unveilings to be each town's highlight of the year, if not the decade. Balls were thrown, school was canceled, Main Streets were draped in red and white bunting, parades were mounted, and one lucky child was selected, with much anticipation and fanfare, to pull the cord that dropped the sheet off the new installation. The UDC invariably mustered young children to lead these ceremonies, which had the happy effect of deflecting accusations of politicization. One UDC motif at countless festivities was the use of thirteen girls, each proudly wearing a sash representing a Confederate state. One unveiling in New Orleans featured a "living" Confederate flag composed of 576 pupils dressed in red and white. In the Confederate Museum of Charleston, there's a hilarious archive image from Richmond, Virginia, of a throng of 3,000 very young schoolchildren laboriously heaving the new statue of Jefferson Davis, toiling like a workhouse's worth of orphans from a bus-and-truck production of *Oliver!* The museum preserves a relic of this civic slavery: a section of the rope they dragged Davis with, tied with red ribbons, presented with the same reverence an Italian parish church might bestow upon the alleged thumb of St. Andrew.

The UDC used a Nashville booster newspaper called *The Confederate Veteran* as its de facto house organ to broadcast and chronicle its assorted drives, folklore, dedications, and condemnations to all of its "camps." Members (and there were more than 100,000 by 1914) saw the *Veteran* as the perfect place to publish opinions and memories that would otherwise be lost to time, which makes it a bonanza, sometimes embarrassingly so, for researchers in Southern history or for anyone who wants to claim the Lost Cause isn't inherently racist. Annual volumes could top 600 pages of sparingly illustrated fine print, each one a back-breaking cornucopia of Southern derring-do and Northern dastardliness. The advertisements contained pitches for temperance products, battle flag pins, and far more damning mail-aways. For many months, this eye-catcher was among its regularly appearing classifieds:

KU KLUX KLAN.

This booklet, published by the Mississippi Division, U.D.C., to be sold and all proceeds to go to erection of monument at Beauvoir, Miss. (home of Jefferson Davis), to the memory of Confederate Veterans, contains absolutely correct history of the origin of this famous Klan. Price, per copy, 30 cents, postpaid.

In an article in the December 1910 issue, Mrs. S. E. F. Rose, the division president who published the booklet, boasted that the *Veteran* had already helped sell the volume in thirty-three states and China. She also furnished a version of her Klan history that was "in suitable form for school study." The sales funded a monument arch in Biloxi that was consecrated in 1917. That memorial was torn to pieces by Hurricane Katrina in 2005, but proud locals took considerable pains to reassemble it. You can still go see it. To this day, Harrison County promotes an annual Confederate Memorial Day there. Bring tribute wreaths for the Rebels and a potluck lunch.

Memorials could be ordered from a catalog supplied by the United Daughters of the Confederacy. If your town didn't have much money, you could order a mass-produced one and the well-placed ladies of the association would charm and hector the appropriate civic leaders until it was installed in a conspicuous location—not in the cemetery where memorials to the dead usually belong, but in public squares where kids were likely to see it on the way to school. The UDC's simplified logic scored high with schoolchildren and at death tourism sites where visitors might be learning about the Civil War for the very first time, so location was everything. In 1922 Greenville, South Carolina, the stone soldier of one memorial, about to be moved to a busy motorway, was literally hidden in a nearby barn for two years until the state Supreme Court pressured the city into relocating his roost to somewhere prominent, where passersby would be more likely to "pause to read the sermon in stone."

The UDC's approved sculptors consisted mostly of European-born artists who cared less about causes than commissions, such as Germans Rudolf Schwarz and Frank Teich, and Italian Pompeo Coppini, who openly criticized anything mass produced. He complained that Confederate societies too often tossed up poor workmanship under the cover of sanctity: "It is easy to influence small communities to give parks or other utilitarian projects for memorials, as the small masses are not educated to art appreciation," he sniffed. In this way, the American landscape was covered with European-styled Civil War remembrances that were purchased out of a book and viewed as kitsch even in their own time.

Corpses cannot speak for themselves. The UDC gave them words, and the method of their ventriloquism was gravestones. This was not merely paying respect. This was PR. Now, as we know, the plan is backfiring, and wide swaths of modern American society are seeing through the subterfuge a century late, a lag time that proves how successful it was. In places where differing opinions are likely to mingle, Confederate memorials are being moved, hidden in storage, explained away. We are amid a great tearing down. One might say that the South's determination to prove its power has always been its Achilles Heel.

When it seized John Brown after his raid, the smart thing to do, as George Templeton Strong suggested at the time, would have been to throw him into the nuthouse where he'd live out his days with the reputation of a loon. Even today, knowing what Brown did, many of us would agree he was a few logs short of a cabin. But instead, Virginia killed him, certifying a martyr, and that in turn unmade their dominion. Time and again, Americans imprudently cave to the temptation to be recalcitrant when compromise is probably best called for.

My favorite figure from the UDC, and there were many self-important showboats, was Mildred Lewis Rutherford, the erstwhile school principal from Athens, Georgia, who now makes her third problematic appearance in my wide-ranging death journey. She's the one who delivered a middling review of Orelia Key Bell's poetry and wrote the impassioned pamphlet defending Captain Henry Wirz on sale at Andersonville. "Miss Millie," as she was called, was ten when the war broke out, and she spent the rest of her life obsessively reliving it. Well into World War I, she indulged a queer penchant for running around in the 1850s hoop skirts of a Southern belle despite her advanced age. Her mother had run an LMA, the constrained precursor to the UDC. When she died, Mildred took that over and also jumped into the UDC with an intimidating intensity, becoming historian-for-life of the Georgia Division of the group, and delivering both speeches and new manuscripts wherever she went. She was a prolific thinker, but not a fair one, building a career writing UDC-approved school textbooks such as *The South in History and Literature,* a reader making a not-altogether unreasonable case for the strength of Southern writers, plus ample detours into the political inculcation of Southern children: "This is the story: The South never violated the Constitution. That instrument conceded to each State the right to conduct its own affairs. The Constitution was violated by the North, as the many amendments necessary after the war proved." By 1911, Miss Millie was appointed the Historian General of the entire UDC. One of Mrs. Rutherford's most ethically acrobatic speeches was delivered at the national convention in Dallas in 1916, in which she assured her adoring public: "What progress has the Negro made in those fifty years? He has as a race, note that I say *as a race*, become disorderly, idle, vicious and diseased...There is no doubt that the Negro finds his truest friends in the South, and that, too, with no social equality ideas to upset him." Miss Millie was also famous for her scrapbooking skills, and in 1918, she made the papers for being thrown off a train. It seems she made a scene trying to force the railroad's African-American porters to cope with seventy hand-made, 400-page volumes of white nationalist Southern history. Miss Millie was a maiden aunt with poison in her heart. For a while, I named my Wi-Fi network after her as a token of my diminishment of the peacocky old biddy.

Activism was one of the only ways a respectable woman such as Miss Millie could flex political muscles. Rutherford was one of the few UDC members not to go by "Mrs." followed by a husband's name (she never married). Even so, many members believed female students should be permitted to achieve the same educational goals as males, yet at the same time, ever-savvy about pandering to the men in power, lobbied against suffrage for women. Why should they need to vote when they could already transform the landscape wherever they wished?

In time, because it was carefully constructed to appear uncontroversial, the UDC's commentary was taken as documentary—and snatching back the meaning of the War was precisely the point of all this. The perfidious arguments of Miss Millie and countless like hers caught fire, and not just in the South. In 1906, a T.H. Mann of Norwich, Connecticut wrote a letter to the editor of the *Atlanta Georgian*: "The best thing for the negro as well as the white man is that the relative inferiority of the negro man should be recognized definitely and clearly in every relation of life," wrote the flatteringly named Mann, proving for the millionth time that our passions as patriots too often trample our feelings as humans. His sentiments were not unique among his fellow Northerners. Ask yourself, for a moment, why the North didn't erect any major statues about black liberation. They fought and won a war to free the slaves—or, depending on your view, to take away the right to own any—and yet can you name a single notable work from the era celebrating the smashing of African-American chains? Other countries, including Brazil, Guyana, Haiti, Mexico, Cuba, and others, have their own monuments to the quashing of slavery, and what's more, they give the former slaves agency in their own liberation. America has mostly paternalistic statues for the white men who fought. So let's not dwell too long on the fiction that Northern memorialists were the nobler ones.

Another favorite theme, one that still powers minorities today, was that the newspapers were unfair, suppressing information and distributing false stories. On May 20, 1895, Colonel Alfred Moore Waddell delivered the dedication speech of the Confederate Monument in Raleigh, North Carolina.

> The accepted history of the late war, like the previous history of the United States, has been written by Northern men, and a Southerner, reading it, cannot help recalling what Fronde said about history generally: namely, that it seemed to him 'like a child's box of letters with which we can spell any word we please. We have only to select such letters as we want, arrange them as we like, and say nothing about those which do not suit our purpose.

His complaint was an early framing of unpleasant coverage as "lamestream media" or "fake news," and it confirms why proponents of the Lost Cause depended on the establishment of a separate network for their memorialization. Yet not a minute later, Waddell followed his North-baiting with this weightless protest: "Let no man say that in discharging this duty I am digging up sectionalism. I utterly disdain any such desire or intention, and I could not if I would, for they are things now buried." As you can see, it was a masterpiece of plausible double-talk that allowed divisive ideas to fly under a scrambled radar, and it was typical of UDC doctrine—avoid discussing the reason the game was played (slavery), and play up the outrage of other rules that were broken (state's rights). Play the victim, complain the other side is being unfair and crowding you out—and once the guilt has been properly stoked, your opponent will think twice before criticizing you again. It's a gaslighting strategy that many of America's retrograde social resistance movements have enjoyed ever since. American political discourse is nothing if not a war of subtext, an ongoing series of dirty tricks that often help a statistical minority win anyway—think Prohibition, think McCarthyism, think the Electoral College.

The UDC's standard poetic rants and abstract vocabulary coalesced against an unspecified danger that an America First activist might cherish today. They marinated in heightened words of "pseudo-heroism"—*valor, honor, principles,* and *glory*—that rarely confessed that the right to own other people was what the battle was about. The lie of false nobility befitted a country whose founding document rhapsodized about inalienable human rights even as it protected human slavery with pen and ink.

A shaft in Monticello, Florida, reminds us the women paid for it:

> "Let the young Southron, as he gazes upon this shaft, remember how gloriously Florida's songs illustrated their sunny land on the red fields of carnage, and how woman— fair and faithful—freshens the glory of their fame."

In Appomattox, Virginia, the place of their ultimate defeat, "still unconquered."

Here on Sunday April, 9, 1865

after four years of heroic struggle

in defense of principles believed fundamental

to the existence of our government

Lee surrendered 9,000 men the remnant

of an army still unconquered in spirit

to 118,000 men under Grant.

Its inscription, along with countless others, was a simple recasting of the motto of the Confederacy: *Deo*

Vindice. In formal circles, that translates to "With God, Our Defender." Really, the South was saying, "God will prove us right someday."

If you doubt just how widespread the Daughters' messaging was, go into New York City's Times Square subway station from 42nd Street. Look up. The tile mosaic trim running under the ceiling throughout the concourse depicts, at regular intervals, a hanging Confederate battle flag. Adolph S. Ochs, the publisher of the *New York Times* from 1896 to 1935, built the skyscraper over the station, which opened on the subway's first day of service in 1904. He was one of the most powerful men in New York City, but also he happened to be the son of Bertha Levi Ochs, a Bavarian-born Jew, Confederate smuggler, and charter member of the UDC. She died in 1910 with full funeral honors from the group, and in 1917, during an expansion of the station, the head architect, Squire J. Vickers, and his head tile man, W. Herbert Dole, appear to have tried to please Ochs by embedding those Rebel flags beneath the very headquarters of New York's "Gray Lady" newspaper. Ochs himself helped develop the system that consecrated the Confederate killing fields at Chickamauga. It's also said that when he died in 1935, the UDC sent a pillow embroidered with the Rebel flag to be placed beside him in his coffin. All of that means that for a century, a Rebel flag saluting the United Daughters of the Confederacy has flown over the heads of unsuspecting Yankees on their daily commutes in Manhattan.

The UDC was the most powerful and prolific of the

revisionist memorial makers, but it wasn't alone. Similar groups sprouted everywhere blood was once spilled: the United Confederate Veterans, the Sons of Confederate Veterans, and among Unionists, the ultra-influential Grand Army of the Republic. They competed to prove who could praise their ancestors with the most luxuriant memorial, but they all traded in the same secret symbols. There may be no sharper rebuttal to their soapy rhetoric than a quote by James Baldwin, who was exactly the kind of man the UDC tried to prevent from existing. Ironically, he wrote it about *Uncle Tom's Cabin*, an anti-slavery novel the UDC hated, too: "Sentimentality, the ostentatious parading of excessive and spurious emotion, is the mark of dishonesty."

But the UDC's sentimentality worked, and it still does. In December 2018, *Smithsonian* magazine calculated that in the preceding decade, at least $40 million in taxpayer funds had been directed to these monuments and their associated Rebel heritage associations, and it found multiple cases of Confederate markers being meticulously restored while all others were defunded and permitted to decay. As the interest in calculating that figure suggests, people are increasingly snatching history back by questioning funding or, in many cases, in removing the UDC's most vulnerable handiwork. Some people want them preserved in museums, some want them melted down, some want signage with better context placed on them, and some will run you over with a Toyota Camry if you even touch them.

My favorite UDC inscription, a masterpiece of humblebrag isn't going anywhere soon. It's back at the Confederate Memorial in Arlington, the same metal memorial that refers to the Roman Cato and asserts itself in a protective ring of Rebels dead. It's elegant in insisting that Confederates not inspect too closely the reasons why they fought, that vague idealistic feelings about duty were more than enough:

Not for fame or reward

Not for place or for rank

Not lured by ambition

Or goaded by necessity

But in simple

Obedience to duty

As they understood it

These men suffered all

Sacrificed all

Dared all—and died

"History will be kind to me, for I intend to write it," Winston Churchill once quipped. But let's be honest. He was still gadding about in breeches when the UDC mastered that skill.

There is now a psychological theory that accounts for the basic human talent for creating enemies. It's called Terror Management Theory, or TMT. It goes back to the first moments we were old enough to interact with other people. The idea is credited to cultural anthropologist Ernest Becker, who laid the groundwork in a 1973 book called *The Denial of Death*. (It's the same book Woody Allen buys for Diane Keaton in *Annie Hall* when she would rather buy a cat book. "I feel that life is divided up into the horrible and the miserable," he tells her after he shows her the cover. "Those are the two categories." She falls in love with him.)

Here's how TMT starts out. Kids freak out when they're scared, hungry, or tired—all biological or emotional needs caused, on an animal level, by an instinct to escape things that can kill us. Yet our reactions to potentially deadly situations are the first behaviors your parents stamp out. To keep from getting kicked off the airline or planted in a back corner of the restaurant, the adults teach children to quit crying, to quit whining out of want, to put aside self-interest and be polite—to stop acting like such babies.

"One of the first things a child has to do is to learn to abandon ecstasy," wrote Becker. "To do without awe, to leave fear and trembling behind...to feel a basic sense of self-worth, of meaningfulness, or power." If we can't acknowledge our mortalities, we must create mechanisms that make us feel psychologically safe.

Becker was committed to demonstrating his theory. Almost immediately after publishing it, he died. It was a brilliant career move because no one could argue with him. He won the Pulitzer—appropriately, posthumously.

Some hip academics took up his work and broadened it into the unified concept of Terror Management Theory. The idea is simple: We all know we are going to die. If you are reading this sentence, you're doomed, and you know it. So everything we do can be interpreted as a move that's subconsciously geared to avoid embracing the inevitable. When humans create groups with a common purpose— our families, our churches, our block associations, our countries, our races, our Trekkies, our baseball teams, our Apple products, probably even the original impulse to carve the planet into countries—we do it because of a desperate emotional need to construct a community that supplies us with the reassurance of universal truths. It takes our minds off the fact that every pulse of your heart is a single missed beat from oblivion. (How 'bout them Red Sox?)

That ideology could quickly transition into psychosis, but we call it something else. "If it's just your belief, it's autism. If it's everyone's belief, it's culture," says Sheldon Solomon, a psychology professor at Skidmore College. Culture gives life a sense of shared agreement and distraction. Sometimes psychologists and philosophers edge dangerously close to confirming that we devote every breath to nothing more than a fantasy that makes us feel better.

Solomon also explains it this way in *Flight from Death*, a 2005 documentary about TMT: "One of my favorite Becker quotes in *The Denial of Death* is that 'Psychology can only take you so far, at which time it drops you directly on the doorstep of religion.' What does he mean by that? His point, very simply, is that, just to get up in the morning, every one of us, whether we like it or not, has to believe certain things about reality. They may be religious, they may be secular, but every one of us has beliefs about reality. And if we're honest with ourselves, there's no way that those beliefs about reality can ever be unambiguously confirmed."

Solomon, who defuses the threat of his theories by teaching in tie-dyed shirts, has a way with words. "You're no more significant or enduring than a cucumber or a cockroach," he's fond of saying. We would be paralyzed with abject terror if we thought about that much. Nihilistic? Definitely. But it's also universal. It's said TMT accounts for nearly every move we make. TMT says that when we lose ourselves in the transcendent joy of being alive, with love, or dancing, or orgasm, or imagination, or vodka, or meditation—as Solomon puts it, "the same Kierkegaardian awareness that you are alive, of being in the moment, of imagination, is the thing that signals you are aware of death, that it's coming, that it could be you." In the all-enveloping theory of TMT—which, like dark tourism, is an academic study that demands scrutiny from a wide variety of disciplines—even the pursuit of joy is an escape from death. We crave happiness because deep down, we recognize that it's a contrast to the actual state of affairs, namely the implacable creep of the Reaper. Or, in the bleating words of hipster troubadour Rufus Wainwright in his song "Matinee Idol": "Whomever has looked at beauty is marked out already by death." It's why we crave wealth, why we have kids, why we create art, and even why we write books (gulp).

And, significantly, it's why we go to war. Here's how that part of TMT works. When two groups come into conflict—Christians and Muslims, Catholics and Protestants, Red Sox fans and Yankee fans, James Woods and everyone else—it happens because someone else's contradictory reality threatens our own carefully constructed defenses. If our rivals are correct about their beliefs, then ours must be wrong, and anyone who threatens our defenses also threatens our control over our latent fear of death. The conflict arises, claimed Becker, in three stages: *derogation*, *assimilation*, and *annihilation*. Take 9/11 as an example. When the Twin Towers fell, American's first reaction after the initial shock was to denounce and dismiss the men who flew the planes, even before anyone had a debate about their political gripes aside from an oversimplified "They hated freedom." That was derogation. "Slaves were lucky they had food and safe homes." That was derogation. Next came *assimilation*, in which Americans, even ones who normally fought with each other, united to demonstrate social consensus about our shared beliefs. You saw that when porches and car bumpers were suddenly and defiantly awash in the reassuring ripple of the stars and stripes. Or the stars and bars. Specifically, that phenomenon is called *mortality salience*, when people amp up ritualistic behavior immediately after any kind of reminder of death. Catholics reach for a rosary, obsessive compulsives reach for the bleach, stress eaters order a sheet cake. Finally came the last stage: *annihilation*. That came in the form of war against the groups that most closely resembled the disruptive viewpoint. Get Saddam. Kill the Yankee. Whenever groups lock horns, it generally follows that three-step pattern.

Becker didn't dwell on the application of TMT to cemeteries and memorials, but it's a logical step. We all want to belong because that gives us a sense of significance, and what could bond us more than shedding tears over the same thing? Monuments make meaning out of a shattered ritual. There's a reason graves say AT REST and not DEAD.

Replacing the wreckage of grief with a proud, clean monument with proud, clean words—that's TMT in action. The act of choosing the materials, the phrasing, and the form is part derogation and part assimilation. If the monument builders like the UDC delete the rival's point of view—and they almost always do—it's annihilation. And if you pay tribute, you are placing yourself in a larger symbolic story about that event in a classic, but entirely unconscious display of TMT. Like church, memorials give us a chance to placate chaos with a sense of ritual. We memorialize death because it helps us control it.

That's why so few memorials—not even all the ones I had seen so far in my journey—are explicit about the visceral reality of blood and breath leaving a young body, but are instead about social concepts like politics or honor, which are reassuringly shared things we can control here and now. These observations are a hedge against emptiness, and if we make them solemnly, we give them the import that our psychological security demands. It's probably no coincidence that the dominant demographic among family research hobbyists is white women who are older than fifty-five, people with their major life accomplishments already in the bag who are facing mortality as an ultimate life goal.

STONEWALL'S LAST YANKEE VICTIM

Wilderness, Locust Grove, and Guinea Station, Virginia

AS STONEWALL JACKSON DIED, HE PROGRESSIVELY left chunks of himself all over Virginia. This is good news for tourists, because they can plan a rich, week-long itinerary tracking his dismantled body across the landscape.

Chancellorsville is his "wounding site." It's buried in the woods off Route 3 in Northern Virginia, near a place named Wilderness. The first hint that I was getting warm was a grey-and-white metal historical sign flashing by my windshield in a blur. Like many of the most important historical signs in the United States, the marker for Chancellorsville is a paragraphs-long essay planted at perilous proximity to a highway with a speed limit of 175 miles per hour, with no way to safely read it without turning your car into a steaming metal ball. I believe there exists a secret federal statute requiring all highway historic signs to be placed to create maximum difficulty for citizens, who, deterred by the inconvenience, find it impossible to stop, thereby saving millions on the erection of future signs and maintaining a pliable, ignorant population. In the rare cases the government has no option but to place a sign within easy view, the information it bears is mandated to dwell on events so obscure (such as the lore of coal-to-coke ovens, or where George Washington dined during a trip to visit his mother—both actual signs in Virginia), that the driver never cares to stop for another one again, thereby saving even more money on civic education. Once I realized I had missed this one, I had to U-turn twice into oncoming light-speed traffic, but still lacking a place to safely pull over to read it, I haphazardly aimed my phone at the fleeting sign and hoped for a clear shot. I would read it in the safety of my own home.

It informed me (I learned later) that Lt. Gen. Thomas J. "Stonewall" Jackson was wounded on May 2, 1863, "just 1.7 miles west on this road." (This is the third bylaw of the federal sign placement code: Signs may not be erected where events actually occurred. A rough "somewhere over there" will do. To be any more specific might inadvertently stimulate historical preservation, and that's expensive.) This sign, dated 1937, reported, "Having brilliantly executed a flanking maneuver against the Federals, Jackson, with eight aides, was returning from a reconnaissance between the lines" when he "was wounded by 'friendly fire.'" Short version: Clever man hit by nice bullets.

A little ways west, the National Park Service has a visitor center. Its signs were noticeably less deferential to old Stonewall, dubbing the incident that took place there a "Confederate Catastrophe." Truly, Jackson's wounding was a pig-pile of hubris: First, Jackson lit into friends who warned him it was too dangerous to head into the woods. Once he was lost in trees, fellow Confederates fired without knowing who was there, and when one of Jackson's party cried out to stop, some hot-head shouted back, "It's a lie! Pour it into them, boys!" Jackson was shot twice in the left arm and once in the right hand, and his horse, Little Sorrel, bolted with him teetering in the saddle like a crash test dummy. Stonewall didn't die here, but the dream of an independent Confederacy did, for no other Southern military leader captured hearts and hopes quite like him.

Two respectfully simple monuments went up relatively quickly. But neither marks the actual place where he was shot. They were only placed there to attract traffic from the nearby Orange Turnpike (now Route 3) and make some cash off acolytes—like a pair of cracker Cracker Barrels. One plain shaft of rough-hewn stones, the Jackson Monument, drew 5,000 people to its 1888 erection, including Jackson's own surgeon, who contributed $25. But the second marker, the Jackson Stone, is the more interesting one, because like Stonehenge, its heritage is unknown.

That stomach-high quartz boulder, your average basic rock, hides unobtrusively down a quiet path at the edge of the woods. Through a thin barrier of reedy trees, the traffic of Route 3 hurtles past, shaking the leaves. Some people think the stone might have come from a stream at a nearby farm, but all we know is it appeared sometime between 1876 and 1885, not long after Reconstruction ended and Southerners felt the coast was clear for Confederate praise. The larger 1888 marker grabs attention, but it's obvious to any visitor that the mysterious Stone holds the talismanic charm. I was there a few days after the anniversary of the shooting. An anonymous admirer had bundled flowers with blue and grey ribbon and laid them on top of the stone, where they decayed mournfully. A small Rebel flag, sodden with dirt and leaves, was planted at the base as if at a grave.

A few yards away lies a stone slab denoting "Unknown Soldier/US Army." It's the only body that's truly here, yet it receives only cursory remembrance. So many visitors walk on the Union man's grave that the grass is dead. Instead, it's the death of the Confederacy that receives the full reverence at Chancellorsville.

The visitor center building is a tribute to the 1960s: a one-level brick-faced ranch-style structure, tobacco brown and flattened like a Texaco station. At the time it was built, the style was called "Park Service Modern," but I can't stand beside old National Park visitor centers without immediately thinking they look like something Mike Brady would have devised in his sunken studio at *The Brady Bunch* house in the Valley. All the Chancellorsville visitor center is missing is groovy bead curtains and an Astroturf lawn.

"This is a Mission 66 Building," explained Katie, the young woman on duty at the ranger's desk, dropping some expert lingo. The National Park universe is a lot like the Marvel Comics universe. Both periodically reinvent themselves, even if it means killing off a few heroes. The Chancellorsville center was intentionally placed nearly on top of the spot where Stonewall's deadly foul-up went down—in fact, it was built over part of the road he was traveling that day. In the 1960s, while Marvel Comics rebooted its image with newfangled characters such as Spider-Man and the X-Men, the National Park Service was prepping for its fiftieth anniversary as an agency by spending $1 billion to upgrade 122 new visitor facilities, like this one. Back in 1955, the government first outlined its plans in a 120-page report that was given the awesomely *Star Trek*-style title *Mission 66: To Provide Adequate Protection and Development of the National Park System for Human Use*. In it, its architects said their central goal was to "help the visitor see the park and enjoy to the fullest extent what it has to offer." The chosen building materials of concrete, glass, and steel, were cost-effective, but had a way of aging quickly, and the "contemporary" architectural style today is constrictive and inadequate—lit by humming fluorescents and using that middle manager of fonts, Helvetica. Politics also change, and funding our heritage fell out of vogue in Washington, forcing a dismaying portion of the Mission 66 additions into the disrepair they were intended to solve.

Mission 66 visitor centers, outgrown and outdated, are endangered nearly wherever they still stand, as the demolition of Neutra's ballyhooed Gettysburg center proved. The centers that do manage to survive another ten or twenty years may eventually be deemed historic enough on their own merit to warrant preservation, but for now, to our current McMansioned tastes, their modest floor space screams of inadequacy. We may sanctify what our grandfathers did, but we tear down what our fathers made.

Chancellorsville's exhibits were conceived in different eras as budgets became available. The Mission 66 stuff clinically outlines troop movements in big blocks like a teacher for the slowest fourth graders. It slavers over the war's brand names, like Jackson, just as crusty old General Grant of the CWCC would have liked it. One of the prize artifacts is a snippet of the coat Stonewall was wearing when he was shot. The old, starchy signs make nothing out of the fact that four other people, including his engineer, James Keith Boswell, were also killed in the volley—it's the Jacksonia that matters.

The newer curatorial additions have more soul. Rather than mire itself in general worship, the newer exhibitions get wrenchingly personal: a curving wall of grizzled photographs of men from both North and South who fought here, each with a description of their fate, presented evenly. Lots of them look like meth cookers on *Breaking Bad*, but now and then you see the ones who are fresh-faced and boy-band young, and when you see hot dead dudes you can't help but feel sad. I never cared much about the Civil War in my teen years. I had to age long enough to realize these guys were only kids.

Katie explains that those haunting ambrotype faces didn't come from government-sponsored scholars. They came directly from descendants. Lacking sufficient federal funding to acquire these histories, Chancellorsville turned to relatives to fill the gaps. In the end, it took budget cuts to bring humanity to the process, and lo, the government-backed *Guns & Ammo* military bias was filtered out so the true awfulness of the matter could hit home. Unsurprisingly, when you remove the military from the storytelling process, it stops praising itself and lets the people do the speaking.

There is a name for how our retelling of history shifts with time, tastes, and pressure—*memory*. The word choice is risible, really, since it's not memory we're talking about, but the willful shaping of it, but that's the name we use. Understanding why we tell our stories the way we do is a study all its own. The Chancellorsville visitor center, hammocked between the spoon-fed, grammar-school-bulletin-board patriotism of the 1960s and our microcosmically personal era, represents the journey of America's twentieth-century memory.

After they pulled Jackson off Little Sorrel, they brought him to a field hospital nearby, where doctors took one look at his mangled left arm—the same one that had been shot when he waved it around at Manassas two years earlier—and decided it had to go. The surgeon sawed it off and dropped it by the door of the tent to be tossed onto a pile with all the other freshly severed limbs. But Jackson had many admirers, and one of them, the chaplain B. Tucker Lacy, couldn't bear to see his idol disassembled in such a way. As what was left of Jackson was rushed across the countryside to recover in safety, Lacy snatched up the bloody arm. It was the nearest thing to an autograph that he could get. He gave it a Christian interment at Ellwood

Manor, which means Stonewall's arm got a better burial than most of his army.

There are unsolved rumors about what happened next. Union soldiers unburied the arm a year later and told everyone they had moved it, but didn't mention where. Others insist the arm lies exactly where it is said to lie. In 1903, one of Jackson's aging staff officers, who had married the daughter of Ellwood's owner, put a fine point on the arm's whereabouts by erecting a granite marker in the family plot, but no one is sure if he was being geographically accurate or just generally affectionate. The National Park Service would rather not dig around to make sure the arm is still there. "It may very well have disintegrated as a result of time, being dug up and aerated, or it simply is somewhere else in the cemetery, long lost, forgotten," park historian Frank O'Reilly admitted to NPR. But Jackson is still a legend in some parts of Virginia, so people come to pay respects to the arm. They are possibly only paying respects to a random slab of granite, but isn't that a fine metaphor for idolatry as a genre?

As I arrived at Ellwood Manor, distant curtains of angry rain were gathering around the Virginia countryside. Despite its grand name, the Manor is just a boxy red farmhouse on an appealing lawn. The aged, canopied trees that surround it were surely not even planted during the war, when this place would have been crawling with military and every living thing trampled to smithereens, but today, as the last shafts of sunlight before the storm lit the farmhouse eaves like a Wyeth painting, it was easy to believe that maybe the Old South wasn't such a mean place after all. Then I remembered I was there to find an amputated arm.

Inside, three elderly volunteer docents, all men, sat around the central hallway shooting the shit. When I walked in, they regarded me with a flutter of annoyance. It was 4:40 in the afternoon, and the Manor was due to close at 5:00. They thought they had been free and clear.

"Here to see the house?" one of them asked. I had to think about why he asked. There was nothing else for a mile in any direction.

I'm a sucker for an enthusiastic senior citizen volunteer. It is the only demographic that can be relied upon to indulge nerdish fascinations. I told him yes, I was, even though the correct answer had to do with the arm. With some difficulty, the fella closest to me hoisted himself to his feet and gave me a quick game plan. Downstairs, restored rooms. In the back, historical display about the family. Outside and down the path, family cemetery.

Not wanting to seem overly ghoulish, I made a decoy of my interest. I would spend five or ten minutes taking in the house, and then, on an idle stroll of the grounds I could pretend to have stumbled across the arm. He showed me the upstairs bedrooms. I asked a few polite questions about how long people lived here until it was a museum, and what strange occupant had the lousy color sense to paint these beautiful wooden floors black.

"Oh, no," he said. "Remember, during the war, this

was used as a field hospital. When the family moved back in, bloodstains kept showing up on the floors. So they painted them black to hide the stains."

I looked at the wood beneath my shoes. The weight of that information was sinking in when, over our heads, the heavy drumming of rain began.

My good manners had cost me my brief pre-storm window of time to check out the arm. We went back down and looked with trepidation out the screen door at the trees. The leaves quivered from the barrage of raindrops.

"I really wanted to go out to the cemetery, too," I sheepishly told my guide.

"Well, we do close at 5:00." He was elderly, so he meant sharp.

There was a flash, and very soon after, thunder's cackle. It was now 4:50. I gazed wistfully out toward the cemetery, but there was a hedged garden in the way and I couldn't see it. I could run out into the storm, soaking myself and risking electrocution, or I could stay here and be satisfied that I had at least made it to the estate. As I considered my options, another flash of lightning lit up the retirees regarding me, and then more thunder rolled in, challenging me to make my choice.

I had come all this way to see the arm's resting place. It was probably a hundred yards from me, but I was on the verge of missing it.

I asked if I could borrow an umbrella.

He fetched me a spare one. I stood at the threshold of Ellwood Manor. "Be careful, now," he said, as if there was a way to sidestep a bolt of lightning. I opened the umbrella, took a deep breath, and ran like the wind. Or at least, given my fitness level, like a moderate breeze.

So there I was, running away from Ellwood Manor into a driving rain, to a destination I couldn't see. Every few seconds or so, another flash of lightning, followed by a louder grumble of thunder, like nature foreshadowing a lethal error. I tore down a gravel path through the hedges. On the other side, there was a huge meadow. I paused to gauge my position. In the middle of the meadow stood a copse of trees encircled by a single-rail wooden fence, the perfect landing beacon for electricity. Linger under a tree in a field during a lightning storm? Why, yes. I was willing to give my life for tourism.

By this time I was well smeared with warm rain, so there was no point in turning back. I hustled myself across the meadow to the cemetery. For many excruciating moments, I was the only structure of height, a speck of idiocy moving across a grassy target, the sole magnet for the electric vengeance that was gathering in the low cloud above me. When I reached the trees, I fumbled my camera out of my satchel and furiously snapped pictures. The marker was the only headstone in the plot, so it made the most of its anticlimax: All it had to say was ARM OF STONEWALL JACKSON MAY 3, 1863. I could mull the details later from my computer screen, but right now, all I could think about was tomorrow's newspaper, which would carry a humorous paragraph about the city slicker from New York who was barbecued while trying to pay a tribute to someone's left arm. I was about to be Stonewall's last Yankee victim.

There would be no contemplation on a quiet corner of tranquil Virginia farmland, no séance or silence. A bolt of lightning struck so nearby that I could make out its sharp jags, and its roar was like a lion that has just had a taste of fresh meat. Once I had my pictures, I retreated back across the field like I was under fire from the Viet Cong.

"Didja see it?" the guide asked when I returned. It was 4:57.

"I sure did," I said, breathless. "Like to have died trying, though."

"Yeah," he said. He accepted his umbrella. "Not much, is it?"

At 5:00 on the dot, I got back in my car and sat dripping. I marveled at the intensity I had just put myself through. All that for just a stone. It only mattered if I cared. It felt a little like the first ten minutes after sex, when you realize how much effort you spent trying to get it and wonder it if had been worth all the time and energy.

Come to think of it, that makes two pointless things you can do with a left arm.

Stone walls can be taken apart, and Jackson was. History took him back in chunks. He was strewn in pieces across Virginia. Without his left arm, he jostled on a springless wagon for twenty-seven miles to the Chandler plantation in Fairfield. There, he was made comfortable in a farm office outbuilding beside Guinea Station, a railway supply depot that bustled day and night with army preparations. It probably wasn't the cleanest or quietest place to stash a man recovering from open wounds, and sure enough, although he arrived in fair shape, he showed signs of pneumonia within two days and slowly expired over the course of six.

Today the site, an outpost of the Fredericksburg and Spotsylvania National Military Park, is green and peaceful, which leads idealistic pilgrims to believe their hero Jackson passed in bucolic grace rather than amid the clamor of boxcars and diarrhea-streaked soldiers. As I pulled up, I had to admit it looked like a nice place to die, and the site's official version of events did nothing to guide me to the truth. The curb of the modern parking lot is equipped with one of those anecdote jukeboxes favored by low-budget tourist sights: press the button for the recorded spiel. I was glad it did, because the narration was so overwrought no flesh-and-blood human could have reliably reproduced it on cue. A reedy, clipped female voice, like the recording that announces elevator floors, painted a tranquil portrait of father, wife, children, and "servants" (she meant slaves) solemnly greeting Jackson's arrival. "From this scene on the fourth of May, he will not return to the world of men and affairs," says the unseen woman, who goes heavy on romantic verbiage so gaseous it would make Longfellow blush: "Sunday, May 10, was a soft day full of birdsong... Surrounded by Lily of the Valley and other spring flowers from the Chandler garden, Jackson's body is placed in the parlor of the big house...The genius of this brilliant American soldier, which pervades the woods and fields of so many battlegrounds, abides here at Chandler's, where he died in cheerful and courageous quiet."

Sounds nice, but (sensing a theme?) it's a lie. The plantation was actually ruined. Most of Thomas Chandler's slaves had fled to freedom the year before, and with three of his sons off with the Confederate Army, he couldn't afford to run it anymore. The muddy, noisy supply depot in their back yard was the last straw, and the family had already sold the property and were preparing to flee by the time the armless Jackson was hauled in on a stretcher. The Chandlers bolted permanently soon after, and subsequent owners went into foreclosure. In 1909, as Rebel revisionist pride was at its peak, the Richmond Fredericksburg & Potomac Railroad—its president, William White, was a Confederate veteran and a Jackson nut—bought the property at a deep discount, demolished the burned-out farmhouse, and renamed the office where Jackson had died as a "shrine." To make back his investment, his railroad charged passengers an extra nickel simply because it passed the place where Jackson had perished. That's why we can even see it today—it was carefully staged to make tourist cash.

A ranger entertained visitors inside the cottage, where the ticking of a clock was audible in every room. Gary had a macabre eagerness that would have made him a good 1950s B-movie director. He took this lightly visited satellite site and wrung it for grisly thrills, chilling the handful of us who had ventured the five miles off I-95. As our wide-eyed gathering cringed, he related how Chaplain Lacy had grabbed Jackson's severed arm "from a five-and-a-half-foot-tall stack of arms and legs." That was a lot more graphic than what I'd been told twenty-seven miles away, but as history click bait, I liked his image better. Gary's storytelling had cinematic sense. One anecdote involved Jackson's couriers dropping him twice "right on his wounded and shattered arm" stump, a visualization that drew flinches from the couple standing beside me. Gary assured us the general's manliness had not been compromised: "He will not make a sound. He was a strict disciplinarian."

So strict, in fact, that the general spent his first days at the Chandlers' relentlessly drilling his attendants on Biblical catechism—for many pompous hours, it seems, his staff suffered far worse than he did. Then things soured. Officers routinely survived wounds more serious than Jackson's, yet he nosedived. Gary explored every theory with gumshoe glee. He was shot wearing all his clothes at once, which might have dehydrated him; his lung may have been bruised; a bullet nicked his artery; his chest was blistered with mustard gas; he was tinctured with antimony and mercury; nothing was sterilized; he drank too much coffee. (I would like to introduce an eighth theory: his staff got sick of catechism lectures.) Any or all could be true, because like the shooting of General Jackson, and indeed like his military style itself, his medical treatment was hampered by confusion and overzealous ineptitude.

Then, to give us the sensation of the very moment of death, Gary directed us to take in the original bed, original covers, "and the ticking of that very same clock, the one you hear today." A squat wooden table clock sat on the mantle. We fell silent to hear. "These will be the last sounds General Jackson hears on the earth," Gary said quietly.

Stonewall's doctor, aware he was attending to the rock star of the Civil War, took careful notes at the time: "A few moments before he died he cried out in his delirium, 'Order A.P. Hill to prepare for action! Pass the infantry to the front rapidly! Tell Major Hawks'—then stopped, leaving the sentence unfinished. Presently a smile of ineffable sweetness spread itself over his pale face, and he said quietly, and with an expression, as if of relief, 'Let us cross over the river, and rest under the shade of the trees.'" ("Ineffable sweetness." I love that. It sounds like what he really wanted was to swear.)

This very bed was the setting of Jackson's big Rosebud Moment. It's one of the most famous death scenes in American history—and no one knows what it means. Historians argue more over his last words than the impact of his command. Some people, the kind who walk in the room and gasp, feel Jackson's last words were mouthed by God and the Book of Revelation. Others, the ones more likely to clutch a Jeff Shaara book, look to his wife, who suggested in her memoir he was merely rhapsodizing about a favorite place he played as a boy. Me, I think he was just slipping into a permanent fantasy nap. His last words meant nothing more than "Gonna go chill now."

Gary drove the general's grand finale home by saying his officers were "openly weeping" upon seeing their commander dead. He meant this as proof that a demigod had passed, because as we all know, men only cry if things get really, really bad. After the death, one of his officers wrote in his diary, "Did we reverence him too much? If so, fearfully have we been punished? He has been taken from us." The sinking feeling that God had rebuked the Confederacy for worshiping a false idol was common at the time, making the railroad's decision to call this room a "shrine" all the more tone-deaf.

The attending doctor was given the original bed, but a huckster in nearby Fredericksburg purchased several of the same model and made a fortune passing off segments of them as relics. After sixty years of misadventures, the real bed finally made it back to the "death room" in the late 1920s. Around the same time, the Chandlers' daughter Lucy, then in her eighties, donated the clock and the bed covers. The recreated shrine is now owned by the very government Stonewall fought. The bed remains made.

Gary told us there was one other place where there's

a war monument to a limb, and could we name it? No one knew (or perhaps raising an arm would be misinterpreted as an offering). It's in Saratoga, New York, where the boot and leg of Benedict Arnold lie. It, too, received an honored burial because according to Gary, the colonials "were reassured his leg was loyal since it came off before he was a traitor."

Jackson's corpse was not reassembled, because Mrs. Jackson didn't want to disturb the Christian burial of the arm—it remained a Rebel before and after detachment. Stonewall and 75 percent of his limbs were buried in Lexington, Virginia. Later, he was dug up and moved beneath an imposing marker topped with a statue depicting him in a more complete state than what lies underground—that event, in 1891 as the UDC was gaining speed peddling its aggrieved version the past, attracted 10,000 more mourners than his funeral did. Virginia's hero worshipers did not forget Jackson's horse, Little Sorrel, either, who is also at rest in two pieces. His hide is on display at the Virginia Military Institute Museum, while his cremated bones repose on VMI's parade ground. The dedication ceremony was in 1997, 111 years after the animal's death.

Even though they lie in pieces all over Virginia, Stonewall and his horse were the lucky ones in that war. They had friends beyond the grave. And after all, what good is a grave without friends to cry on it?

HOW HORACE GOT TO FRANCE

Grant's Tomb

IF YOU PLAN TO DIE, TAKE SOME ADVICE: GET YOUR friends to build your tomb.

Ulysses S. Grant had lots of friends. His 1885 funeral in Manhattan was the Super Bowl of its epoch, and it had some stiff competition, if you'll pardon the phrase, in the funeral department. Before people had cinemas to amuse them, they got off on send-offs. Manhattan hosted some heart-stopping funerals—Abraham Lincoln's World Tour '65, a progressive grief party of fourteen stops starting in Washington and ending in his resting place in Springfield, Illinois, was one such black-banner occasion. But Grant's funeral made Lincoln's look like a winter picnic. His drew a million spectators in a city that only had a population of about 1.3 million. To put that into perspective, America has seen only one gathering of a million souls at a single event in our lifetime: Barack Obama's inauguration. (A free concert by Rod Stewart in 1996 attracted 3.5 million, but that was in Brazil, and it *was* Rod Stewart.) The funeral's 60,000 marchers took five hours to pass and stretched seven miles down Broadway.

What none of the million people lining Broadway knew (and people still don't know) was that their esteemed General Grant was being carried to his eternal rest on a beer cart. It was a green and red Ehret's Brewery cart pulled by two dozen brewery horses. It was the only vehicle the funeral parlor could find that would support his ridiculously heavy catafalque. This was unfortunate because General Grant had a nagging reputation as a fall-down drunk. The undertakers carefully festooned the wagon with $500 of crepe, no small expenditure in 1885, so that spectators, many of whom were given the day off and were drunk on the very same beer, wouldn't recognize it.

They loaded poor Ulysses, tucked into his coffin with silver handles and a solid gold nameplate, on top of ten tons of crude pig iron. "Had to do it," the funeral company's president confessed nearly sixty years later to writer Meyer Berger, "or those horses would have run away with the funeral. They were used to big loads."

It's a good thing the identity of Grant's makeshift beer bier was so concealed, otherwise the throng might have also spied the other dirty secret of his cortège: the huge Star of David painted on the wagon. Ehret's Brewery, at the time the country's largest, was founded by George Ehret, a German Jewish immigrant, and it took the Jewish star as its logo so millions of illiterate, but thirsty laborers could recognize its product without words. Problem: the only thing more infamous than Grant's insobriety was his rap as a raging anti-Semite. That black mark stemmed from Grant's General Order No. 11, which in 1862 banned Jewish people from his military district in Tennessee, Mississippi, and Kentucky. The intent was to stem the peddler's black market, and Lincoln revoked the order three days later, but a stain like that isn't easily washed off. Tales of Grant's alleged anti-Semitism dogged him during the election of 1868. After he won, he responded by appointing more Jewish leaders to office than all presidents before him combined, and he was the first

American president to attend a synagogue. But he also made Christmas (and not Hannukah) a national holiday, and there were still plenty of Jews who despised him, so catching sight of the Star of David under his casket in a city teeming with Jewish immigrants might have elicited a confused uprising. So while organizers held their breath, horses dragged the reputedly drunk Jew hater uptown on a Jewish booze wagon.

The parade deposited Grant's body in a temporary brick vault on a bluff over the Hudson River just west of Harlem. His real tomb didn't exist yet. (Neither, at the time, did Abraham Lincoln's, who also politely waited thirty-six years in a reception vault until his memorial was ready, in 1901). Grant's body languished on the empty site for twelve years while organizers publicly promised, and noticeably failed to deliver, the most elaborate edifice in history. Behind the scenes they begged, wheedled, and eventually shrank plans to meet lowered expectations in tough economic times. By the end, some 90,000 people had pitched in and a slenderized tomb was dedicated on April 22, 1897. The modern eye fails to detect any restraint: Grant's Tomb, 150 feet tall, is a monolithic white cube of 8,000 tons of granite topped by a colonnaded cupola, a proud riverside temple based on the lost Mausoleum at Halicarnassus: "It will be everywhere known and will be everywhere accepted as the great typical example of American art," *Century* magazine gushed, but then, late-life Grant had been one of its star writers, so then, it would.

His admirers carved LET US HAVE PEACE above the door. That was Grant's catch phrase. The trouble there is, no one can find a time he actually uttered it. He did tag it onto the end of his letter accepting the nomination of his party for president in 1868, but he didn't mean it with any more force than we might scribble "sincerely" or "XO." In fact, in the preceding sentence, Grant wrote we needed peace not because it's humane, but because it keeps taxes low—but "Let us have peace so we can keep our money" does not make for a snappy epitaph. The shorter version also reminded Confederates of all the ways he hadn't crushed them like cockroaches once they lost, and lest you doubt the words carved over the tomb's portal weren't meant to admonish, note that they face south.

Americans are fond of monuments that remind them of temples, if only to make a god out of the man (it's always a man) they tribute. We built an entire capital that way. The neoclassical (it's always neoclassical) Lincoln Memorial and the Jefferson Memorial can still jerk a tear even if you failed eighth grade social studies, because the edifice makes you feel something vaguely stirring and you know just enough information about what's inside to fortify the sensation, one of the most American things about it. This theatricality is the essence of Western memorial making. But when history forgets the figure, these echoing glory halls become majorly creepy. For years, Grant's Tomb was the king of American death tourism sites. At the start of the twentieth century, it attracted nearly a million tourists a year, more than even the Statue of Liberty. But when there was no one left alive from the Civil War, it became unloved, even for a tomb. It became one of those things you swear you'll do someday, but don't, like skydiving or peyote.

In the 1930s, under the control of a civilian booster group, it was lavished with money to keep people from forgetting, and that's when custodians remade Grant's Tomb from a cleanly classic resting place into something militarized. It had been built with nearly no overt war symbols since, after all, Grant had also been president for two terms. The tomb's Depression-era booster group abandoned such even-handedness. Gas-flame lanterns that cast moody shadows were replaced with busts of unblinking Civil War leaders. In the "reliquary rooms" on either side of the circular gallery, where tattered memorabilia from Grant's life had faithfully tortured generations of children, WPA muralist Dean Fausett added map murals depicting the Civil War battle theatre. (As proof of how poor civics education has always been, he misspelled the 1864 Battle of Monocacy as "Monocaly.") After 1959, the National Park Service thought the neoclassical design could also use a splash of vandalism, so it added "lunette mosaic murals" by artist Allyn Cox. According to the NPS' Master Plan, the intent was to foster "an understanding of the basic facts of his career," and another death tourism site was reshaped into a lesson. But they turned out as two-dimensional and as blithely literal as illustrations in a Cold War children's textbook. The central mural, the one you see first when you enter, now depicts General Robert E. Lee at Appomattox Court House. Poor Grant. After everything he went through, even being elected president twice, and after all the trouble his benefactors went through to build a graceful tomb, America's militarized mentality prevailed and his nemesis assumed pride of place hovering above his eternal rest.

By the 1970s, the only reason anyone ducked inside Grant's Tomb was because being in a crypt was a lot less scary than being in its neighborhood. That area of upper Manhattan had deteriorated into an episode of *Kojak*: pimps in velvet chasing hookers, naked toddlers bathing in fire hydrant water, and people driving Lincoln Continentals through piles of empty boxes. The entry staircase's stone eagles, hand-me-downs from the city post office when that was torn down in the 1930s, had their wings pocked with bullets and their beaks blown off with explosives. Rangers routinely discovered evidence of animal sacrifice on the grounds. Some defeated civic leader decided that if they couldn't clean up the area, they could at least junk up the tomb to match. So with the help of, apparently, some hallucinating schoolchildren, they encircled it on three sides with a barrier of Gaudí-esque, multicolored mosaic benches, which instantly disintegrated. The idea, bizarrely, was to make the neo-classical tomb evoke the community's Caribbean and Puerto Rican residents. Things got so ugly that in the early 1990s, some Illinois lawmakers demanded the National Park Service dismantle the whole thing and ship it to their state for safekeeping.

Routine animal sacrifice in the mausoleum of a national hero could be tolerated, but New Yorkers knew they'd sunk to a new low when the Midwest said it could do better. The NPS turned things around. By 2008, the graffiti was power-washed away, the plastic bags disengaged from the tree branches, and the leaky roof patched. The National Park Service rewrote the website to promise thrills and revelations: "He's not just the man on the fifty dollar bill," it crowed. The eagle's bullet hole was permitted to remain as a warning of the city's savage past, and the multicolored benches were, miraculously, deemed to have acquired their own civic cachet, so they stayed, too. Which leads to today, when a double-decker Gray Line bus packed with sightseers, including me, halts nearby, and no one else gets off.

"I'm just curious," I said to one of the young rangers whose primary duty appeared to be ringing up paperweights; it's my standard icebreaker for museum guides and docents. "I'm just curious. I saw the tomb was once the biggest tourist sight in America. Can you tell me about that time?"

"Well, if you have any simple questions, I can answer them for you," said the junior ranger.

"I would love to find out more about its popularity at its peak."

The junior ranger considered my question. "I know something that can help you," he said, and he wrote a word on a slip of paper and slid it across the gift shop counter to me.

"GOOGLE," it read. And he turned away to resume ringing up paperweights and chatting with his colleague.

An older ranger appeared—all vacationers know the sort; he was the kind who coolly wears his Smokey Bear hat like a crown, even in Upper Manhattan, and confronts new visitors with a broad chest and stiff chin, ready for any trivia challenge. I took the hatted ranger to be the Alpha, the silverback of Grant's Tomb, because when he strode into the small presentation room to deliver his introductory speech, the junior rangers fell silent, in the way middle-schoolers are becalmed and edgy when their teacher arrives.

Silverback Ranger made a striking claim. "If Abraham Lincoln had not been assassinated at a place called Ford's Theatre in Washington, DC, (Grant) would have been the first civil rights president." This was a brain-bending, alternative-reality history lesson, sort of like saying Dick Sargent was the first guy to play Darrin on *Bewitched* except for the fact Dick York did it before him. What he meant, I think, was that Lincoln never got a chance to implement freedom for the slaves, and his successor, Andrew Johnson, was a virulent racist, which meant Grant, the third president after emancipation, was the first to properly defend laws that treated black people like 5/5ths human beings. Whatever Silverback meant, I knew he was aptly performing his role as a custodian of a national memorial: he was convincing us why it was important.

The more he spoke, the clearer it became that there

was a wide chasm between Grant the Man and Grant the Honoree. If you look at the facts—a corrupt presidential administration, financial ruin in a ponzi scheme, his Jewish problem and booze problem—no bar was low enough for Grant. He failed at farming and even at saddle selling. Grant's corrupted presidency was a dismal point in American politics, at least until today. Grant's only skill, in fact, was war. So it was ironic, and probably distressing for him, considering his few God-given gifts, that he detested the sight of blood. Imagine being Julia Child, but fainting at the sight of butter. He refused to go hunting and always demanded his steaks be cooked until they were nearly charcoal. But his memorial, as all memorials must, doesn't permit interpretation that falls too short of deification.

Which presents another contradiction, because Grant was not one for boasting. An early biographer's description of him is borderline derisive, writing he "had a girl's primness of manner and modesty of conduct. He was almost half-woman. He was small and slender. His voice was always soft, clear, and musical, and his hands had the long, tapering fingers of a woman." Grant refused to brag despite being one of the biggest celebrities alive, and he only agreed to write his memoirs so he could stop asking friends to pay for his meals after he went broke. Even then, his buddy Mark Twain had to beg him to do it and undertook the hard work of publishing it for him.

As I stood in his marble memorial, it all begged the question: If Grant was this modest and his record so questionable, who let his polished granite tomb become so grandiose? It was because Julia Dent, his cross-eyed wife, wanted it that way, and by that time he was too dead to argue. Grant wanted to be buried in St. Louis, where three of his kids were born, or in Galena, Illinois, where he'd lived. In fact, he had purchased cemetery plots in both places. (If he had met the messy end he delivered to his rival Stonewall, he could have used both of them.) "It is possible that my funeral could become a public event," Grant wrote on June 23, 1885, with characteristic miscalculation. But Galena bored Julia, who as First Lady had grown accustomed to Manhattan's high life. She helped decimate the family savings by traveling with Ulysses around the world in luxury (he was the first American president to visit Saigon), and then she insisted they live near friends, which meant off Fifth Avenue. Washington and West Point would have welcomed Grant's grave, but they wouldn't accept wives, so that wouldn't do, either. When her husband the legend passed, Julia Dent became the keeper of his book fortune and of his reputation, and nothing's as stubborn as a rich wife with a husband to champion. Because his tomb would also become her tomb, she was in the enviable position of being able to shop for her resting place knowing other people were paying.

So when we call it Grant's Tomb, it's more accurate to think of it as Julia Dent Grant's Tomb, which also had a spot for her late husband. He's a sort of a subletter.

At Les Invalides in Paris (finished in 1861), Napoleon

Bonaparte was entombed in a lower gallery so visitors would be forced to bow their heads to behold the great leader. So Julia displayed her husband in the style that was fashionable among political demigods: Worshipers would have to bow their heads to view the twin sarcophagi of Wisconsin red granite gleaming in the low light below. From location to design, Dent got everything she wanted, including a mind-boggling dedication day speaker: Varina Davis, the wife of none other than Confederacy president Jefferson Davis. The widow of the man who unsuccessfully plotted for Grant's death twenty-five years earlier was the person chosen to consecrate his soul because these days, Julia and Varina flounced arm-in-arm on the New York social scene.

Besides Julia, there was one other person pulling the strings. If it weren't for Horace Porter, as the Silverback Ranger pointed out in his introduction, we wouldn't have Grant's Tomb at all. Porter was Grant's loyal war aide, whose superhuman efforts in the final years of fundraising finally made this tomb a reality rather than the pipe dream it was turning out to be. Porter canvassed every corner of New York with appeals for donations. His dedication was frenzied and tireless—which, as all students of politics know, also made it suspicious.

Good old Horace Porter had a dog in the fight: As Grant's personal secretary in the White House, he was implicated in one of the president's most deplorable scandals. Even its name sounds crooked: the Whiskey Scandal. Porter's legacy depended entirely on the burnishing of Grant's. When Porter noticed donors losing interest in the memorial and Grant's legend tarnishing as his body languished by the river in a cruddy brick crypt, Porter led the final push to collect the last third of donations. He did everything he could to reshape the memorial into something more affordable, but no less grand. He theatrically proclaimed that New York was about to lose its hero to the likes of Ohio, which would be a galling prospect to any New Yorker even today—and just like with the memorials at Chickamauga and Gettysburg, stoking state jealousies was a more effective fundraising tool than, you know, mere mourning. Porter also convinced the bus companies to slash fares to Riverside Park to ensure the ribbon cutting would be a shoulder-to-shoulder smash. And it was. Immediately after the lollapalooza dedication, Porter cashed in with a tell-all bestseller, *Campaigning with Grant*, which wisely stuck to the War and skirted his scandalous stint in the White House. Now with his rehabilitated reputation as a constant servant and the mastermind of miracles, he was offered an appointment as ambassador to France, a position previously held by Benjamin Franklin and Thomas Jefferson as one of the cushiest government jobs on record (and, it bears noting, the same one Charles Guiteau assassinated President Garfield over). I'm not saying Porter's scheme was necessarily Machiavellian, but as he boarded the steamer to France, it was clear he got more out of Grant's Tomb than the satisfaction of a job well done—and so did Julia, and so did the military boosters who renovated it later. Grant had dreamed of something simple. But he had no say.

You can call it a perversion of the purity of mourning if you want, but from Fort Sumter, to Arlington, to the merry revisionists of the UDC, there has always proved to be great power in the successful manipulation of negative events. As Horace Porter and Julia Dent both found to the satisfaction of their personal legacies, if you have a group of true believers to harness, the American Myth is a tool that can open every door for you.

I returned to Grant's Tomb at night. The NPS deems itself too fact-based to host something as déclassé as a ghost tour, so this was billed as "a night tour." But everyone knew we were there to get freaked out. Silverback Ranger, or probably his junior minions, had switched off the lights and laid a circle of LED votive candles on the circular ledge overlooking the twin coffins, which were barely discernible below in the shadows. No other lights were on except a corona of pale yellow in the cupola far above, like a halo.

Silverback carefully led our small group, including a yuppie couple chauffeuring an uncontrollable carriage so big it almost required a license plate, down the stone stairs to the enclosed corridor encircling the sarcophagi, and as the stillness gathered around us in chilling plumes, Silverback told us to turn our backs to Ulysses and Julia. Now defenseless against their zombies, we heard the story of Grant's death, about how one day in the spring of 1884, he was eating a peach and felt a sharp pain in his throat. How his physician was on vacation in Europe, so he ignored it until the fall when it was too late. How the doctor gave him a year to live, but all he really had was nine months, all of which he spent feverishly recording his life story as the cancer grew. By the end, he couldn't swallow at all.

"He weighed around ninety pounds," said Silverback Ranger. The echo swarmed over his grave and faded into silence. "He starved to death."

Someone among us exhaled through teeth in appreciation. At least I hope it was one of us.

Silverback pressed his fists together and lifted them in the direction of Ulysses' body, just a few feet behind us. "The cancer that took over the roof of Grant's mouth, the back side of his tongue, and the right side of his throat was the size of my two fists."

He left his fists upraised, representing Grant's tumor. This he let settle in. "Okay?" he said. Five seconds, ten seconds. Thirteen seconds. Something creaked on the upper level of the tomb.

"Grant's suffering made a lasting lifetime impression on everybody who saw it," he said solemnly. "Remarkably enough, one of the last full sentences that Grant spoke, about twenty hours before he died was, 'I don't want anybody to be uncomfortable on my account.'"

The sound of his final request echoed around his chilly granite death palace.

THE MEMORIAL
IMPULSE

HERE LIE THE POWERS
OF REMEMBERING

"There's the story, then there's the real story, then there's the story of how the story came to be told. Then there's what you leave out of the story. Which is part of the story, too."

—MARGARET ATWOOD, *MADDADDAM*

"Men will not understand us...and the war will be forgotten."

—ERICH MARIA REMARQUE, *ALL QUIET ON THE WESTERN FRONT*

"A man is not old until regrets take the place of dreams."

—JOHN BARRYMORE

$77,000

Northeast Georgia

Photo: Tracy O'Neal Photographic Collection, Georgia State University Library

TRAIN ENGINEERING RUNS IN MY FAMILY, LIKE BIG butts. My Confederate veteran great-great-grandfather, Will O'Neal's dad, was also a train engineer. He was part of the team that got the South running again after General Sherman's march. The North had removed every rail between Atlanta and the Carolinas, heated them, and bent them around poles and trees. When the surrender was signed, locals heated the rails and straightened them up as best they could, but they were amateurs at this and their mills were all destroyed, so for a long time, the trains in Georgia ran wobbly. They derailed constantly, but at speeds so creeping—often, just twelve miles per hour—that riding a train was an incessant annoyance, not a mortal threat. For years, Will's dad would often arrive hours late, all because of those damn Yankees. Even if you were on the fence about who was right in the Civil War, a late train has the power to make you despise a million souls.

Will and three of his brothers took up the family business on the Southern Railway, but by the time they were running the engines, the wobbles had been ironed out and they were permitted more perilous speeds. Ironically, things had been much safer after Sherman, as Will would learn. In researching the passing of my derailed forebear, I ran across a clip someone had cut out of the *Atlanta Journal*—the paper that gossiped about Rosa's health and later paid her traumatized son Tracy to photograph crime scenes. Judging by the typeface, it's midcentury. In the clipping, a man named Pierce Harris, a Methodist preacher who sidelined as a columnist, wrote a chicken-soup piece about Southern life, something to be read in the warm bass tones of Garrison Keillor, fuzzy with shameless nostalgia. It was set about forty years before, wrote Harris, "when I was a little barefooted kid up at Buford, GA, living in the Methodist parsonage, with just the highway between us and the railroad tracks, and waving at every train that passed." Lord, all this clipping needs is a rocking chair and an old sleepin' dog.

> One day the engineer of No. 38 pushed the long bill of his peaked cap back on his head, leaned out of the window of his engine with a big smile on his smoke-smeared face, and threw me an orange. I know how the children of Israel felt in the wilderness when they saw the manna coming down from Heaven.

> An orange! The only time we ever had oranges was at Christmas. After I rolled my orange out of my stocking on Christmas morning I spent the first week just SMELLING it. Then I peeled it sadly, and ate it—but saved the peeling... We'd put them in a biscuit pan in the stove and parch them crisp. Then chew them! And the old engineer threw us an orange.

> One night when I went up to meet the Air Line Belle to get my Journals to deliver over on Spring Hill, I went into the depot and asked the agent who the engineer on No. 38 was. He told me, "Will O'Neal." From that time on, Will O'Neal

was my hero, along with Ty Cobb, Jim Jeffries, and Santa Claus. After that, nearly every day Mr. O'Neal would toss off a little gift and we'd wait for his train every day.

One Sunday, some bad boys put an iron spike on the tracks and engine 1231 didn't make the curve. It piled up in the weeds by the tracks with its engineer, Ben Dewberry, caught under the wreckage.

I was one of the first to get there. It was terrible! A living man caught down there under all that hot iron and escaping steam. Somebody said they'd sent for Mrs. Dewberry and about an hour later we heard an engine coming up the tracks from toward Atlanta and we could tell it was coming fast. Along about Sugar Hill crossing it gave out a mournful blast that sounded like the wail of a lost soul, and I said, "Boys, I bet that's ol' Will O'Neal at the throttle," and it was.

Being a little boy, they didn't let me get very close to the wreck, but folks said Will O'Neal was down at the station getting ready to go out on his run when the news of the wreck reached the station and he volunteered to take the special out—with Ben Dewberry's loved ones aboard...

Later, Will O'Neal was killed in a wreck at Mount Airy. His fireman died in the same wreck, which made eighteen firemen who had died in wreckage which Will O'Neal escaped until the last time. He was my hero and still lives in blessed memory because of his kindness to a little boy.

It was a premonition, a confirmation, and a eulogy, all in one—even if he got the train number wrong and Mount Airy was about seventeen miles west of where Will actually met his maker. If there was one lesson that touring America's major death tourism shrines taught me, it was that praiseworthy feelings don't have to be accurate to be defining. Nostalgia is better soft, as sweet and as perishable as an orange. So that clip, like so many American remembrances, was more myth than documentary, but I quite enjoy the image of my great-great-grandfather tossing fruit to me from a locomotive as he hurtled toward his fate.

Along with that clipping in my feeble pile of clues was a photo I had taken of Will O'Neal's grave. It was carved with a symbol of some kind, a seal with a compass, like something Masonic. I posted it on Twitter asking for help, and a follower identified it as the insignia of the Brotherhood of Locomotive Engineers, a group that fortunately still exists today. I called John Bentley, a public relations officer there, and he said although most of its archives had been purged years ago, he knew that somewhere in his building, a few bound copies of the old membership magazine, the scintillatingly named *Locomotive Engineers Journal*, were dejectedly gathering dust.

"Most of the time, researching the *Journal* is like looking for a needle in a haystack," he confessed. But because I knew a date, I was in luck. "At the time," Bentley told me, "the B.L.E. had its own life insurance for members. Railroading was deemed too dangerous of an occupation and no regular insurance company would provide coverage to our members." Train engineers turned to their own for coverage, and Will, "member of Div. 696," held a B.L.E. policy. Bentley showed me the result.

Name: W.J. O'Neal; age 49; Date of Admission, April 22, 1893; Date of death, Feb. 22, 1909; Cause of death or disability, killed; Amount of insurance, $3,000.00; Payable to: Wife and son.

In those days, the railway was one of the most prestigious jobs a man with a basic education could take. Trains enabled a worker to see the country in a way that, at that time, relatively few people could. The locomotive and its rails were the cutting edge of technology, and literal and figurative engines of American power, expansion, and boundless wealth.

But in my family, trains just overturned. Even though Rosa's husband had one of the longest careers on the entire Southern Railway, the new widow was only paid the equivalent of $77,000 in today's money to raise her kids. (Incidentally, the engineer Casey Jones, whose own heroic 1900 wreck death was immortalized into folklore by the popular ballad, had also been a B.L.E life policyholder. Mrs. Jones was paid exactly what Rosa got.)

The *Journal* didn't editorialize any more about Will's wreck and who caused it ("mainly because they were all too common," Bentley explained), and no one ever wrote a song about it, which was hardly fair since Will hadn't been snorting cocaine on the job like Casey Jones had been, if you believe the Grateful Dead version. Will died the same death, but it was the junkie who became the legend. Worse, fifteen years after Will's crash, the balladeer Vernon Dalhart recorded the tragedy tune "Wreck of the Old 97," by G. B. Grayson and Henry Whitter. Engineer mortality was so routine that the song was virtually identical to Will's story: a heroic Southern Railway locomotive engineer was scalded to death in a crash. "He was found in the wreck with his hand on the throttle/Scalded to death by the steam." That gruesome toe-tapper became the first American song to sell more than a million copies—maybe because everyone knew someone who had succumbed to the country's miraculous, but prodigiously chancy rail system. That song ultimately went on to sell more than five million, a death attraction manifest as consumer product. Later it became a song by another train wreck, Johnny Cash. I wish my ancestors had gotten a piece of that sweet, sweet train crash ditty cash. Even though Will departed the same way as Casey Jones on the Old 97, all Rosa got was a few thousand bucks and chronic drug stupor.

The Civil War and its wobbly-railed universe of woe are behind us. Like my grandfathers, we move out of that dark period into a climactic future, furiously attempting to straighten the rails as we go. New questions emerge for the last of my odyssey, which covers the years outside that war: Why do we immortalize some losses, and why do we let others die a second time? And when is national mourning just something we pursue to achieve a theatrical effect?

At this point in my explorations, as I moved toward my own era, the answers started hitting a lot closer to home.

REALLY NOT REALLY

Ford's Theatre

Appomattox

Harpers Ferry, West Virginia

Buffalo, New York

Sand Creek, Colorado

Wounded Knee, South Dakota

IN ANY MOVIE STARRING ABRAHAM LINCOLN, JUST pick one, whenever he has something important to say, he inevitably rises and says it as he stares out a window. More than any president America has had, Abraham Lincoln was unmatched in his proficiency at haunted window staring. What he saw out his many sad windows was why he required diversion at the theatre. There, he stared out of his box seat instead, and it was during the last such staring he ended.

I said I'd be going to no more sites from the Civil War, and I meant it. But there's a reason I'm permitting Ford's Theatre to make an appearance. For one, it's now a legitimate performance house for paying audiences again. Productions share space with toddling tourists who hope to gawp at the fateful presidential box where Lincoln himself, we're reminded, found himself too absorbed in a performance of *Our American Cousin*. Ford's' first season after its 2009 renovation was a flop musical called *The Civil War,* cowritten by Frank Wildhorn, the same Lite FM balladeer who inflicted pop culture with *Jekyll and Hyde* starring David Hasselhoff. *The Civil War* is conspicuous for smothering accuracy in a thick frosting of wistful pseudo-pop. It's a Mad Libs musical in which the lyricist filled every blank with *glory, brother,* or *home*—come to think of it, much like the death tourism attractions about the period. It also includes a requisite scene of Lincoln staring out a window. Mercifully, Abe doesn't break into a power ballad. He just stands there, being the penny. Instead, a slave called Harriet does the work—no obvious jokes, please—by planting her feet on the stage and rendering the barn burner (if that's the phrase, given John Wilkes Booth's fate) "Candle in the Window." "Every evening I can see his shadow on the shade/And I don't feel so alone or afraid/There's a candle in the window every night/Reflecting all our hopes and dreams...Burning like the yearning to be free." It was hammy nonsense, but then again, so was *Our American Cousin*, up to one extremely uncomfortable point.

On the night I was at Ford's, though, there was a more appropriate musical in production: *1776*, a mostly accurate rendition in which Adams, Jefferson, and Franklin sing their way toward drafting the Declaration of Independence. After the show, the friend I attended with talked with Brooks Ashmanskas, the guy playing John Adams, and we asked him what it felt like to play an American president in the same space that Lincoln had been shot. "There's a place in the show where slavery comes up—and the fact that it was one of the big compromises that was excised from the original document, sadly," Ashmanskas said. "And there's a line that Adams has. I say to Franklin, 'Mark me: if we give in on this issue, posterity will never forgive us.' And where I'm standing, I'm literally looking at Lincoln's chair. At times I have to not look because it's so moving and upsetting. It's so heavy being here."

On a lower level near the stage, you'll find the museum. You can tell the type of visitor a site wants to attract by the intellectual depth of its informational signs.

Most American signs wouldn't challenge a third grader; they keep the *howevers* and *meanwhiles* of history to a minimum and stick to the A plot. But you can tell who *really* comes to an attraction by what its gift shop sells. Like Gettysburg, Ford's Theatre is controlled by a public-private partnership, the National Park Service and Ford's Theatre Society, which, also like Gettysburg, contracts its sales to Event Network. The souvenirs shy away from John Wilkes Booth bobbleheads, but they're still questionable for a murder scene: Merchandise has included *Haunted Theaters*, *Abraham Lincoln: Vampire Hunter*, a t-shirt of Abe visiting Antietam with the legend "Does this top hat make me look too tall?" and two varieties of chocolate peanuts: Democrap Donkey Dung and Repooplican Elephant Dung. My tacky takeaway: a $4 Ford's Theatre key chain filled with colored goop that slowly oozes down each time you turn it over. History is fun!

Tourists are not treated to a free performance at Ford's. They have to pay if they want to see a show, and his presidential box is off-limits (a little too late). But the museum visit includes the multimedia section in the basement, the Petersen House across the street (a few doors down from Lincoln's Waffle Shop—"Bus Groups Welcome!"), where he died and where the faded bloodstain on the pillow is the star attraction. That was only preserved because its landlord, William Petersen, recognized its commercial value amid the fevered moment of national grief—what a true American. The bed, bloody sheets, and the Lincolns' eveningwear found their way to Chicago by way of caramel maker Charles Gunther, who also knew there was cash to be made in presidential gore. He also purchased the notorious Confederate POW camp Libby Prison, moved it stone by stone from Richmond to Chicago's Wabash Avenue in 1889, and displayed his assassination quarry alongside Barnumesque balderdash such as the "Skin of the Serpent that Tempted Eve in the Garden of Eden." The Republican National Convention was hosted in a hall behind the Libby Prison facade for five presidential nominations running, from 1904 to 1920—we chose Taft in a Confederate POW camp building serving as a death tourism attraction—and now the Chicago Historical Society owns the clothes.

Ford's Theatre is one of Washington's must-see tourist stops, and it churns through the coachloads and school groups hourly. Tickets are timed to manage the flood of mostly unengaged tagalongs, and I didn't have nearly enough time to take in the exhibits crammed into the cellar. Despite a fine design that gives the impression of a spooky, half-dismantled mansion, mostly people milled about looking lost. Some managed to watch only a few seconds of documentaries that were already only a minute or two long, and some skimmed what amounted to a respectable *SparkNotes* version of Lincoln's life. A few posed for cheesy vacation photos with dopey Instagram-ready figures intended to represent a "swarm of office seekers." The prurient details of Lincoln's shooting, including a case containing John Wilkes Booth's tiny Derringer pistol and images of the coconspirators, were discreetly placed in a dimly lit nook behind a partition, where the squeamish could avoid stumbling across them. This created a traffic jam of picture snappers around the murder weapon. But many others wanted nothing at all to do with education and sat petulantly on the floor until it was time for their tour of the assassination zone upstairs.

In due course, we were flushed out of the museum to go upstairs and sit in the mezzanine of the theatre. There, the National Park ranger pointed to what everyone came to see: Lincoln's box seat, decked out with bunting and a portrait of George Washington, as it was in 1865. He devoted most of his twenty-minute talk to a detailed timeline of that dark day, usually in the present tense, like a 1950s episode of *You Are There*. Lincoln "sat there," Booth leapt "and landed about there."* He repopulated the night of April 14, 1865, right before our eyes in Ford's Theatre's latest performance.

But then, in the very last seconds of his engrossing retelling, as we were reaching for our bags, he dropped his truth. After the Civil War, he said, the government acquired the theatre. "The government, doing what they do, has property they utilize. So they turned this building into an office warehouse for war records. In 1893, the third floor collapsed all the way to the basement, killed twenty-two government workers, injured about seventy,"

---

* Speaking of throwback CBS TV shows, the last surviving eyewitness to the assassination, Samuel J. Seymour, appeared on the panel game show *I've Got a Secret* in 1956. That's right: someone who saw John Wilkes Booth shoot Lincoln appeared on television at age ninety-six. "I was scared to death," he told Jayne Meadows. So worth Googling. But also so not the point, hence its relegation to this rare footnote.

he said. "In 1965, President Lyndon Johnson signed a bill to restore Ford's Theatre to exactly the way it was the night President Lincoln was here."

So, surprise, tourists: Lincoln did *not* sit there, and Booth didn't land there, either. Everything inside the brick walls was put there in the 1960s. The facade is original, but the interior of Ford's Theatre is as fake as the sets of the plays on its stage, but pilgrims aren't told until the final seconds of a ninety-minute visit, when they're fatigued and unlikely to retain the bombshell.

What, now?

"Thank you for your attention. Please be sure to collect all of your belongings."

The materials in the theatre lend the impression it's been preserved for a century and a half. The way the wood creaks underfoot might have you believe it, too. But Ford's Theatre is a fabrication derived from architects' best guesses from the scanty records that exist. It's meant to capture Lincoln's night, but there isn't so much as a plaque for the twenty-two people who perished in the collapse of the original Ford's. They selflessly gave their lives to secretarial services, but Lincoln earns the only eulogy—and he didn't even die on the premises.

The Ford's Theatre we visit is not from the Civil War. It's not even as old as the Korean War. Ford's *Bewitched*-era provenance was one of the biggest shocks of my tour of death tourism landmarks, but it doesn't stand alone as a faker. Many so-called historic sites weren't historic at all, but were recreations to provide a stage for your feelings. Take the White House. In the Depression, it was declared at risk of collapse, so in 1950, Truman gutted it to the brick walls. For a while, it was held together by scaffolding. He installed steel support beams, reinforced concrete columns, and a new sub-basement, but most of the dry-rotted wood had to be tossed. So he rebuilt everything (this time, happily, without slave labor) using replicas. The White House imitates the White House. That means Lincoln never slept in our Lincoln Bedroom, either.

Retelling the past in and of itself seems subject to the Heisenberg Principle: If people know a place was important enough to share with future generations, then it cannot be observed honestly, because they know it's important enough to stage. The simple act of recording history, because you recorded one thing and not another, is already defined by a bias for what's important. Even Matthew Brady, held today as the pioneer of gritty photojournalism, rearranged his corpses for effect.

Quite a few landmark buildings went missing because of road shows designed to make cash off dark tourism. The McLean House in Appomattox, Virginia, where Robert E. Lee surrendered to Ulysses S. Grant and ended the war, was torn down in the 1890s. The owner intended to tour the structure as a traveling attraction, but he ran out of money, and its pieces were left to rot outside. It was reinvented according to original plans around World War II. I visited on a foggy spring morning. My tour group was encouraged to feel awe at being in such a hallowed chamber, but when I asked the docent if everything was original, a pall fell over her face. "This is very much like what the two generals would have experienced," she said sourly. Only the vases on the mantel and the frame of the horsehair couch in the corner were even in the real room at the time. It's all simulated for imaginative effect—making Appomattox less of a museum and more like the set for a movie that can play in our minds. Same for the cabin at Abraham Lincoln Birthplace National Historical Park in Hodgenville, Kentucky. It doesn't even fit in the Memorial Building that protects it. When I went, it was stuffed in there like a thirty-pound turkey in a two-quart pot. You're not allowed to enter it, and I couldn't fit it all into my camera lens even if I pressed my back to the wall. When I asked what was going on, I was told that in 1909, Americans were eager to mark one hundred years since Lincoln's birth, and federal authorities were all too eager to acquire this cabin, which was being passed off as Lincoln's as it toured the country, and chop it down to squeeze in their neo-classical shrine. The cabin's dubious origins were evident from the start, but not publicized because it would dent tourism numbers. It took decades for rangers to openly admit that this shack is a faker. It was actually built in the 1890s by a New York huckster to cash in on pilgrims (he also bought another cabin he claimed belonged to Confederate President Jefferson Davis—to appeal to the other side of the aisle). Recent tree ring tests dated the wood to 1848, when Lincoln was already in Congress. Now the National Park Service gingerly dubs it the "Symbolic Birth Cabin." That didn't stop the US Mint from putting the fraud on the 2009 Lincoln penny, engraved with no such caveat. You may have the hoax in your pocket right now.

Not all reconstructions are arranged for strategic political use, but as long as no one is aware of the truth, all reconstructed places can be used politically. Most of Harpers Ferry, where John Brown's gang martyred themselves in an attempt to kick-start the Civil War, was essentially destroyed within eighteen months. You can blame the war for that: the town changed hands more than ten times over the course of it, bombarded all to hell. (Will O'Neal's father, Joshua, fought in the Battle of Corrick's Ford, which delivered Harpers Ferry and West Virginia to the Union once and for all, where it stayed.) Only the old guard house, where John Brown's final stand took place, still stands there, where it attracts visitors as a de facto memorial to the visionary agitator. But surprise—even that's a reconstruction. In 1891, the original battered shack was sold, dismantled, and sent to Chicago for the World's Columbian Exposition, after which its pieces were abandoned in a vacant lot. Benefactors saved what they could, moving it to a spot three miles out of Harpers Ferry and then to a nearby college campus. Only in 1968, around the time Ford's Theatre was being fabricated, did the building, now known as John Brown's Fort, wind up back in Harpers Ferry—which also lost its apostrophe in the intervening years—and not even in the right spot, since its rightful home is 150 feet away, under what's now a railroad embankment. When you're on a tour of your next allegedly preserved historical shrine, always ask what's original. It's fun to watch guides strain to be optimistic while they tell you most of what you're seeing is a wild guess, "typical for the period."

The original Federal Hall in New York City, where George Washington was inaugurated and Congress first convened? Demolished in 1812 and sold for $400 in scrap. Teddy Roosevelt Birthplace National Historic Site in Manhattan? Torn down in 1916, then rebuilt three years later out of severe regret. The simulated interior contains "family furniture." Guides know this, but to unquestioning guests, they still proclaim physically impossible things such as "the charter for the Museum of Natural History was signed in this room."

Embarrassment is another good way we lose track of history. I parked my car in an unremarkable Buffalo neighborhood and wandered its streets past conspicuously shifting curtains until I located the place where William McKinley was assassinated in 1901. Now it lies in the median of a street, marked only by a half-hearted plaque stuck on an ankle-height rock. The humiliated city fathers, in his time, were horrified they let the crime happen, and because war between the classes was in the air, they were terrified that a proper remembrance would become a shrine for those who sought to upend the social order. Even the home where his vice president, Teddy Roosevelt, was sworn in got turned into a turkey restaurant.

The place where John Wilkes Booth died is also under a road, and so is the spot in the train station where President James Garfield was shot, or maybe it's under the National Gallery—no one is quite sure anymore. But no one wanted to aggrandize Booth, and Garfield's assassination was the act of a madman; it righted no wrongs, attained no political purpose, and required no official defense. So both were swept away. JFK's final stand is *literally* in the middle of the road, smack in a traffic lane, but Dallas, humiliated like Buffalo, never cared to uphold the event by roping off the location; it's still used by cars to this day. If you're counting, that means 75 percent of assassinated US presidents' attack sites are now found under a road. That's how much we want to forget—or how much authorities, always keen to preserve the peaceful political order, don't want us to dwell on them. Hotel managers aren't keen to attract nosy parkers, either. The rooms that saw the last of Sid Vicious, Whitney Houston, and Anna Nicole Smith, have all been subdivided, gut renovated, or renumbered.

The site of the 1890 massacre at Wounded Knee (as many as 300 more Native people, by US troops) is without a federal attraction of any kind. That land, at the southern edge of the Badlands, still belongs to the Lakota Sioux, where the US federal government has no jurisdiction to carve out a National Park unit. It's a National Historic Landmark, a distinction on paper, but its designation beyond the bureaucratic margins prevent it from becoming a popular tourist sight. There's a roadside museum that feeds off traffic from the famous South Dakota truck stop Wall Drug, nearly two miles' drive north of the actual site on I-90, and I was repeatedly encouraged to satisfy my curiosity by going there instead. In fact, every white person I met along the way told me to be careful if I insisted on going to Wounded Knee itself.

I insisted, and it was a shock. The Pine Ridge Reservation is one of the poorest areas in the entire nation, plagued by chronic alcoholism, murder, and poverty. Those who dare to pay their respects at the actual Wounded Knee, site of the event that helped usher all that despair in, may do so at a makeshift museum run on an erratic schedule by locals faithful to the audaciously independent American Indian Movement. A hand-painted sign declares the facility is "pledged to fight White man's injustice to Indians, his oppression, persecution, discrimination, and malfeasance in the handling of Indian Affairs." Although I am most certainly white, no one I met was poised to avenge injustice. As is so often the case at places I've been warned against visiting, the people there were friendly and happy to see I was interested. We chatted about how many guests they get ("some, not too many") and what winters are like ("really cold"). Many of the victims are buried in a hilltop cemetery encircled by chain link fence tied with streams of colored fabric and marked by a stark iron-and-cinder block arch straight out of Tim Burton. The wind was fierce. Wanting to leave something positive behind, I bought some handmade bracelets from a woman who hung out in a minivan wearing a parka and would jump out, smiling to signal a clear welcome, whenever an out-of-towner like me showed up. I was the only person there, and her only customer.

To the eye accustomed to manicured Arlington and Gettysburg, the encroaching dry grasses are ignored and unkempt, so my instinct was to feel anger at the disrespect, but in fact, allowing a grave to overgrow is part of the Lakota tradition. I was told by a South Dakotan that it would be a sign of respect to leave tobacco. The only brand I could find at the convenience store on the way was the chewing kind called Red Man. The package was adorned with a stereotypical drawing of an Indian, tribe unexplained, wearing a warrior eagle feather war bonnet. I sheepishly looked upon the carved names of the murdered, such as Afraid of Bear and Scatters Them, and not wanting to simply dump the tobacco—it would just fly away in the wind—I propped the pouch against the main memorial. As I hastily darted away to take shelter, the Red Man caricature watched me go, wholly unimpressed by the white man caricature tossing the wrong offering and beating a sheepish retreat in his rental car. I hoped that when it comes to pilgrimage, it's the thought that counts the most. I did not feel absolved.

Deep in remote Colorado, down unpaved brown roads that seemed to have no ending, the American government does a lot better than usual at the site of 1864's so-called Battle of Sand Creek. Some battle—it was really just an out-and-out slaughter by United States troops. As many as 163 Native American people, most of them kids and women, were murdered. There, in a landscape as windswept and desolate as your nightmares might paint it to be, you're filled in on the gory scene, not in a lush Mission 66 visitor center, but in a cheap trailer-*cum*-museum with the wind leaking in. Here, far from cities and off the radar for nearly all Americans, you finally find frankness that's unusual for a National Park unit—lots of talk of bashed brains and entrails courtesy of Uncle Sam. This far into nowhere, there's no point in sanitizing shame anymore. The US did it, so there's no take-backsies or spinning this one. The few visitors who come are acquainted with the harrowing truth, plus some morsels about the fragility of cottonwood and prairie grass because national parks can't help themselves. While I was there, no one else showed up except a busload of Cheeto-fragrant middle-schoolers (the same age as some of the victims) who shuffled robotically toward the placards. No one is allowed anywhere near the spot of the actual murders, given that it's considered sacred ground—again, that's more respect than we give to a lot of these places—although there are a few mounted binoculars you can peer through at the rumpled prairie, trying to figure out exactly where you should be looking. You may only consider the scene respectfully from an impossible distance—a fitting metaphor for how we view any of the Native American massacres.

COMMANDING PEACE

Triangle Shirtwaist Factory
General Slocum
Colfax, Louisiana
The Lorraine Motel
Haymarket Square Riot

RECOGNITION IS UNFAIR BECAUSE NOT EVERYONE
can have it. We like to think we pay tribute to the greatest sacrifices, but it's just not true. Far more places are
neglected than are canonized, and when you consider the
ones that get passed over, a pattern emerges that tells us
more about society than it feels polite to admit.

At the outset of my journeys, I made a list of the
most awful American events I could think of. But when
the map was out and I began planning, time and again I
would learn that most of my ideas didn't attract groupies
in appreciable numbers. They endure mostly in textbooks or on lonely plaques. For example, there's nothing
significant in Chicago that commemorates the Great
Fire of 1871. That killed some 300 people and irrevoca-
bly transformed the city's trajectory, and locals never
tire of bringing it up, but there are no vital museums
or attractions for it. Michigan Avenue's Water Tower
and its pumping station are rare and precious survivors
of the fire, but the tower contains an art gallery and
the station houses a theatre ensemble with Ross from
Friends as a member. Likewise, in San Francisco you'll
hear unrelenting references to 1906's horrific quake
and fire, but you'll see no single pedigreed attraction
chronicling the 3,000-or-so people killed nor the way
the disaster reshaped the entire West. It defies logic that
both cities wouldn't dwell on the one thing that the residents *still* can't stop talking about, but if you flip the
pages of time backward, you come to understand that
in the wake of such calamities, the victims only wanted

to look forward and rebuild as fast as they could. In both places, idealistic city planners tried to take advantage of the moment to introduce new plans for radial avenues and parklands that would rival the aesthetics of Paris or Washington. They were drowned out by businesses that didn't want to pause for a moment and risk losing power to competition. New streets were laid right on top of the old ones, rubble was plowed into landfill, and that mentality of forward motion appears to inform their tourism approaches to this day. You could say that those cities, like Katrina-wasted New Orleans or London after the Blitz, did not care to be defined by their heartache, so there were never serious social movements to build altars extending it.

A death might have been a major cause célèbre in its era, and thousands of people might have marched in protest of it waving a hundred newspaper headlines, but if prosecution attorneys ever managed to sully their names in the public mind—like Sacco and Vanzetti, like Julius and Ethel Rosenberg—they earn no beatification in their afterlife. The accused witches of Salem, Massachusetts, are mostly remembered with honky-tonk vacation amusements that fetishize torture, the steamroller of injustice, and the occult rituals that none of them actually practiced. The Wall Street bombing of 1920 killed thirty-eight and wounded 400, but with no suspects, there was no one to blame and therefore no one to be indignant about, no one to tell our children to vilify. No one pays pilgrimage there, either. In fact, Americans have forgotten it so completely they may assume terrorism arrived with the World Trade Center.

Moreover, events that happened out of government failure are enormously unlikely to be memorialized with any thoughtfulness. There's nothing of specific substance for 1894's seminal Pullman Strike riot in Chicago (killed: thirty, maybe more); although the buildings themselves are preserved, it's as milestones in urban design. Same for 1914's Ludlow Massacre in Colorado, where some twenty-five people (thirteen of them women or kids) were snuffed out in their tent city because they supported unions—the site exists, but no one really goes. (Admit it: you hadn't even heard about it until now.) In New York City, more than thirty-three times as many people died of AIDS than in the Twin Towers—that's more than 100,000 lives. You'd think a number that overwhelming would merit a substantial museum of deep investigation—Antietam, with a quarter the casualties, sets aside five square miles and has a busy interpretive center. Yet outside Greenwich Village's onetime St. Vincent's Hospital, ground zero of that losing battle, the only remembrance that can be mustered is an abstract, skeletal canopy on a commercially unviable wedge of a traffic island, marooned by busy streets. And even that poor showing, which teaches nothing that a marker of loss of that magnitude should, took thirty long years to come up with. Meanwhile, the hospital's death wards where the tragedy actually unfolded were converted into luxury apartments. We all know why money won out over those people.

Commercial fires have been wiped away. Take the horrendous 1903 conflagration in Chicago's Iroquois Theatre, which consumed more than 600 people at the children's play *Mr. Bluebeard* and forced fire exit standards that protect you and me today. That theatre was rebuilt into a popular house for Broadway road shows, but the only signs you'll find outside the lobby doors are the ones reading "No smoking." The Brooklyn Theatre fire of 1876 snatched 300 souls, primarily in the family section, who are now only recalled in a graveyard. Similarly, although 146 people were set ablaze in the obscene Triangle Shirtwaist Factory in 1911, an event that transformed labor rights in the United States and changed the way you and I do our jobs, there's no place to learn about it. The floors where those abused workers were trapped aren't even consecrated; they're working laboratories at New York University. All we get is a plaque over a section of sidewalk where flaming women hurled themselves to their ends. On the anniversary, a few people come to stand in the cold, read the names of the dead, and ring a bell, but that's the annual extent of the tourism facilities. It's even worse for the victims of the sinking of the steamer *General Slocum* in the East River in 1904. That took 1,021 people, mostly women and children, and it revolutionized transportation safety. Until 9/11, it was the deadliest disaster in New York City, yet there's no landmark for that other than a shabby, antique, hard-to-find drinking fountain in Tompkins Square Park on the Lower East Side. Those two paltry memorials can be visited, or more likely overlooked, within a few blocks of each other. When I passed them one spring afternoon, it struck me that until this point in my cross-country adventures, a majority of the important dark tourism sites were the outcome of boys trying to prove they were men. These events were the only sites that claimed mostly female and child victims—and they barely register.

But when a mess culminates in dead soldiers or police officers—oh, yes, when it's the government that suffers the loss—memorials spring up like mushrooms after a rain. This commemoration bias happens throughout history—government dead strongly tend to be more remembered than the death of mere civilians. If you want to have a memorial dedicated to you, then you'd better be a soldier, a politician, or a cop. In Chicago, there may not be much dedicated to the Great Fire, but you can bet there's something for its firefighters. Chicago had a leading role as a crucible of modern US labor rights, but misses most of its logical landmarks. The one major memorial it did attempt to erect quickly devolved into an outrageous, century-long saga of insult, hilarity, and rogue public transportation.

I'm talking about the much-persecuted Haymarket Memorial, the Rodney Dangerfield of death markers. Come with me as we follow this bombastic statue's uproariously messy journey through time, as it fails again and again to put observers in the mind of anything except bumbling mayhem.

It was 1886, yet another moment when Americans,

as they routinely do, panicked over an obsession that foreign-born terrorists were trying to destroy us all. As it so often does, it was our trigger-happy anxiety, and not the immigrants, that brought the tears. On May 3 of that year, police shot and killed two (maybe six; reports vary) workers who were striking for an eight-hour workday. The next day, foreign-born labor activists, the most harmless rung on the pay scale, responded by organizing a mass protest. In retrospect, the German organizer probably shouldn't have headlined his protest announcement flyer with the threatening exclamation "Workingmen, To Arms!!!" and its unnamed typesetter probably shouldn't have added the word "REVENGE!" in bold letters across the top. Some 1,500 protesters showed up, well pissed off, and the cops, also in a froth, were ready for anything. Their fury fast fizzled. It was raining, the protest was a dud, and the crowd thinned out. The mayor told the police they could start going home, too. When there were only about 300 stragglers left, a group of 200 policemen abruptly advanced on them and someone—no one knows who—lobbed a bomb. The cops opened fire, mowing protesters down, and by the end, the explosion and melee had bloodied sixty officers, killed seven of them, and resulted in the shooting deaths of countless workers—at least four, but no one knows for sure, because once again, the proletariat goes uncounted. The courts' solution was to go after the protesters because broadly, labor agitators had a reputation for violence, so one of them was deemed most likely to have thrown the device.

Seven men were given the death penalty, not because of any solid evidence against them, but essentially because activism made them suspicious.

Within three years, Chicago's police forged a memorial—not to the bystanders who were gunned down, but to themselves. It was a nine-foot colossus intended to shame, a preposterously manly cop with feet apart and right arm upraised as if to halt all movement, looming atop a pedestal taller than any mortal below. The inscription rebuked all who approached: "I command peace." Frankly, in later years, you could have labeled it LENIN or FRANCO and shipped it to war, so plainly fascistic was its aspect, but the cops had the funds to make the statue and therefore the funds to claim the meaning of the riot for themselves. The public was, to put it pleasantly, unimpressed. Considering the atmosphere, in which popular opinion—rightly or wrongly—revered the put-upon protesters, the monstrous cop was declared to be heavy-handed, tone-deaf symbolism, and a bald attempt to redefine the incident. This authoritarian art was installed squarely in the middle of Haymarket Square, the scene of the tragedy, where it blocked traffic to assert its fiber. That did not go over well, either. The Cop quickly assumed the role of the city's favorite canvas for vandalism. Annoyed by that, the government decided to move it to a less busy spot on a nearby intersection, but largely because of its largeness, its reign of irritation continued, and for Chicagoans, defiling it in ever-more creative ways evolved into a kind of sport. In 1927, on the forty-first anniversary of the bombing, a streetcar jumped its tracks and rammed the pedestal, knocking it over. The motorman shrugged and told cops that gee, his brakes must have failed, while privately, he lustily bragged that he was "sick of seeing that policeman with his arm raised."

At this point, the Chicago Police might have realized it was time to retire the old lightning rod, but instead, as Americans do, they chose entrenchment over compromise. The Cop moved again into a park, a secure distance from rogue trolley attacks, but it continued to get painted, chipped, and bashed by fresh new generations of eager police hecklers, until it was relocated to yet another home alongside the grimy Kennedy Expressway, its fourth spot in seventy years. That's when the fun really began. On the eighty-second anniversary, it was doused in black paint. The city retaliated by declaring it a monument. The next year, 1969, a bomb exploded between its ankles, blowing out one hundred windows and sending chunks of cop akimbo, not unlike the poor policemen it was sculpted to honor. The mayor ("an attack on all the citizens of Chicago!") put it back together again and rededicated it. Five months later, another bomb sent it flying once more in different pieces. Furious, the major fixed it *again* and ordered the expense of round-the-clock protection. But in 1972, as the Vietnam War dragged on, the art enforcement corps finally recognized it was time to surrender. Stripped of its pedestal, the battered Haymarket statue finally found refuge inside police buildings, stashed first in the HQ and then in a locked courtyard of a training building. Not until 2004, 118 years after the Haymarket Bombing, did the city try to balance its inflammatory pro-police statement by chipping in for a separate, inoffensive memorial that would pay token respect to labor unions. Only after that, in 2007, did the battered Haymarket cop feel it was safe enough to show his face in public again. Today, he gingerly risks a renewed thrashing a few short feet from the police headquarters, his seventh location, and so near the entrance that he could almost dart indoors at the first hint of agitation.

Massacres usually reveal a weakness in the victors, and the Haymarket cop is just one example of many in which people's movements were elbowed aside to sing praises of the establishment. There have been countless locations in US history where the death of the powerless made life and work better for the rest of us, their contributions as worthy as those who perished in uniforms. In a truly healthy democracy, you might say, the machinery of government would never be permitted to be wielded to obscure its most vulnerable citizens.

Historian Shelby Foote, like many flowery writers who churned out nectar for Civil War buffs to endlessly gather, thought the likelihood of memorialization depends mostly about what the subject means to the population. I think yes, that may be a factor, but mostly it's about who's paying. It's quick work for the government to authorize budgets to tribute its own, but if you died opposing the status quo, you were always by definition struggling to make a mark. Foote also thought memorials are all about finding a common truth to heal us, but I think the UDC's double-talking inscriptions prove that's naïve. Memorials are too often about stanching further debate. Mounting one can simply be about claiming the final victory by commanding peace.

WHITE HOLY BONES

Navy Yard and Fort Greene Park, Brooklyn
Dealey Plaza

SOMETIMES, PEOPLE JUST STOP CARING. AMERIcans are good at many things, but for us, especially, forgetting is a forte. That's especially true of the death tourism sites that concern our freedom itself: the American Revolution. There are nearly none. Except the one that contains nearly 12,000 bodies in a single room in the middle of the city.

Mel Gibson's cherry-cheeked son never rushed into a cloud of musket smoke for our independence. It only happened in the movies. What the die-hard patriots skip over, besides the fact that France won us the Revolution, is that during that war, more people died in British prisons than the relatively lucky 4,400 who died on the battlefield. Three times as many, in fact, although Americans far prefer to imagine their liberators perishing bravely by the magnificent impact of a musket ball.

These were no ordinary prisons. They were decommissioned ships that had outlived their seagoing usefulness. The British would strip these leaky vessels of fittings, leaving behind what were called *hulks*. In later years, the Redcoats would ship undesirables to Australia, but in the 1770s, Australia hadn't been invented yet, so the Brits anchored their hulks off colonial coasts and stuffed thousands of enemies—spies, captured sailors, visiting Spaniards, anyone who displeased King George— onto them without light, air, or adequate provisions. They were no less than floating concentration camps. The worst of them (there were at least fifteen) were in Wallabout Bay off the Brooklyn shore, around the bend from where the Brooklyn Bridge now touches down.

The ships were operated with morbid efficiency, which is to say they were surpassingly efficient at morbidity. If you watched them, you'd see them produce a steady haul of corpses. Every day, under the command of a Scots-born royalist from Philadelphia with the mordantly Dickensian name of David Sproat, Hessian mercenaries would press-gang a few of the strongest prisoners to row the day's dead to shore and hastily sprinkle their newly departed comrades with a few inches of sand. As many as eight lifeless men a day were removed from the most notorious prison ship, the *Jersey*, a vermin-infested hulk which held 1,000 convicts at a time. We wouldn't have known the true body count at all if it hadn't been for a Dutchman and his daughter who kept count from the window of the nearby Remsen's Mill in then-pastoral Brooklyn; but with help from their records, we now guess that some 11,500 corpses accumulated this way from 1775 to 1783.

Despite this horrific eight-year orgy of suffering, not one prisoner is known to have recanted his allegiance to the colonies and to have joined the British. One capitulatory word would have freed any man from his agonizing sentence. "Promises of pardon and gold were made to them if they would but submit to 'good King George;'" recounted *Harper's Weekly* ninety years later, "but they sadly shook their heads. 'Then rot!' said the British officers; and rot and die they did." Terrified of disease, no clergy came to pray, no civilians sent aid, and no farm delivered food despite the fact that there was plenty of fresh crops and water within sight on shore. Making matters worse, George Washington, who headed up the Continental Army, refused to lift a finger to rescue the impounded, not only because the prisoners could unleash smallpox upon the general population, but also—as Lincoln feared with Andersonville—mainly because a prisoner exchange would put healthy enemy soldiers back on the lines. Washington let them suffer and die because he thought the prisoners were a necessary sacrifice.

After Independence, the pestilent hulls bobbed in the East River for years until the worms took them under. Into the early nineteenth century, Americans still lamented the mass slaughter of "the Martyrs." Anyone who lived in the booming metropolis of New York after the Revolutionary War would have had a hard time forgetting: When least expected, corpses would resurface from the shallow sludge with uncivilized regularity. For a while there, the East River looked like Carol Ann's swimming pool in *Poltergeist*. Skulls lined the shore like seashells. In 1808, in an effort to reform their harbor of horrors into an international seaport of a more professional caliber, New Yorkers pinched their noses, poked around the mud for all the leftover human remains they could scrounge up, and redumped them, with just enough solemnity to make it seemly, in a shoddy hut, and then got back to the business of making money. The Martyrs were saved from the vacuum of history just in time, or so Brooklyn thought.

The new wooden crypt caved in almost immediately, exposing the prisoners' bodies to the elements once again as if they were still yearning for the freedom of fresh air. Meanwhile, crowds of new, uncharted skeletons kept turning up when Wallabout Bay was dredged to eventually build the Brooklyn Navy Yard shipbuilding area. (This tiny patch of Brooklyn developed a funky way of pumping out some of history's biggest people eaters. The shipyard that built the first iron-clad warship, the USS *Monitor,* was established in the same inauspicious spot where the Martyrs died. Then the ill-fated *Maine* was christened there. A few decades later, it became the birthplace of the USS *Missouri*, which survived Iwo Jima and Okinawa before hosting the surrender of Japan in World War II. It's now permanently docked at Pearl Harbor.)

As Brooklynites plucked bones from the soil, a few conscientious people noticed we were forgetting. Walt Whitman, bless him, was one. In what may have been the last American political movement incited by poetry (that is, until Clinton gave Monica Lewinsky a copy of *Leaves of Grass*, also Whitman's), he composed verse meant to inspire construction of a proper, durable memorial to the Martyrs. One ode was to be sung to the tune of the national anthem (though I can't see how) at the newly created Fort Greene Park, Brooklyn's first park, in 1846. Quoted in an old *New York Times* story:

...How priceless the worth of the sanctified earth

We are standing on now! Lo! The slope of its girth

Where the martyrs were buried; nor prayers, tears or stones

Marked their crumbled-in coffins, their white holy bones.

Anyway, Whitman finally saw his dream come true. The remaining remains were quietly placed in a luxury stone crypt dug into a tiered, one-hundred-foot-wide staircase in the hillside of Fort Greene Park. After he died, in 1908, the government and civic groups including the Sons and the Daughters of the American Revolution chipped in to embellish the burial place with a structure so remarkable that no one could *possibly* forget the Martyrs again. They engaged the world's most famous architect horndog, Stanford White, to raise the most gracious commemorative phallus ever: a 149-foot-tall granite column fitted with an eternal gas flame in an eight-ton urn that could hold thirty-five men, should that strange requirement ever arise. From the column's pinnacle, which could be reached by metal staircase or in a new Otis elevator, future visitors could gaze a few blocks north to the area where the Martyrs perished. Stanford White would have proudly escorted the opening-day dignitaries to absorb the view himself, but he had recently been shot in the face by his underage girlfriend's husband, so he was freshly interred on Long Island by then. It was to be his last work.

At the time, White's final New York erection was the tallest freestanding Doric column in the world, which in that simpler era was ample cause for celebration. The ceremony was orated by President-Elect William Howard Taft and attended by 20,000 onlookers despite proceedings that were, in the grumpy words of one sleet-soaked onlooker, "much marred by the unfriendly elements." The souvenir program, however, promised sunshine and rainbows plus a veiled dig at the borough of Brooklyn: "This monument is not placed here to fill the eye with a sense of beauty and contrast with surroundings," it lied. "It represents, so far as cold stone may, the love, affection, the eternal gratitude of a free people, enjoying untold blessings of liberty and equality, wrung from a despotic government by blood, by suffering and by treasure." At that time, in 1908, there were still royalist-leaning Americans whose grandparents had fought in the War of 1812, so at least in the speeches, anti-Crown jingoism was suppressed out of courtesy. "The conditions were the result of neglect, not design," Taft told the assembled by way of excusing the British. Then he went so far as to gloat that thanks to agreements reached at The Hague the prior year, the sufferings of prisoners of war were forever banished. "This great Memorial, which we dedicate today, the condition of things which it records and their contrast with present conditions, properly call to mind the human advance which has been made even in so cruel a thing as war."

He was wrong. Orators frequently are. Turn your back on American history for a mere moment and it will not have wasted the opportunity to bypass you. Yet again, gratitude to the Martyrs didn't stick. Like its contemporary, Grant's Tomb, Fort Greene Park became dilapidated and encircled by housing projects for society's have-nots. The "eternal flame" atop the column was snuffed, every stone surface was tagged with graffiti, the prim Japanese hedge planted with such precision by the 1908 design committee died, and the four bronze eagles on the flanks had to be uninstalled and stored until New Yorkers decided they knew how to take care of nice things—"removed for their safety in 1962 by the Parks Department" is how my 2002 Blue Guide put it. The exhaust-soiled column, once touted as a beacon of remembrance forevermore, now looked a lot like a smokestack rising from a factory that manufactured poverty.

In 1995, Henry J. Stern, the head of the city parks, wanted funds to save the neighborhood, so in a modern echo of Whitman, he invoked the Martyrs to get it. He told the *Times* it was "New York's Washington Monument." (A little too true since they were only there because George Washington had forsaken them.) Today, the column looks terrific, with new gold leaf to simulate the not-so-eternal flame, and a fresh POW-MIA flag flying beside it in stark counterpoint of President Taft's premature declaration that POWs were obsolete. A placard credits it as "America's greatest mass grave," and the message may finally be catching on a little bit; one dark night in 2015, some rogue artists installed an official-looking bust of controversial patriot Edward Snowden near the column, telling *Mashable* it was "as a continuation of a story that began at the beginning of this country." The city impounded it by lunchtime.

The crypt is always closed, but I visited on a rare day when the door at the base of the Doric column would be open for visitors. A cherubic city ranger named Paulie showed me inside. There wasn't much to show me. It was as hollow as a brick pipe. He told me the eternal flame had been doused since World War II because someone feared a German bomber could use it to pick out New York City and then that persistent Martyr's amnesia kicked in and no one remembered to turn it back on. Eventually the unused elevator simply collapsed within the column in a rusty bramble. Just as he finished that story, two young boys appeared in the doorway, both wearing LA Lakers T-shirts. Neither one could have been older than six.

They wanted to know where the bodies were. Paulie pointed down. "Kind of underneath," he said. "Through a door in the stairs over there." Through a tarnished green panel, the bones of the 11,500—or at least minor tidbits of 8,000 or so, since the nineteenth-century search had been half-assed—are jumbled together in an ossuary of twenty slate coffins. A twenty-first-century coffin contains a nineteenth-century caretaker who wanted to be buried with his charges and got his wish.

"Can we go in?" begged the older boy.

Paulie said no. No one is allowed in. They scampered away to have a look at the door anyway.

When they were out of earshot, Paulie told me that wasn't exactly true. If you can somehow prove you're related to someone inside, you can petition for a peek. Other than that, it's locked tight. They did once let a cable TV history program in for a few minutes. And there was also the time they gave a contractor the key so he could fix something, and he accidentally left the crypt door open. In the middle of the night, some curious neighborhood kids who didn't know what that green door hid wandered inside, but they ran out screaming when they found a loose jawbone. But other than those macabre lapses, Paulie promised, admittance is very strict. I guess you have to be rigorous when you run America's greatest mass grave.

The surrounding brownstones and housing projects, meanwhile, are hot real estate all over again, but almost no one knows what the column marks. If a fifteen-story Doric column can't jog people's memories about the deaths of 11,500 heroes, nothing ever will. Three times recovered, three times abandoned. In recent years the only donations made to improving their mass grave came from Spike Lee, who understood that tennis and basketball are much more important to us nowadays and paid for Fort Greene Park's new courts. Instead of junkies, the park attracts oblivious skateboarders and joggers who hit their cardio goals by stampeding up and down the stairs above the white holy bones. I'll leave it to a sociologist to explain the character of a country that forgets its founding saints three times and then dribbles on their corpses.

"Have a great visit!" the perky young docent chirps as I enter the Fifth Floor Depository Museum.

"A great visit? Do you realize why the hell we're all in this place?" I want to ask. But I don't.

Dallas is infamous for one particular killing. But to prove that Americans do not always pay attention to all of the tragedies we ought to, perhaps I should talk about the *other* one. The forgotten one. The one perpetrated not by a mysterious rifleman, but by the entire city.

In the winter of 1910, Dallas was suffering a crime wave of purse snatchings and assaults. The police didn't know how to stop it, and people were hungry for blame.

One night amid this crisis, a sixty-eight-year-old servant named Allen Brooks was discovered in a barn outside of town in the company of three-year-old Mary Ethel Huvens. The record doesn't state they were doing anything more nefarious than playing patty cake, but Ethel had been missing, and Brooks was a black man. And then there was the matter of the blood smeared on her legs.

Fearing a mob, the authorities did the fair thing: they hid Brooks away for a week while they waited for his trial. The day of Brooks' hearing arrived. But the people of Dallas were enraged and turned against the police. Feeling terrorized by the crime wave, they blamed police for dragging their feet. They demanded action. In a building facing what is now Dealey Plaza in downtown Dallas, more than seventy officers were needed to escort him to a courtroom on the second floor.

Before Brooks could respond to the charges against him, the mob stormed the courthouse, snapping the heavy chains that had been strung across Grand Staircase to stop them—this kind of thing happened quite a lot, so police came prepared. Nevertheless, furious citizens, insane with rage, filled the courtroom, heedless of the police's shouts for them to stop, and found Brooks shielding himself in a corner. They tied a rope around his neck. The other end of the rope was fed through a window to the braying throng below, which hoisted it until Brooks was dragged kicking and clawing across the courtroom floor. He jerked through the glass and was yanked head-first to the sidewalk below.

If the fall killed him, we will never know for sure. Because once they had him, the stamping mob "crushed his face into a pulp," as a bystander reported, and dragged his body for blocks behind a car down Main Street—past Market, past Lamar. They stopped by an arch at Akard Street that was left over from an Elks convention two years before. Never pausing, they hanged his body from a telephone pole. The cheers of 10,000 people, many of them children, rang through the streets of Dallas' central business district, as they sliced patches of fabric from Brooks' clothing as souvenirs.

The mob felt empowered by the police's ineffectual response. It surged back down Main Street to the jail, also on today's Dealey Plaza. They seized steel rails to batter a path inside, braying for the execution of four more accused criminals, three black and one white.

"The firemen were called out and attempted to disperse the crowd with water," reported the *New York Times*, "but the threat to lynch them caused a quick withdrawal. Then dynamite was displayed, and the word passed that the jail would be blown up if the garrison held out much longer." Officers had just enough time to race the four prisoners to safety by automobile in Fort Worth.

"Man, you're talking about the bloody teens and the bloody '20s," said Darwin Payne, a journalist who researched the Brooks lynching, to the *Wilmington Morning Star* in 1999. "This was home to Klan Chapter Number 66, the largest in the country." Texas was, after all, a slaveholding state, and in 1860, a third of its population was in bondage, which is not something Texans generally brag about when they're boasting about their ten-gallon heritage.

The city's hangover was swift, but not too serious. The mayor shuttered all 220 of its saloons and mobilized the Texas National Guard. Out of that shame, perhaps, the incident was minimized. Despite 10,000 witnesses, no one was charged with a single crime. A photograph of the mob surrounding Brooks' broken body, dangling in the middle distance from the telephone pole, became a popular postcard traded by white supremacists—postcards of Negro murders were considered powerful declarations of warning by white nationalists. Brooks' lynching became not a lesson, but a souvenir.

No one bothered to put up so much as a plaque. Hardly anyone living in Dallas today even knows it happened.

Racial slaughter fares poorly among major death tourism attractions. Although some 150 people were executed in Colfax, Louisiana, when two rival Reconstruction governments—one white, one black—claimed superiority, once again, you only get a plaque, the equivalent of a footnote in national memory or a card in Trivial Pursuit, that implies permission to not have known something, because if it were more important, we would all know about it. Not that Colfax could support an actual tourist attraction, since most children aren't taught it to begin with. There's also nothing for countless race riots in Memphis, Detroit, Atlanta, Chicago, Tulsa, Seattle, Wilmington, Los Angeles, Denver, or any of the dozens of other places minorities were attacked in a frenzy; those get lumped into "civil rights" museums, a sweetened stage name for "African-American social cleansing" if ever there was one, and most of these institutions opened only in our time. Some people take Los Angeles' Watts Towers as a remembrance of solidarity amid racial violence, but in fact they were begun in 1921, decades before their neighborhood exploded. They were adopted as a symbol of racial reconciliation because nothing else existed. In 2018, a generalized memorial for all African-American lynchings was built on some land outside Montgomery, Alabama, but the common thread is clear: The powerless remain powerless, and when a horrific event springs from moments of insanity among common people, it rarely gets its due, even if we all agree about its importance in the development of our society. The Lorraine Motel, where Martin Luther King, Jr. was assassinated in 1968, descended into flophouse status for almost a quarter century, determinedly protected by its discerning owner at great personal cost, before private citizens, and not the government, came to their senses. It was converted into one of those "civil rights" museums, and a very good one, in 1991.

With civil rights violence, it usually takes years for the truth to become widely available, even in the case of Allen Brooks in Dallas. Years after the horror of the lynching, in our own times, the journalist Darwin Payne, digging around in some neglected archive, made a chilling discovery.

He hit upon a stray fact that had never surfaced until then, not for decades, largely because what happened to Brooks was just one of many hundreds of similar headlines that happened across our free country, and the people in power didn't care. He learned that one of Brooks' rival servants, a cook in the same house, had, many years later, privately confessed to doing something terrible. He had smeared chicken blood all over Mary Ethel Huvens' legs in a plot to frame his enemy. The crime Brooks died for had never happened.

In 2016, scores of Dallas citizens took to the streets again, swarming through the same neighborhoods of the Brooks lynching for a different social protest: to express outrage for the continued killing of black suspects without charges or trial. In the confusion, Micah Xavier Johnson, a lifelong Texan and a black man, stalked and shot five police officers.

"The suspect said he was upset with white people and wanted to kill white people, especially white officers," the police chief told the TV cameras. The hairdos on the news channels shook their heads, as if it was utterly bizarre that anyone could possibly feel that way in our golden land.

INSPIRATION (NOW LOST)

The *Maine* Monument
The Alamo

BY THE TIME I WAS BORN, MY COUNTRY HAD already given up on sending men to the moon, so I don't know why it expected much out of me. By the time I was born, my country told me segregation was solved, yet in grammar school, I couldn't play at my black friends' houses because they were all bussed. By the time I was born, my country convinced a generation of baby boomers to be heroes like their fathers, but then crushed them in a pointless war. Governors and presidents were actors and crooks, yet I was expected to be a patriot, right hand always ready to go over my heart. By the time I was ready for sex, even my most natural impulses could kill me, and my leaders wouldn't even mention it. My country never won a real war in my lifetime. My country demanded my taxes, but made it harder to vote. Seventeen kids in my brother's town were shot up in a high school gun massacre. I achieved more education than my parents, but have always owned half of what they had at the same age. When my country innovated by filming its first twelve-reel motion picture, it chose to make it about superior whites killing inferior blacks. In my country, we get dumber and meaner and more selfish by the day and despite unimaginable wealth, allow the most vulnerable among us to suffer and die. It's so hard to keep up with the disappointment and willful self-destruction. The baby boomers fumbled everything.

It's enough to make a man look for what his country's ideal was supposed to be. I couldn't tell anymore. I had gone to death tourism sights that made death seem swell.

I had seen ones that translated history into an imitation of team sports. Some fudged history. I had found many more that seemed more about profit than education, or about shaming someone, or about shrewdly twisting distant events to manipulate my politics. The one disappointing thing they all had in common was an identity crisis. They all concealed their theatrical tricks behind a beatific mask of sanctity and reverence.

That mask was sometimes literal. There is an actual face that I saw repeating at many of the country's most pious places. As I conducted a search for identity in my mighty, confused nation, there was one face I saw more than any other. It's not the Statue of Liberty. It's not Abraham Lincoln. It's the ethereal visage of the same woman on sculpture after sculpture—strong, rounded cheekbones like on a Michelangelo archangel, Roman nose allowing for no weakness, proportional forehead to soften the vigor. It feels like the same woman followed me wherever I went. This woman's face is enshrined as a visual shorthand to denote abundance, and justice, and strength: surveying Wall Street atop Manhattan Municipal Building, on the dome of Wisconsin's State capital, on South Carolina's Women's Monument, gracing the palatial New York Public Library, above parading girls on the proscenium arch of Ziegfeld's New Amsterdam Theatre, validating success on a tapestry at George Vanderbilt's Biltmore Estate in North Carolina. The owner of this face was the model for as many as 75 percent of the 1,500 works of art at the Panama-Pacific Exposition of 1915 in San Francisco, earning her the nickname of the Exposition Girl, and (some say) she appeared on both the Winged Liberty dime and the Walking Liberty half dollar. And dozens of other places besides.

The face gazing at us from the emblems of our best intentions is Audrey Munson, the muse of some two dozen Europe-trained Beaux-Arts sculptors, male and female. Her face became a literal icon of national benevolence. Munson was the most famous artist's model in the United States. She is everywhere. Her career began when she was only a teen. From a chance sighting on Fifth Avenue, a photographer convinced her mother, a worker at a corset factory, to allow her pubescent daughter to strip nude for cash as a model. Mom delivered her daughter's pretty body to the artist's eye, and for a while it turned out fine. Her supple form, dimpled lower back, and sturdy jaw were embraced by the in crowd of architects and sculptors as a visual embodiment of the American spirit and were reproduced on dozens of pedestals and pediments. Audrey was installed in the finest structures of the age. Such beatification is liable to embolden any ego, and Audrey, who experienced it in an age of feminine empowerment, seized her self-determination. She wrote newspaper columns and, courageously, even appeared nude in films—she was the first leading actress to do it, in *Inspiration* (now lost) for Mutual in 1915; she played a model. Audrey was known nationwide by the swoony sobriquet "The American Venus." In 1915, Pennsylvania's *New Oxford Item* had already assessed her value to the future, predicting, "Long after she and everyone else of this generation shall have become dust, Audrey Munson... will live in the bronzes and canvasses of the art centers of the world."

But Audrey's fate was too much like her nation's. She became the perfect metaphor, first in refinement, and then in the perishable qualities of potential. The Beaux-Arts boom faded before her beauty did. As her work dried up, a fan killed his wife (unbidden) so he could pursue Audrey (unasked), and the innuendo, stoked by salacious newspapers, extinguished what was left of her career and her celebrity. Still striking, and perhaps even familiar to some, she was reduced to selling kitchen utensils door to door, a situation no doubt made more humiliating by the dismal potential of being paid in coins that bore the image of her own faded beauty. In May 1922, at thirty-one years old, she tried to kill herself by swallowing mercury bichloride tablets. She didn't take enough. Instead, the embodiment of American perfection became irretrievably insane. "Miss Munson has been calling herself Baroness Audrey Meri Munson-Monson, though the derivation of the title is as much a mystery as her effort to commit suicide," the *New York Times* reported piteously, and more than a touch derisively.

Her neighbors renamed her "Crazy Audrey." A judge remanded her to an institution in Ogdensburg, New York. And there the paragon of US virtue remained discarded and forgotten for sixty-five years, until 1996, when she died in that institution at the wizened age of 105. Her face defined the American ideal, but ultimately she amounted to no more than an advertisement for a catchy notion, as allegorical and as nonexistent as Parson Brown of the songs. Her face still stares at American citizens from many angles in many halls of justice and power, but the representative of so many idealistic national intentions was herself dropped into an unmarked grave, which is a more astute metaphor for the unspooling of the twentieth century than any artist could imagine.

Among her many metaphorical appearances, Munson was the model for the figure of Columbia Triumphant on the extravagant *Maine* memorial on Central Park's southwest corner—one of America's purest examples of a monument purporting to be about mourning that was actually a weapon for a cynical political power grab. The 1898 explosion of the *Maine* in Havana harbor gripped Americans as perhaps no other international incident did before Pearl Harbor and 9/11. Spain was instantly blamed. Just two days after the explosion, newspaper owner William Randolph Hearst, a young newspaper owner of extreme political ambition, began lathering the readers of his sensationalistic *New York Morning Journal* into a paper-purchasing frenzy by concocting fables of Cuban atrocities, diabolical Spanish masterminds, and plausible fibs about torpedoes. Most importantly, he peddled a prescription: "The American fleet can move on Havana today and plant the flag of the Cuban Republic on Morro and Cabana," the very first editorial raved as the wreckage still sizzled in Havana. "It is still strong enough for that in the absence of further 'accidents.' And if we take such action as that, it is extremely unlikely that any other accident will happen." It was an argument for preemptive war, novel at that time because the United States had never been capable of it before. His success led America into many a misadventure in the century hence. That idea didn't turn out so well for Cuban-American relations, as we know, but it did for Hearst, who bolstered his newspaper sales with noisy campaign for donations for a grand memorial on the edge of Central Park.

Whipped up by Hearst, monuments that openly scorned Spain were erected with intense speed. They went up so fast that if you had been thinking, you would have been suspicious. Dead *Maine* servicemen were buried right away at Arlington and in 1900 in Key West. Spain swore up and down its hands were clean, but American politicians—led by President William "Barista" McKinley, amplified by Hearst, and cemented by stone monuments—howled that it was an act of sabotage worthy of starting a war over, and so we did. Many died, but in the aftermath America snatched the right to govern Puerto Rico, Hawaii, Guam, the Philippines, and naval dominance of the Pacific in the aftermath, a critical factor in dragging us into World War II. "Remember the *Maine*!" went the war cry, though the fact no one does should tell you about the legitimacy of its origin. Much like "Remember the Alamo," which omits the fact San Antonio's Alamo was only occupied in the hopes that Texas would tip the national balance of power toward slave states so there could be wider adoption of human bondage. And that it was a spectacular flop for the ages. The Texans couldn't have selected a more unsuitable holdout position than the Alamo, which had few windows to shoot from, and as a consequence, the Mexicans couldn't have executed every last American with any more ease. Today, this pitiful moral and tactical failure is revered mostly as a notional symbol of Texas' lingering recalcitrance over the matter. By day, it cycles through busloads of disappointed tourists, and by evening it's mildly enlivened by a projection show that makes the old beige Waterloo seem more eminent than it was.

Arlington displayed the *Maine*'s mast and an anchor while other relics from the wreckage were enshrined from Ohio, to Maryland, to California so people could pay respects wherever they lived (and spread the imperialist movement). But the exuberant fountain on Columbus Circle at Manhattan's Central Park was the main *Maine* event for its political and artistic overreach, and just looking at the thing screams volumes about how artifice has always fed America's worst appetites.

I sat on the edge of the *Maine* monument. Once you know it was built to justify war, it's hard not to feel dejected by it. The whole stone circus, held together by gold leaf and confidence, is a monument to jingoistic yellow journalism, funded by lies from stem to stern. No one reads the inscription, and no one mourns or fumes at Spain even though that was the objective. It's a glorified park bench beneath a rictus of victory. This harbinger of woe from Cuba to Asia is now a popular spot for meetings and lunch breaks, and at night, drunken pees in its fountains. Which proves that once a false cause is forgotten, if its monument is properly bombastic it can always endure as an elaborate urinal. It's still festooned with sad hooded figures, supple naked men, prostrate figures with outstretched arms, seashells, dolphins, and the teeth-gnashing lament "By fate unwarned/In death unafraid"—once again, senseless death being laundered by a posthumous portrait of bravery. Its forty-four-foot pylon is topped with a gilded sculpture cluster of, as the Central Park Conservancy describes it, "Columbia Triumphant leading a seashell chariot of three hippo-campi—part horse, part sea-creature and are said to be cast from metal recovered from the guns of the *Maine*." That would be Crazy Audrey, made of guns.

In 1974, a Navy study determined that the explosion probably wasn't sabotage after all, but an accident. The *Maine* wasn't blown up by anyone, at least not intention-ally. Never mind. None of the memorials were amended. At least 17,000 more lives had been snuffed out in result-ing battles, but by then, the battle for minds had been won. Military misadventures enriched a lot of merchants and industrialists, and the new clash of forces in the Pacific eventually culminated in World War II. The *Maine* Effect not only ultimately delivered Cuba to the communists, but it also anointed the United States as an international power, a crown that we wear heavily to this day, much like Crazy Audrey does atop the folly that inspired it all.

Audrey penned some newspaper columns herself, not to foment war and conquest, but to muse to her fans. Perhaps she foresaw that the false perfection she embodied would soon unravel into an unhealthy destiny. "I am wondering if many of my readers have not stood before a masterpiece of lovely sculpture or a remarkable painting of a young girl," she wrote in 1921, "her very abandonment of draperies accentuating rather than diminishing her modesty and purity, and asked themselves the question, 'Where is she now, this model who was so beautiful? What has been her reward? Is she happy and prosperous, or is she sad and forlorn, her beauty gone, leaving only memories in its wake?'"

The molding of the American ideal was not just a Gilded Age inclination. Take, for example, the willful reconfiguration of the image of Martin Luther King, Jr. His National Memorial in Washington, DC was largely paid for by corporate donors including General Motors and Verizon. A swooping "inscription wall" encircles sculptor Lei Yixin's idol-like likeness of King, which looks (more than a little) like Han Solo encased in carbonite at the end of *The Empire Strikes Back*. On that wall are fourteen beautiful King quotations. They testify to his wisdom, and reading them, I was reminded again that it was no wonder that this man, who traveled to India in 1959 to study the methods of Mahatma Gandhi, was worthy of the Nobel Peace Prize he earned in 1964. "Injustice anywhere is a threat to justice everywhere," began one of them. And from his Nobel acceptance speech: "I believe that unarmed truth and unconditional love will have the final word in reality. This is why right, temporarily defeated, is stronger than evil triumphant." King's essential tenets had been boiled down to some pleasing maxims and carved into stone for permanence. But they are all vague bumper stickers. Nowhere on the monument do King's words reflect his persistent and pointed criticism of American foreign policy, and nowhere do the words "racism" or "slavery" appear. It was as if America's most profoundly effective civil rights leaders had never said anything about civil rights. I asked Dr. Ed Jackson, the executive architect of the memorial, about it.

"Okay, but you see, therein lies a narrow view," he shot back. "We did not necessarily put a memorial to Dr. King because he was a civil rights leader."

While I concentrated on trying to keep my eyebrows from flying to the ceiling, Dr. Jackson told me the design committee spent eighteen months looking at King's work to find just the right quotations. "We champion the moment because it is etched in the minds of people in history. But you try to leverage that as an opportunity to inform them about things that they don't know. I think that we in essence have championed his legacy by moving it to the next level so that other folks that come behind, other generations, can read the wall and be inspired by it."

"I can see the point in that," I said. "So many memorials from the distant past are so fixed in their moment that when we pass that moment, we don't understand the significance anymore. Is that one of the reasons you've done it this way? It's a broader thing that people will be able to understand even one hundred years from now when they're not in the same climate anymore?"

"You're right on target," said the architect.

The Martin Luther King. Jr. Memorial omits racism because the people who paid for it wanted to revise his reputation.

Meanwhile, the King family had asked for, and more appallingly received, nearly $1 million in licensing fees for the right to use his image and words on *his own memorial* on the National Mall.

If even MLK has been mined for profit, no lore can be trusted.

OUR SCARY MARY POPPINS

Johnstown

STARTING DURING THE CIVIL WAR, THE NURSE known as Clara Barton was present at nearly every massacre, human calamity, epidemic, and natural disaster that befell the United States. She arrived to puzzle a solution to any nasty mess you can think of from the late 1800s: she is the Jessica Fletcher of American misery. One of her biggest successes was in the Pennsylvania hills east of Pittsburgh. That's where the most well-fed titans of industry, including Henry Clay Frick, Andrew Mellon, and Andrew Carnegie, owned the South Fork Fishing and Hunting Club, where they could get away from the filthy hoi polloi to whom they paid wages of pennies on the hour. Up in the hills, they could idly catch expensive game fish in an old reservoir, which their club had modified for that purpose without the inconvenience and expense of qualified engineers. At 3:15 p.m. during a fierce rainstorm in May 1889, their jerry-rigged fishing dam crumbled. "The entire lake began to move," said one witness, and twenty million tons of water raced downhill, shaving the valley town of Johnstown off the face of the earth. Those who didn't drown outright were carried along by debris, but to the relief of many, the jumble was prevented from flowing out of the valley when it wedged against a bridge, amassing a thirty-acre field of jagged wooden debris full of people clinging for dear life. Just when it looked like rescue was imminent, the wreckage caught fire, and over three days that traumatized everyone who witnessed them from shore, a huge population of the town roasted alive. Fatalities totaled 2,209, including ninety-nine entire families.

Clara Barton—who years before had exhumed Andersonville victims with luckless Dorr Atwater, as you know—sprang to the rescue. She stayed for five months, feeding, clothing, and nursing an estimated 25,000 afflicted survivors with a team of fifty volunteers. She had been caring for tragedy victims for years (she found the battle at Antietam, in progress, by following the sound of artillery and rushing toward the noise with bandages), but Johnstown was the first showing for her American Red Cross. Until then, despairing onlookers lacked a worthy outlet for their donations, and by its creation Barton, then aged sixty-seven, once again earned the appreciation of a grateful nation, which up to then had been mostly left to fend for itself when horror came a-calling.

The lobby wall of the Johnstown Flood National Memorial visitor center, beside the broken dam, is pierced by a mammoth, fake tree, the better to jolt new arrivals with the sensation of being crushed, for at this death tourism site, appreciation must begin with imagination. A cadaverous mannequin clings eerily to simulated debris, and if you press a red button near it, you realize the figure is supposed to be young Victor Heiser, who recounts the terrible day on tape as an old man. Inside a sparse cinema ("parental guidance recommended"), the orientation movie continues the haunted-house effect, opening with long-camera pans of gravestones. (The closed captions, which are required to appear on every National Park video nationwide, describe the eerie sound effects as "Strange sounds and echoes.") The film is long on mood, but short on facts, milking every piteous moment for its pain and chaos, and throwing in stock deluge footage from black-and-white silent films to flour the goulash. "They all died equally in the eyes of the Lord," we are told, one of a surprising number of references to the Last Judgment for a federal institution. "I hear them weeping through a chorus of falling tears." In the gift shop, along with Clara Barton coloring books, rangers sell locally handcrafted soaps—an odd souvenir choice for a site where thousands perished by water.

Andrew Carnegie and his fellow fishing club investors, who included future Attorney General Philander Knox, were legally untouchable. They were shielded from personal liability by the incorporation of their pleasure ground, and without a paper trail, no one could pin responsibility on them. Mary Anne Davis, Frick's great-granddaughter, told park rangers that the silence was preserved at home, too, that the family never spoke about the disaster. Lawyers kept everyone clean. As it is, Johnstown comes close to being our only death tourism site that blames a mass slaughter on wealthy entitlement—but if you look closely, the messaging is more about the woes of lousy engineering than about the dangers of social inequality.

Yet even this site, which shies from boldly pointing fingers at the upper class, would not be what it is without the backing of the rich. From the moment of the flood onward, Carnegie behaved like a man burdened by culpability. After Johnstown, he embarked on a lifetime program of aggressive philanthropy, building some 3,000 libraries for communities across the country between 1885 and his death in 1919. No one can prove that his boundless magnanimousness arose from guilt for his role in the extermination of those 2,200 people, but it's a telling truth that one of the very first libraries he built, in 1891, was for Johnstown itself, to replace the one his club's flood destroyed. Today, his Cambria Public Library Building houses the Johnstown Flood Museum, and inside those Carnegie-built stone walls, you can still view bottles of dirty flood water, the contents found in victims' pockets, and tattered debris. Johnstown is the rare American death tourism attraction devoted to a natural disaster—even if the disaster wasn't natural at all. It found its tourism groove partly thanks to an anarchic political undertone that prevailed among the working class at the turn of the last century.

Although she's known as a nurse, Barton rarely

worked in hospitals. She did her work on the spot, shin-deep in gore, the first responder at many of the same death tourism sites I saw, only at the very blood-curdling moment they qualified for the label. She was the original death tourism groupie. She didn't just dig up corpses at Andersonville. She was also at Manassas, Wilderness, and Richmond. At Antietam, a boy was shot to death while she gave him a drink of water (yet it was post-presidential McKinley who was rewarded with a statue for brave beverage serving). She camped at Petersburg. She rushed to Havana to straighten up the aftermath of the *Maine*. She arrived out of the blue to clean up after forest fires in Michigan, tidal waves in Texas, hurricanes in South Carolina, and epic floods on the Ohio River—she was a scary Mary Poppins. She may have been the best person in history to give you the eyewitness truth about the utter gnarliness of what Americans are capable of doing to each other.

You can still take a tour of her final home (sadly, few do, but I did). Somehow fittingly, it was built beside a roller coaster in Glen Echo, Maryland, at the end of the trolley line from Washington. Perhaps the sense of stomach-juggling mayhem and the faint aroma of vomit felt reassuring to her. Her house was fashioned out of one of the mobile dormitories she once used to shelter the homeless of Johnstown. So much of formative American misery has a connection to that frugal shack, where this virtuoso of kindness personally redeemed so many of the dreadful scenes I had seen for myself in their sanitized versions. And if you look closely at her ceilings, you'll notice she papered them with bandages to save money so that she'd have enough funds left over to save even more people. She died in bed in 1912, swaddled like a wound within that wallpaper, just as *Titanic* was steaming toward New York City, missing by hours her chance to help out there, too.

APPOGGIATURA

The Murrow Building and the Twin Towers
Vietnam Veterans Memorial
Martin Luther King, Jr. Memorial

I THOUGHT THEY WERE THROWING FURNITURE out of the burning towers.

I lived in Lower Manhattan on September 11, 2001, and like many of us who have seen days so terrible they seem as distant as hallucinations, I still don't like going into it much. I don't need to. I heard the second jet buzz over my apartment roof, and out on the street, I saw the drip-drip-drip of debris from the black gash in the side of the North Tower. I saw tiny specks falling from the windows, plummeting down, vanishing behind other buildings to collide unseen with the earth. They're throwing their burning furniture out of the windows, I thought, they were making more room for air until the helicopters come for them.

The one aspect of 9/11 that I can't explain to people who only experienced it through their TVs is just how nonsensical and out of control everything felt. The primal disturbance, the wave of anxiety that arrived and never left, has lingered with us ever since, sometimes overtly and sometimes covertly. True terror, and not just the theoretical dread of it or the observation of it on a screen, gets woven into your bones. In the frenzy of the moment, we didn't know what was actually happening, whether there were poison gases in the smoke, bombs beneath our feet on the subways, fleets of additional aircraft flying in low to plow us all flat.

Sealed off on our island by the military, we could only submit to fate. We could have been snuffed out in a state of high confusion, and some of us were. This is what the death moment is, truly—an animal calculation to survive, the fleeting thought that "this is the kind of thing that could kill someone," right before it does. For us, both fight and flight were eliminated as options; we could only calmly breathe through each minute, and our main survival trick became gentleness for one another. Soldiers will tell you they got through battles the same way, through brotherhood. Once the danger was over, our enemies became abstract; all that mattered to us was our care for each other and our embrace of a peace we would no longer take for granted. We had seen war firsthand. We wanted no more of it.

But in the days after September 11, we New Yorkers stood by helplessly as our exquisite, tender human brushes with the eternal, our searches for meaning within guttural suffering, were seized by outsiders and refined into fuel for the war machine. While we put flyers on walls and fences in search of the missing, outsiders arrived at the scene of our profound violation to stand atop the rubble and declare it for another use for the cameras. While we replaced those posters with handmade tiles that sanctified the lost, outsiders were sharpening their bayonets, unasked, in our names. Most of us in Lower Manhattan realized that now we had joined an unlucky club of those who understand the sensations of war, and that by witnessing it, we would never clamor for war the way mere observers did. We spent the next weeks lining up at Hell's Kitchen's Afghani restaurants to show we did not blame them, and then we spent years marching by the thousands in the streets, begging the government not to attack more innocent people, the way we had been attacked. They ignored us. Our mourning was converted into someone else's weapon. I guess you could say I would never see war, or my country, the same way again. Nationally, many people picked up a gun because of the amplified drumbeat following 9/11. Locally, many of us stepped back from flag waving and saw how mourning can be so quickly processed into a caustic toxin of idealism.

This was perhaps the true catalyst for my dark tourism endeavor, long before I stood in front of Will O'Neal's grave and wondered what it was all about. My frustration with the uses of mourning sprang out of a desire to get distance from how I felt when I looked up on that Tuesday morning and how I felt when I heard our sobs orchestrated into war drums. The most visceral experience of my life to that point plundered my reality, my breath, and my fears. It revealed true apocalypse without screens or scripts, larger and more real than mere jingoism, but seemingly before I could gasp it was seized, simplified, and woven into a flag.

Anyone can understand the delicate nature of tragedy when it happens in your own life. For so much of the past, memorials were about generic heroes—the soldier, the leader, the underdog—sacrificing the self in the name of the group. But in our lifetime, there has been a shift. Our memorials are not the same as they have been for hundreds of years.

Starting with Pearl Harbor, America's major memorials are no longer about valor, but about surprise—the moment violence pounced. Modern disaster museums present a stunned forensic reconstruction of events, as if organizing our state of shock into an orderly queue of concurrent incidents. Our shared trauma is storyboarded like a movie. *But we're* American. *How could this happen?*

Oklahoma City's bomb site is bracketed by two gates, one labeled 9:01 and one 9:03, to saturate the ghost of the Murrow Building with a trenchant admonition that 9:02 was our point of no return. The entire site dwells forever within 9:02. The narrative begins with an introductory room that recreates the peace of how blissfully mundane life was just before the moment, the better to wrenchingly shatter them with an excruciating audio of the moment played in a darkened room, where your imagination can run with it. Once the retelling of the mayhem begins its cascade, the struggle atomizes into tiny fragments, accumulating, exhaustive to the last scrap of salvageable detail, each shard of evidence picked up and inspected before being put back on the shelf of time for all to remourn. They rip open the wound so that it can heal again. The latest death sites emphatically remind us that once it's spilled, we can never put the glitter back into the box. The misery is the message.

The effect is cinematic, and that's on purpose. When I told a friend, a dresser for Broadway shows, that I was thinking about embarking on this book, she clucked her tongue. She grew up in west Honolulu, watching tour buses disgorge hundreds of slow-moving tourists at Pearl Harbor each morning. "It's a grief factory," she said. Her youth was spent watching people dutifully amble from tour coach, to sightseeing boat, to gift shop before being hauled back to Waikiki in time for the Polynesian-themed floor shows. My friend makes illusion for a living, so she knows a well-oiled performance when she sees one. There's a solid link between Pearl Harbor and popular entertainment, and I don't mean that bombastic Ben Affleck movie: The USS *Arizona* memorial itself was largely paid for by an Elvis Presley benefit concert. When you take the boat to the *Arizona* shrine, over blue tropical water that beckons for a margarita and a fishing rod, you are soon enveloped in a faint oily funk of diesel fuel. It rises all around you, leaking from battleships that took bunkrooms of boys down with them, and hugs them underwater even now. When the odor of fuel fills your nostrils, there is no doubt about what happened in Pearl Harbor, despite the efforts to stage manage everything else into an antiseptic peace of grassy lawns and waving flags. In a way, as the fumes rise, the attack is happening still. It's unique among the death landscapes I visited, because unmistakable evidence of the event, something rangers haven't been able to manipulate, is always leaking through the rest of the carefully arranged tableau. The shrieking smell of incinerated metal that clung to Manhattan for six months after the attacks can no longer be detected at Ground Zero, and the dust has been swept away in Oklahoma, but at Pearl Harbor, the elusive whiff of oil is the only true thing to lend credence to the stories you read on the signs. It has become part of the show.

Modern Americans insist that their new museums engage them viscerally, too. Silence and dusty signs will no longer do; we have been Disneyfied. The soundtracks at these new attractions have been consciously arranged to feature timpani and bugles. In the old Mission 66-era national park sites, the fife and drum were the musical voices for American soldiers because that's what they actually used, and in the middle twentieth century, recorded spiels were sonorously redolent of James Mason. That's what we thought historical authority sounded like back then. But the new unofficial sound of sentiment, heard in the videos everywhere from Gettysburg to Ground Zero, borrows from our new models of emotional understanding, the movies of Steven Spielberg and John Williams.

A talented composer and arranger can orchestrate an emotional response, and they do. A British psychologist John Sloboda asked people to tell him about songs that made them feel teary or inspired, and he used his data to identify a musical device called *appoggiatura*. A psychologist from the University of British Columbia took that idea and ran with it, isolating four features of songs that elicit physiological proof of emotion such as increased heart rate or goose bumps. Think of Adele's "Someone Like You," a James Bond theme, or Samuel Barber's "Adagio for Strings," used in *Platoon*: Music must start quietly and crescendo. It should include the sudden introduction of an additional instrument or harmony. It might be embellished by something jumping an octave or two higher. And it should throw in some unforeseen jackknifes in the melody or harmony, something that deviates from what went before. Taken together, it elicits subliminal tension, a personal carnival ride of emotion. Scientists have also concluded that when music stokes emotional intensity, it's often accompanied by the release of dopamine, which doses the listener with an effect similar to sex or drugs. It's neuroscience. We learn to crave the emotional manipulation. And because we lose ourselves for a moment in the face of death, it's also perfect Terror Management Theory. Present-day multimedia museums curate music to encourage an intentional sense of mourning—in the lobby at the September 11 Museum, it's "Taps" and "Amazing Grace" on a loop—and they set their exhibits not under impartial fluorescent lights as in olden national park days, but under professionally designed lighting that plucks exhibited items out of darkness the way a cinematographer tells you how to feel by the angle of the shadows.

Oklahoma City's experience also painstakingly uncovers the individuality of the dead. Each victim (and finally, women are just as much a focus as men) is named, and their personal possessions, no matter how mundane, are gathered under glass as a reminder of their irreplaceable personhood. The most meaningless tchotchke sears the heart with loss. Wristwatches, keys, memos. It is the opposite of the memorials of the past, in which all personal dramas melted into a single stoic stone—2,111 unnamed Union soldiers stuffed into Arlington's pot of honor—fitting the fortitude of their ages. Instead, we retrace in minute detail the victims' paths forever, for them. They were real, we're told. It's we who are now the ghosts at their fateful moments.

Hyper-individualization is now the only way. We expect it. You might be tempted to blame a mindset engendered by social media, but the trend had been bubbling on the local level for years and was scaled to the national stage back in 1983 by Maya Lin's design for the Vietnam Veteran's Memorial in Washington. It was, as art critic Robert Hughes put it, "a monument without figures, only names—completely the reverse of traditional depictions of heroism in war." While countless small towns, universities, and even companies frequently enumerated their own dead from older wars on civic plaques, Lin's project tackled personal recognition for an entire country by carving every known American victim in Vietnam by name, more than 58,000 of them. The design was tacitly intended to castigate a government that had lied about its intentions with the conflict—listed there is the cost, itemized like an invoice, a seething warning of the potential of mass revolution if it happened again. The visual style embraced modern theatricality, too. Lin's design was dug into black granite slabs in a gash in the earth off the National Mall. Prior to the Vietnam Veterans Memorial, America's shorthand for proud democracy was classical, post-Roman architecture—we even built all the important buildings in our capital in that image. In halls built by bygone classist societies, like the sanctuaries of London's Westminster Abbey and St. Paul's Cathedral, the death tolls of whole battles are represented by a sculpture to a single military leader. Honor him, and thousands of nameless dead of lesser class are noted by implication. Lin's concept trashed class. Losses were jumbled together without regard to status, Turner's *The Field of Waterloo* rendered in Optima typeface.

With Maya Lin, the model for classical symbolism and group redemption was replaced with a Facebook's worth of names—democracy by the masses, having failed to stop the war, would still get the last word. To read even a single name is to acknowledge waste. Like the UDC's Lost Cause messaging, there's a utility in that futility. But in fifty years, as memory moves on, they will become only names. Like all memorials, the Vietnam wall is most meaningful to contemporaries. Like the grave of Stonewall's arm, it's a rock with no resonance except for the personal meaning a pilgrim brings to it. It's a trigger only if a visitor's heart comes loaded.

My heart came loaded to Lower Manhattan. I can still smell the burning metal, and whenever I pass a construction site and smell it again, I'm inevitably struck silent for a few minutes. For a long while, I put off going to the memorial. It was too much for me to contemplate reabsorbing the fear and the suffering I felt and witnessed. The design of the twin fountains—two great black square maws into which cascades of water incessantly vanish, with no visible bottom—reminded me too much of the plunges from the top floors of the towers. Those people's landings, like the vortex of the fountain's waters, only lived in our most terrible imaginations. The planners of the September 11 Museum expected trepidation like mine. In 2012, before it opened, a *New York Times* article fretted that the sunken granite memorial pools, dug in the location of the two Twin Towers, were very likely to attract self-harm. "Someone could be visiting the memorial and be overwhelmed by the thought of suicide," reasoned one psychotherapist to the newspaper.

But that's not what happened. The fountains were consecrated first, while funds were still being gathered for the indoor museum, and after they opened, the complaint shifted. Visitors didn't seem depressed *enough*. "Tourists Treating 9/11 Memorial Like a Playground" lamented a *New York Post* story. "People laughed and took pictures smiling," complained the head of one civic group, "and so many people leaned on the tablets with all of my friends' names engraved in them, holding Starbucks cups, like it was a kitchen table."

Further editorials chastised couples for making out by the pools. The sister of one victim expressed amazement to the *Times*: "I have always assumed that as time goes by, people will come there for gentle recreation—walking, sitting in the dappled sunshine, even picnicking." Why she thought they'd stop at necking is a gross underestimation of the human capacity to get aroused by anything, anywhere.

People also shamed the gift shop for having the gall to sell souvenirs—ignoring the economic reality that purchases are a foundational source of income when government funding is absent. Like the Oklahoma City memorial, the September 11 Museum was built from private donations, not federal management. "They're marketing the headstones of our loved ones on key chains," a victim's family member complained to the *New York Times*. "How disgusting is that?" They would shudder to know what they sold over at Oklahoma City: stuffed versions of the German Shepherds that sniffed for survivors and corpses alike in the rubble. I bought one. I'm glad I got it when I did. Now the Memorial Store has switched to a $22 Golden Retriever puppy, which must sell better because it's cuter. It wears an orange work vest bearing a white emergency cross that reads RESCUE.

Many months after it opened, I finally went to the National September 11 Memorial and Museum, but I brought my family with me. I warned them I might get emotional, but I didn't. Maybe I have exhausted all possible emotion over the attack. But more likely, seeing a different recounting of that day could never come close to the way I felt living it. "It felt like my innocence had been taken from me," says the voice of one recorded witness at the Twin Towers. It was the precise metaphysical undercurrent that had unsettled me, too: Everything can disintegrate in an instant, nothing can feel safe again. Like Oklahoma City, large signs denoting the advancing time lead visitors through an exhaustive narrative of the mayhem. I didn't notice anyone making out in front of the twisted fire engines, airplane fuselage, or the video loops of Matt Lauer and Katie Couric, but I did see plenty of kids too young to care. The furrowed brows of introspective parents were consistently ignored by their kids, who are constitutionally unable to connect with anything that hasn't happened in their lifetimes. They have seen worse violence in Fortnite or Avengers movies. They hunch over smartphones while screens around them project an endless loop of showering shrapnel. I want to stop them, to tell them how it was like a portal to hell had torn open like an ulcer and vomited horror into our lives. And then I realized: If I did that, I'd be trying to make future generations see an event the way I thought they should. I'd be exactly like everyone who ever erected a manipulative monument at every death attraction I visited. So I let them enjoy their obliviousness. Perhaps it's better that they're not contaminated by such an awful experience.

The most telling messages at the 9/11 museum in Lower Manhattan weren't about the fear. They were the broad statements. One sign, "AMERICA IN SHOCK," finished with this line: "Even in the absence of consensus about military action, many Americans supported the nation's armed forces and affirmed patriotic resolve." All the survivors who didn't want to answer freelance terrorism with war, and there were many, were summarily shut down with that line. The other message that distressed me was on sale. It was a souvenir t-shirt sold years before 2016. It read: HONOR REMEMBER REUNITE.

I didn't think much of it at first—those words of chin-up cheerleading are as prevalent on granite as they are on cotton, and we're used to this kind of emblematic message now—but then it struck me: Why *reunite*? Why not UNITE instead? To assert we came together again, you must first accept that we started broken apart. The t-shirt gave away the source code of America (we are perpetually in a state of unraveling) and of every memorial site (to ward off discord by enforcing peace). LET US HAVE PEACE, as Grant says. I COMMAND PEACE, as the Haymarket cop says.

Museums at both Oklahoma City and Ground Zero, comprehensive as they try to be, conspicuously avoid asking what we could have done to prevent this woe. When we think about the Oklahoma City bombing, the first thing we know is that it was homegrown terrorism, fully made in America. An entire room of its museum dissects the brilliance of the FBI and law enforcement for catching him; there isn't a single panel that explains why Timothy McVeigh wanted to do it to begin with.

I asked a volunteer docent, a sweet former grade school teacher, why there was nothing about McVeigh's worldview in a museum that, I couldn't help noticing, covered everything else in such exhaustive detail.

She considered my question.

"Well..." she said. "We just tell people that he was a bad man."

"A bad man," I said.

"Yes," she said. "He was just very troubled."

It seems immoral to leave a multimillion-dollar facility documenting a critical event and still feel the need to Wikipedia what happened. At the 9/11 memorial, visitors also come away with a rock-solid appreciation for first responders, as they should, but nearly no understanding of what made the foreign hijackers enraged about the United States' international policy to begin with, which, regardless of your politics, would also be informative to at least know. We will never prevent a new crop of aggrieved madmen from sprouting if we don't inspect and smash the hothouse environments that nourish them. Eliminating the perpetrators' grievances is an accepted curatorial norm. "We are not interested in talking about the Allies' story and certainly not the enemies' story," the president of New Orleans' National World War II museum told me once over lunch. "This is *our* story."

There is one conclusion that modern death tourism sites are all eager to make, because they all make it. It can be summed up in a single word: redemption. After United Flight 93 crashed into southwestern Pennsylvania (just a few miles from Johnstown, incidentally), Congress took only a year to dedicate the land as part of the National Park system, one of the fastest federal handovers of land in American history—despite their importance, some Civil War sites took a half a century or more. From the get-go, the Act was as explicit about its intent to shape minds as Hearst's *Maine* monument, declaring the site should be preserved not because it was the resting place for forty passengers and crew, which it is, but for its use as a "profound symbol of American patriotism and spontaneous leadership of citizen-heroes." Once the unit was up and running, the takeaway remained as sectarian as it was reverent. When I visited, the guest comments included this one, for some unconscionable reason pinned to the wall by a ranger: "I can still remember this tragic day and cannot get over the hate that some Muslims feel toward us. Although I do not understand it, they will pay in the end."

The final panels of all modern memorial museums inevitably assert that ultimately, we were brought together. They state union as historical fact, as if it can be proved: The bad guys left us stronger. Both Oklahoma City and Ground Zero even have their own "survivor tree" that lived through the respective cataclysms (in Oklahoma, an American Elm; in New York, a Callery pear) and are explicitly presented as motivational symbols. They survived. They made it through, stronger. We all did.

That's bunk, of course. No one alive can honestly claim 9/11 healed our nation; just look at us. But to say otherwise would be like insulting the deceased at his funeral, and just like an old Civil War monument, it's unheard of to confess how much we actually lost. Or worse, how maybe how things were never as solid as we thought they were. It's a comforting takeaway of an event to say that God is on your side, which is why nearly every American memorial tries that line. If we give ourselves enough labels—*united, honor, together, remember, stronger, hope*—then perhaps they'll be as good as true. So why do we feel so broken?

Standing there in the gift shop at the World Trade Center, a spot that only a few years prior had been at the heart of a tangled inferno of burning steel and fleshly annihilation, the phrase finally came to me. It was a realization that had eluded me throughout my journey, but which summed up, in six words, why so many of the supposedly sanctified sites I visited lacked the definitive holiness I sought.

Every memorial is propaganda for something.

"THE MEMORIAL IMPULSE"

Forest Lawn Memorial-Park

AFTER THE UNHEALED ANXIETIES AND FRUSTRA-
tions dredged up by Ground Zero, I knew I had to end my
extinction expedition on a lighter note. So I chose to fly
to Los Angeles and do it glamorously. My first stop was
the creaky old Oakland Cemetery in Atlanta, so my final
stop would be a bookend of sorts: where the biggest stars
of Hollywood fell to earth in America's most fabulously
touristy cemetery. It turned out to be the perfect choice. It
was there that I finally learned, once and for all, the clear-
est explanation for why Americans do what we do with
our tragedies, and what happens when we are permitted to take our memorialization instincts to their purest
extreme, with no history lessons or politics to muddy the
glory. Forest Lawn is the apotheosis of American death
tourism. It truly is the Disneyland of Death.

Hubert Eaton knew that to have a good life, he had
to own death. He found the place in Tropico, California.
It was an ugly graveyard of mismatched headstones and
eucalyptus trees where few people lived and fewer still
wished to wind up. There were only 115 arid acres, and
many of those were in title dispute, but when thirty-year-
old Hubert Eaton saw it for the first time in June of 1912,
he saw a life's work in the demise of others. Today, Forest
Lawn Glendale is the king of tourist cemeteries, and its
origins introduce the meaning of memorials better than
anywhere else I could end my journeys.

No one changed American graveyards as much as
Dr. Hubert Eaton. Walt Disney built his dominion in
the citrus groves past Los Angeles' southern limits, but

here, at the northern end of the trolley line from the city, Eaton created his own kingdom. He spent decades obsessing over how to shape his acquisition into something that would instinctively appeal to all ages. Eaton carved his ideals in marble at the middle of his newly acquired graveyard so there would be no mistaking the intention of this kingdom: His "Builder's Creed" towers on a slab outside the central Great Mausoleum at what is now called Forest Lawn Glendale. Knee-high statues of two small children and a bulbous-headed Precious Moments puppy stare up in admiration of his ethics. To take in The Creed, you must look skyward with a similar bemusement that I imagine Moses felt upon discovering the Ten Commandments. The Creed is 357 words long, or nearly ninety words longer than that other timeless meditation on the proper mode of cemetery memorialization, the Gettysburg Address.

Every memorial is propaganda for something, and Eaton's message was pleasantness. In his Creed, he rejected "the cemeteries of today" as "unsightly stone yards, full of inartistic symbols and depressing customs" and "misshapen monuments." He discarded the conventional dreariness of burial. "I therefore prayerfully resolve on this New Year's Day, 1917," he carved, "that I shall endeavor to build Forest Lawn as different, as unlike other cemeteries as sunshine is unlike darkness, as Eternal Life is unlike death."

Dr. Eaton envisioned a getaway more like a Danish pleasure garden than a boneyard. "Forest Lawn shall become a place where lovers new and old shall love to stroll and watch the sunset's glow," he rhapsodized, "planning for the future or reminiscing of the past; a place where artists study and sketch; where school teachers bring happy children to see the things they read of in books;"—yes, we're still talking about merry jaunts into a graveyard, not Knott's Berry Farm—"where little churches invite...where memorialization of loved ones in sculptured marble and pictorial glass shall be encouraged but controlled by acknowledged artists..." He didn't sign his pledge with his name. Instead, he signed it like a deity: "The Builder."

"This is the Builder's Dream; this is the Builder's Creed."

Eaton dismissed the word "cemetery" and coined the term "memorial-park." Tombstones were banned. Instead, he insisted on uniform, flat plaques that allowed the hilly vista to roll uninterrupted except for choice works of art. These he selected for their evocative powers. Besides solace, each masterwork had a second purpose. Years before Disneyland did it, Eaton divided his grounds into themed districts, each variously priced to segregate the frugal funerals from the spendy send-offs: The Vale of Memory, Inspiration Slope, Mystery of Life. He removed age-old symbols of pain and mourning, visually arranging everything in his deathlands to impart exaltation, a pleasingly vanilla oblivion for all who had the money to enjoy one.

He had started his career as a young metallurgist, and

when he failed to extract money out of the ground, he found a dozen angles to profit from by putting things into it. Until Eaton came along, Americans would probably have been buried simply in a churchyard. But with Forest Lawn, everything was groomed to divert attention from its true purpose, the true purpose of all cemeteries, which is to dispose of corpses before they poison the rest of us.

Eaton eagerly bounded over the low hedge that separates a cleric from a showman. But if idealism inspired him, pragmatism rooted him. In 1954, the Interment Association of California published the fifty-seven-page *The Comemoral: The Cemetery of the Future*. This breezy little treatise on the bereavement industry illuminated his motivations. In it, he insists the urge to build lasting things is not only biological, but ancient. "The first sculpture was a rude pillar placed to mark a grave," Eaton asserted, taking the liberty of validating his business plan with ancient examples.

> The world's first book was a memorial. It was printed in China on crude handmade paper from blocks in 868 A.D. by Wang Chieh to perpetuate the memory of his parents. Architecture started with tombs that housed the dead...The oldest engineering triumphs in the world, the Pyramids, are tombs...The glorious Gothic cathedrals of the Middle Ages housed crypts and monuments.

"The Memorial Impulse," he dubbed it, hailing it as "the father of art and architecture." We all yearn to leave something positive behind, he reasoned.

It has nourished literature, music, sculpture, and painting...our churches and cathedrals, our libraries, parks, colleges, hospitals, orphanages, and museums. Through its expression we can trace the advance of civilization. To the Memorial Impulse is due much that man has accomplished in his progress from cave dwellings and mud huts to our modern mode of living.

That's a heady declaration for a pamphlet, and something a tweedy psychoanalyst could juice for years: We make nice things because we know we're going to die.

This hereditary urge, Dr. Eaton confessed, is also what gave him a business edge, since all cash-carrying humans unwittingly obey that Memorial Impulse. "Let every salesman's motto be: *Accent the spiritual!*" (The italics are his. When Dr. Eaton lacked evidence or eloquence, he expressed his life force through italics.) And he had two additional, deeply moral reasons for cramming Forest Lawn with eye candy. One was to protect his customers' final resting places, because, as he put it, "Society rarely tears down that which is beautiful." The other reason was a sensible reaction to two World Wars and the Great Depression: Curated collections cushioned him against the depreciation of the American dollar. If "the interest on the endowment care fund (at the time $4 million, California's largest for a cemetery) is not sufficient, Forest Lawn may then charge admission to view its art treasures," he wrote. If he could forge a parallel identity as a tourist attraction, the graves wouldn't decay—his own Memorial Impulse manifested on a balance sheet. His idea bore fruit, too; on the 1937 Hollywood Starland map of the celebrity homes and hangouts, Forest Lawn was marked along with fame magnets like the Brown Derby and the Cafe Trocadero. Hubert Eaton had built Forest Lawn Glendale into a theme park for mourning.

The similarity to Walt Disney's model was no accident. In fact, Dr. Eaton and Disney were friends. Both were born in small-town Missouri at the end of the 1800s and became crucial figures in Los Angeles' development. Both were driven by a firm Midwestern belief in hard work, patriotism, and the American Dream. Both built their brands by appealing to people's fantasies about their better natures. Both despaired of convention so obsessively that they innovated at great personal and financial risk. Disney wanted to elicit a suspension of disbelief of fantasy, while Eaton wanted visitors to suspend belief of reality. Whereas both dreamers once endured derision from colleagues and loan officers alike, their risks wound up creating a new mold that revolutionized their respective sectors. We play and die by their respective visions today.

Like Disneyland's "cast members," Eaton's sales force was carefully groomed to elicit soothing emotions. He obtained workers through classified newspaper ads seeking "clean cut, forcible men only," so customers would feel becalmed, like they were contemplating their doom with the local minister's son. Meanwhile, he milked latent anxieties. Money flowed strongest not in death, but in the inexorable expectation of it. Dr. Eaton calculated the interest to be accrued in selling consumers their own demises before they had so much as a sniffle. Buy space early for "peace of mind," he said, because it's your duty to spare your loved ones the burden of your final arrangements.

Once he perfected his cemetery's style into something doleful, but not dolorous, he busily gussied up his "memorial-park" with tourist-friendly oddities. He styled himself into a post-mortem Barnum: he trawled Europe to amass more than 1,000 stained glass windows. He commissioned copies of all of Michelangelo's sculptures. He opened a museum for fine art and antiquities. He installed seven links of "the Liberty Chain," said to have kept British warships out of New York Harbor during the Revolutionary War. He transported the canopy of the Temple of Santa Sabina, under which Napoleon is said to have written in his diary, from Rome to the road that leads to the niches of W.C. Fields and Jean Harlow. On Memorial Day, he'd dispatch blimps to scatter flowers over the gathered bereaved. He styled every assiduously meandering drive with pastoral calm and warmly invited the world to come play in his wonderful graveyard.

And his late clientele responded. Celebrities spent dearly to be counted among the so-called treasures, and a roster of pop culture fixtures gathered to spend their eternities there: Harold Lloyd, Clifford Odets, Theodore Dreiser, Louis L'Amour, Errol Flynn, Aimee Semple McPherson, Tom Mix, David O. Selznick, Gillette of the

Gillette razor empire, all three Andrews Sisters, two of the Marx Brothers (Chico and Gummo), and one of the Three Stooges (Larry). The Freedom Mausoleum, in the corner of the property, contains a firmament of extinguished stars: Nat "King" Cole, Mary Wells, George Burns and Gracie Allen (epitaph: "Together Again"), Clara Bow, and Dorothy Dandridge. Mary Pickford, once the most famous woman on earth, chose the locked Garden of Memory to make her inaccessible glamour permanent, beneath the inscription "America's Sweetheart." The burial plots were an eternal extension of their occupants' lifetimes of role-playing.

The first thing a visitor encounters within the property's twenty-five-foot-tall wrought iron entry gates is an incongruous English Tudor-style complex, a pitch-perfect imitation of a cozy village inn at Stratford-upon-Avon—or, at the very least, a restroom outbuilding at Epcot. Like Disneyland's train station, it sets the mood. This inviting nook is Forest Lawn's arrival station, too. It's the onsite mortuary, a 1930s addition of which Dr. Eaton was justly proud, because until then, cemeteries outsourced bodies to be prepared off premises and then delivered, like take-out dinners. Dr. Eaton's obsessive vision of death management wasn't merely pastoral. He had the revolutionary brainstorm to expand burial business vertically, such as it were, so families could essentially drop off the remains of their loved ones and spend the rest of their energies crying and laying flowers—which, conveniently, Dr. Eaton also now sold. This novelty, Dr. Eaton told the

American Cemetery Association during his ascent, was not only "economically correct," but also his contribution to "the sorrowing purchaser."

Dr. Eaton threw in nonsectarian chapels to corner the event market, too, and his society buddies stepped up. In 1940, Ronald Reagan married Jane Wyman among the dead, a fact that may have been a portent of the fate of their union, in the Wee Kirk o'the Heather, which was inspired by a chapel that once stood in Glencairn, Scotland. Another chapel, the Little Church of the Flowers, was a pastiche of a village church in Stoke Poges, Buckinghamshire. Its sanctuary was built with sunlit alcoves so plants would grow and birds would sing alongside services. In 1918, the year before L. Frank Baum's funeral was held in it, *Popular Science Monthly* hailed its "peculiar charm" as "the latest thing in churches."

Nuptial bliss wasn't nearly the limit to Dr. Eaton's ambitions. You can baptize your infant in his cemetery, too. School groups bus themselves to see art shows in its gallery (Picasso and Braque are on a typical docket). Memorial Day may be marked with Civil War reenactors and Abe Lincoln impersonators. Forest Lawn would probably rent you a party clown for an eighth birthday party if you asked. From womb to tomb, it has Angelenos covered, and once a spirit is gone, it'll sell grief seminars to the survivors. An early advertising slogan promised, "Forest Lawn: Where one call does it all!" which is the vow of a diversified necroverse if ever there was one.

Although these tactics bordered on false coarseness—

the wrong side of the border, many might say—Dr. Eaton's innovations became industry standard. Your own arrangements will probably be handled the same way, if they haven't been already. Dr. Eaton changed the way we die.

When Walt Disney expanded his own empire by constructing a new studio in nearby Burbank, Eaton staked out a spot on the hillside above his buddy's property—perhaps not coincidentally, Walt originally planned to place Disneyland between the two. The slope had long been used as a filming location for the pictures, including for the battle scene of *The Birth of a Nation*, but now it was disused. While neighbors dithered about how to halt the plan, Dr. Eaton raided the county morgue and quickly deposited six unidentified bodies, meeting the state threshold for declaring it an official graveyard—a dirty trick to secure eternal rest that might also have encouraged Walt to find a smarter location for his play park than beneath a new graveyard. Forest Lawn-Hollywood Hills, as Eaton's ill-gotten cemetery sequel is now known, also revels in a patriotic theme. Still overlooking the Walt Disney Studios, attractions include a recreation of Boston's Old North Church and the glass "Birth of Liberty" mosaic measuring 160 by 30 feet. (Contemporary additions include Bette Davis, Liberace, John Ritter, Carrie Fisher, and Debbie Reynolds.) More Forest Lawns followed, including in Long Beach, the Covinas, and Cathedral City. There are now ten Forest Lawns scattered around Southern California, all cut from the same Renaissance-Redux style.

In 1948, British novelist Evelyn Waugh wrote *The Loved One*, a scathing mockery of the Forest Lawn way. Although he prefaced his work with an unconvincing assertion that he had made everything up, Waugh's talents as a satirist were barely tested since he didn't have to change many details. His Eaton, "Wilbur Kenworthy," was called The Dreamer instead of The Builder, but his cemetery, "Whispering Glades," was possessed of the same cultish mission and pretentious signage. Or, as Waugh wryly put it, its "failing credulity was fortified by the painted word." Whispering Glades promised the same thing Eaton did: a disciplined inner peace through "before-need" mortuary planning. "Many people let their vital energy lag prematurely and their earning capacity diminish simply through fear of death," pitches a saleswoman at Waugh's not-so-fictional cemetery. "By removing that fear they actually increase their expectation of life."

In 1966, *Time* magazine named Eaton "The Millionaire Mortician." He built himself a mansion down the steep hill on the back side of Forest Lawn, with a chauffer's quarters, maids' quarters, and a funicular that carried him daily to his mountaintop to fulfill his life of death.

Not requiring mortuary services, at least not yet, I drove deep into its grassy expanse, passing whitewashed statues situated tastefully along swooping hillside lawns. Somewhere to my right, lying six feet beneath an attractive slope that Dr. Eaton probably thought was ideal for potato sack races, was Jimmy Stewart.

The first living thing I saw was a coyote. It must have crept up from the hillside below, near Dr. Eaton's old funicular track, and it halted midstep by the Kinsey family crypt as I stopped my rental car and rolled down my window. Part of me wondered if it was clever robotic fabrication to elicit a soulful appreciation for nature. It seemed possible. After all, portions of Forest Lawn are wired with hidden speakers that play contemplative music on a gentle and imperceptible loop. But no, the coyote glared at me with slattern eyes, waiting coolly for me to die, or at least for me to drive past so it could continue its advance on a nearby trash can, which, like all trash cans at Forest Lawn, was hidden in a hip-high canister sculpted to look like a tree stump. A nearby sign chided: FLOWER THEFT IS A CRIME PUNISHABLE BY IMPRISONMENT.

I passed the goliath knockoff of Michelangelo's *David* in Carrara marble. Originally near Mary Pickford's forbidden grave, it was installed in 1938, scandalizing Eaton's Art Committee, which insisted on shielding visitors from unseemly nakedness with a plaster fig leaf. The David, genius sculpture though it is, conceals a catastrophic flaw. It's weak at the ankles, a failing Michelangelo tried to remedy by joining his right leg with a tree trunk. What barely worked in Florence was no match for the San Fernando fault, and Forest Lawn's copy was toppled by the Sylmar earthquake of 1971. That David was replaced at great expense, and times having changed, the new one was permitted to fully display his form in its admittedly modest glory. This time, Teflon was inserted into his pedestal to mitigate tremors. The Teflon David, too, was felled at the ankles, more like Achilles, by the Northridge quake in 1994. The third David now stands near Humphrey Bogart, awaiting the moment the fates yet again rebuke those who had the temerity to demote a Florentine masterpiece to a Glendale garden gnome.

I made my way to the central Great Mausoleum, a sprawling citadel modeled after Pisa's Camposanto Monumentale, or perhaps subconsciously, after Hearst's San Simeon. Like Hearst, Eaton mimicked classic European aristocracy to class up the joint. The Great Mausoleum is to Forest Lawn what Sleeping Beauty Castle is to Disneyland: a dreamy focal point pastiche containing nothing alive. It does contain more royalty, or at least Hollywood royalty: Sid Grauman, William Wrigley, Theda Bara, Clark Gable (who was entombed beside Carole Lombard despite being married twice after her plane crash), Lon Chaney, David O. Selznick, and Irving Thalberg, to name just a few shakers of the early twentieth century, are all somewhere inside.

As I entered the complex, I hid my camera under my jacket and grimaced wanly at the attendant in her booth, uneasily trying to find a face that was both unthreatening and moderately mournful. For despite Dr. Eaton's intention to fashion a world-class attraction, anyone caught sleuthing around for celebrity resting places is collared and ejected. When Michael Jackson's family announced plans to invite fans to gather his tomb on the first anniversary of his death, the family of Clark Gable, who lies nearby, reportedly vetoed the plan since it "wouldn't be sacred." The objection is bizarre on the face of it when you learn that the Great Mausoleum also contains Forest Lawn's oldest blockbuster attraction: a full-scale reproduction of da Vinci's *The Last Supper* executed entirely in stained glass.

Tourists are permitted to troop into the Mausoleum for thirty minutes at a time to see the window. I took a few lingering minutes to nose around the cathedral-like innards, trying falsely to look mildly sorrowful, but not in obvious need of directions so the hidden cameras wouldn't detect me as I stole quick photos. The mazelike niches, most of which were blocked with ropes, seemed better suited to Vincent Price's cackle than to the frisbees and picnic baskets of an Eatonesque family outing. The central alcoves, dimly lit by hanging lanterns, were lined with imposing classical sculptures that observed me with blank, beatific expressions. It didn't feel so much like a luxury crypt as it did the foyer of a reclusive Newport tycoon.

This was the Hall of Memories, and at its focal point, towering ten feet, was a sublimely sculpted angel, wings spread regally and arms outstretched in preparation for the final embrace. It was beautiful. This was the closest thing to something authentically moving I had seen here—sculpted from Porracci marble by an Italian Ermenegildo Luppi. Its official name was the *Angel of Memory*. But on the chest-high plinth supporting the angel, another name was carved: ELIZABETH ROSEMOND TAYLOR. So *that's* where she wound up: steps away from her pal Michael Jackson, who earns $145 million a year in royalties even as he lies here, the two inseparable beyond the end. We can all take comfort in the fact that Liz, a woman who lived life in the limelight, selected a final resting place where every half hour, people grope their way toward the Last Supper in stained glass.

This Lite Brite da Vinci, as I call it, was dedicated in 1931 by Gov. James "Sunny Jim" Rolph (a politician of such poor judgment that his main legacy would turn out to be his approval of the lynching of two accused murderers). The stunt made for an exuberant MacGuffin for Forest Lawn. When it debuted, the Great Mausoleum had lines 'round the cemetery. Some 11,000 people a month came to view the window during its first year. Now it was time to see what the Depression-era fuss was about. The hall lights dimmed, and I took a seat amid the crypt's shiny marble floor. Not much can distract a man from the gnawing realization he's sitting alone in a tomb surrounded by thousands of corpses. Except, I found, one thing: Tinny recorded music began to play and a mechanical curtain triumphantly revealed the thirty-foot-long glass artwork. The dull monaural sound worthy of a forgotten Charlton Heston picture filled the mausoleum as Jesus and his banqueting buddies soaked me in lurid color. A narrator's voice came in, gamely stoking my approbation by explaining how the thing had taken seven painstaking years to assemble, and—wouldn't you know it—how that scoundrel Judas Iscariot shattered in the kiln five times. The artist, the disembodied crypt voice told me, was about to give up and scrap the whole seven-year project when lo, her prayers were answered and Judas baked properly! Robotic shutters behind the window slowly closed on cue, simulating a sunset, so that I might be as duly amazed by the window's nuance as Dr. Eaton's investment had intended, but for a long moment I was wondering how, in the name of research, I managed to strand myself in a mausoleum without the lights on.

When the lights finally came up, I could see a row of burial niches directly underneath the stained glass. These were the elite "Immortals" as determined by the Council of Regents of Forest Lawn. Only the most prestigious people were invited to be dead there. Their number includes composer Rudolf Friml, Mount Rushmore sculptor Gutzon Borglum (his epitaph pointedly asserts "he toiled for equality in the rights of man," which would seem an oddly defensive assertion for a sculptor until you remember he joined the KKK to get the Stone Mountain gig), and a tablet for Dr. Hubert Eaton himself. How we define our past in stone is the last and most enduring fib we are permitted to tell about ourselves. Eaton's fib was his entire career. If the crest proclaiming ETERNITY above Forest Lawn's entry gates didn't impress you when you drove in, Dr. Eaton's marker sums up the profound motive for every investment The Builder made.

"IF YOU WOULD SEE HIS MONUMENT

LOOK ABOUT YOU."

In Forest Lawn's gift shop—what's a graveyard without a gift shop?—I selected a $16 copy of a 134-page, full-color guidebook, *Forest Lawn: The First 100 Years*, a glossy omnibus of praise for Dr. Eaton. Inside were images of The Builder himself: an unremarkable, round-faced, bald man in practical, midcentury plastic-rimmed glasses. He grinned unconvincingly, looking like someone whose hot air balloon was about to whisk out of Oz. In every photo, he wore a suit.

Mustering the solemnity that I assumed was appropriate for souvenir browsing in a cemetery (who can say?), I also brought to the cashier a sporty over-the-shoulder tote bag emblazoned "Forest Lawn Memorial-Park," which I planned to stuff with suntan lotion and cold beer for the most depressing beach day ever. The girl behind the counter chattered as she rang me up, as blithely as if we were at the mall.

"Don't miss the giant painting of Jesus!" she chirped as she handed me my bag.

She meant Hubert Eaton's other tent-pole cemetery

blockbuster attraction: *The Crucifixion*, a 195-foot-by-45-foot panorama depicting Jesus Christ's final moments. The Polish painter Jan Styka completed it in 1897 mostly as a ballsy way to sell tickets to the devout across Europe. Styka eventually lugged his behemoth canvas to America in time to be displayed at the Louisiana Purchase Exposition in St. Louis in 1904, but his efforts went nowhere: when unfurled, it wouldn't fit in the hall, and to make things worse, the other paintings he brought were consumed by fire. Styka returned to Poland, tail between his legs, but he had to leave his most spectacular work behind because he couldn't afford to pay the duty to get it back across the Atlantic. It wound up rolled around a telephone pole in the storehouses of Chicago's Lyric Opera where Dr. Eaton's men, seeking a tourist attraction to lure the penitent masses, tracked it down during World War II.

On Good Friday in 1951, after first revealing the restored painting at Los Angeles' Shrine Auditorium (then, also home to the Oscars), Dr. Eaton opened the neo-Gothic Hall of the Crucifixion, which he built at a cost of $1.3 million, most of it borrowed. The Hall of Crucifixion has a name that promises a show that might *really* sell tickets, but I'm sorry to report the interior is no scarier than a high school auditorium with rows of purgatorial hard-back seats. The canvas is unveiled six times a day. I caught the spiel with eight other people in a house that could fit one hundred times our number. A pompous recorded narration echoed, the music swelled, and the curtains peeled away.

Dr. Eaton's piety must have confirmed his conviction that he had stumbled across a masterwork, because Styka's compositional talents were powerless to do it. *The Crucifixion* is all sky and crowds, and as with all Victorian-era blockbuster panoramas, tries to stuff an epic into a single frame: soldiers draw lots, Peter looks nervous, and every New Testament player lines up as if in a curtain call. The script is as garish as the artwork: "This masterpiece might never have been seen again were it not for the vision and tireless effort of one man: Dr. Hubert Eaton, founder of Forest Lawn. This man—this *visionary*—who signed his first and boldest work, his Creed as The Builder, had an even grander idea..." And so on. For an interminable half hour we, again trapped in the dark, were then regaled with an unexpurgated retelling of the Gospel, as if we would be unable to appreciate a painting the size of a soccer field without an accompanying lecture about the Good News. Sometimes it tossed in some sound effects or crowd noises for color, but the time we got to the snidely whiplash snickering of the Roman soldiers, I could hear the couple nearest to me snoring softly. They were jolted awake by the queasy and entirely too realistic sound effect of nails being hammered through flesh. It was the only place in all of Forest Lawn where death was treated as a reality.

When Dr. Eaton, Superstar Mortician, died at the age of eighty-six on September 20, 1966, Walt Disney himself was an honorary pallbearer (and so was Herbert Hoover). Ronald Reagan, who emceed the opening day of Disneyland on ABC, also attended as they laid Dr. Eaton to rest in the Memorial Court of Honor by his beloved glass da Vinci. Walt Disney joined Eaton permanently in Forest Lawn's Court of Freedom sixty-three days later.

Forest Lawn is American memory in microcosm. It is not just an audaciously stage-managed reliquary of consumerist proportions—although it is that. It's also a theatrical embodiment of controlled feelings, catastrophe consummated as something splendid and palatable. It's quintessentially us, and this false image endures wherever idealism is a more preferable takeaway than suffering—in the perfected lawns at Pearl Harbor, in the cheerful families skipping on the cover of the Gettysburg tourism brochures, in Survivor Trees and "United We Stand." Dr. Eaton's brilliance was in spackling over suffering with aesthetics, in varnishing the fury of grief with store-bought decorum, and in recognizing that there shall be no commemoration without commercialization. Just as Disneyland is the essence of American fantasy, Forest Lawn is the essence of American memory: a Hollywood ending.

After all, it's the finale that contains the meaning of the performance.

MY LAST TESTAMENT, AND WILL

HERE LIES AMERICA

"After all, what is reality anyway?
Nothin' but a collective hunch."

—JANE WAGNER, *THE SEARCH FOR SIGNS OF*
INTELLIGENT LIFE IN THE UNIVERSE

THE AVENGERS OF TUGALOO

Dugilu'yî

AMERICA CHERISHES LEGENDS, BUT FORSAKES HIS-
tory. In trying to find out something, anything, final about
the murder of my poor scalded Engineer and absentee
patriarch, Will O'Neal, I roused civil servants from their
tax-supported naps across the city, the county, at the
coroner's, and in police stations in both South Carolina
and Georgia. No matter who I asked for paperwork, no
one had kept any records of the crime scene, the witness
statements, the testimony, or the evidence.

Research is a team sport. You can't do it alone. The
sidewalk of the internet ends just a few years in the past,
so to foray further into the hinterlands of time, you will
require the benevolence of a librarian guide. Archives and
historical associations are tasked with preserving history,
but that doesn't mean they make it easy to obtain. First
you have to figure out who might hold what. Then you
have to find out if the document you need actually still
exists, then you have to rely on someone to fish it out
of the warehouse or, worse, fly somewhere to fish it out
yourself, and before you can do any of those things, you
need a clerk to help you navigate an endless variety of
peculiar reference systems, most of which are offline and
only hint at potential holdings, and all of which are more
effective at hiding things than locating them.

In Europe, they throw a rope around anything that
gathers a cobweb, and you can't so much as wiggle a cob-
blestone without obtaining seven levels of government
clearance. But in the United States, the land of perpetual
forward motion and retrenched funds, preservation is left

to luck. Governmental archives are often represented on the web by flimsy hand-coded HTML pages, in the stacks by storage systems better suited to time capsules or coat closet shelves, and in person by office hours restricted to thirty minutes on the fifth Saturday of every other month. Meanwhile, local historical associations subsist on uncatalogued boxes from old ladies' attics. This is how history is allegedly retained in America, which is to say how it's so routinely forgotten. In most cases, particularly in my family, as much was recorded about the lives of average Americans in the early 1800s as was recorded about the daily lives of serfs in feudal England—which is nothing. Most of our days float into oblivion as soon as they're lived.

As I went from office to archive in the rural South, government desk clerks were reliably unimpressed by my interest. Civil servants provided nothing. But volunteers at historical societies were fascinated by Will's tale, and begged for every detail—but in turn could provide even less. The ravages of the twentieth century and bureaucratic ennui had conspired to destroy every vestige of Will's accident, right down to the location: I still couldn't find an antique map that pinpointed beyond generality the exact spot of the flag stop at Harbin's. I just knew it was somewhere in a certain patch of woods.

In desperation, I sent a letter to the South Carolina Archives and History Center, another random analog repository I'd miraculously found, asking for advice. I received a formal response from Steven D. Tuttle, its supervisor of reference services. Mr. Tuttle politely informed me that his office had found a few papers regarding the trial, which he would send me.

The day the envelope arrived, I was so excited I took a photo of it waiting on my kitchen table. Then I stared at it, unopened, wondering if the whole story of the wreck was sealed in front of me, a happy Pandora.

After some wine, I opened it and pulled out a stapled sheaf of forty-four single-sided papers, seventeen inches by eleven inches. They were copies of the original indictments of the kids accused of causing the wreck, from 1909: THE STATE VS. JIM LEWIS AND JOHN TERRELL.

Court documents are rarely as illuminating as you imagine them to be, and at first glance, these didn't fail to disappoint. Most of them rehashed, in pompous legalese, what I already knew: Jim Lewis and John Terrell stood accused of "obstructing and wrecking train No. 35, Southern Railway" by which "Will O'Neal then and there died." (Will's black assistant, Joe Clay, once again, wasn't mentioned. Probably he didn't rate a trial.) And as I leafed through the filled-in legal forms, something unexpected happened: real human beings took form.

The papers were drawn up mostly without typewriters, and with every curve and dot of inkwell scrawl, for the first time I was gripped by evidence that living people had named my great-great-grandfather as a victim worth avenging. There, on the ninth page, the one listing the $1,000 bail set for Jim Lewis, was a short list of signatures. The first one was in the same hand as the court clerk, but it read "Jim Lewis," and between those two words was an X labeled, in tiny cursive, "his mark."

Jim Lewis, one of the "two negroes" accused of murdering Will, was a backwoods lad who could not read or write. That little X took me where blurry newspaper articles hadn't: to South Carolina in the spring of 1909, when a black kid accused of trying to kill a ranking white man would be lucky to make it to the courthouse alive, let alone survive the verdict. This fragile little X was scrawled on a form at the command of some drawling white lawyer—he was represented by names right out of Welty: R.T. Jaynes, Stribling, Dendy, and J.E. Boggs.

John Terrell, the elder boy, was able to write his own name, so he appeared to have been privy to an education. It appeared in tall, trembling script, like a thing he had never been made to write before. His bail was twice Lewis', $2,000, or about $50,000 today, which meant he was probably seen as the guiltier of the pair. Tiny type at the edges credited the *Keowee Courier* as having printed the court forms. Probably the only press in town. It was also the same newspaper that declared these "two negroes" were sure to swing in a noose. The rest of the paperwork cataloged the names of the nearly two dozen witnesses slated to be called by the defense and included warnings of $200 fines—$5,000 today—if any of them failed to show up for the proceedings. If you live somewhere your major newspaper is named *Farm and Factory*, that's a life's savings.

The packet contained no statements, no evidence,

no photographs—nothing that could shine light on the circumstances of Will's death, or what the defense would argue. So I got to work on the only thing I had: names. I wrote a list of the ones who paid bail for Terrell and Lewis before the trial, and then I made a list of defense witnesses. There was nothing listing prosecution witnesses—that must have been in another bundle of documents, long since lost—but half the story was better than none. Some of the words were a challenge to transcribe—penmanship evolves like bacteria—so I wrote a few possible versions. When I had enough names, I turned to a copy of the 1910 Census, taken a year after the trial. From this I could match everyone's age, address, gender, and occupation.

The census contested its own legibility. Where it said "place of birth," the census taker had written "South Carolina" repeatedly in glowing, proud curves, but when it came time to record the names of the "negroes," she could only muster an atrophied tangle of ink strokes. But there were enough common letters to show me human lives at stake. The Terrells made their home in a place the census called Tugaloo Township, South Carolina, in a neighborhood where residents were predominately marked B, for black. As I researched, they silently filed into my imagination and stood staring at me in the half-light, awaiting the inevitable firing squad.

John Terrell was just eighteen years old at the time of Will's murder. He was a boy—which is what a white Georgian would have patronizingly called him, but I mean an actual kid—and yet even at eighteen he was already married to a sixteen-year-old girl the census called Beaulah. John worked as a laborer in "odd jobs." The couple lived with John's five young brothers and sisters in the same house as his parents, Katie, age thirty-six, and King, forty-one, who were also called to testify. Nine people under one South Carolina roof. King Terrell was a farmer. King also marked his Witness Recognizance with an X. Their household was racially mixed: King was a B for black, while Katie, the children, and Beaulah were all MU, for mulatto. John's little brother Walter, twelve years old, was summoned to testify to save his brother's life, hauled from his farm to the county seat to swear before a room full of powerful white men, who were only too ready to break his brother's neck with the tap of a gavel. Siblings Jessie and Rosana, aged six and seven, were spared that trauma.

One by one, the townspeople of Tugaloo also stepped out of the shadows, and a community worthy of Harper Lee began to form. The first witnesses I located were neighbors. A few yards down the road from the Terrells lived a seventeen-year-old girl named Myrtie Johnson (B), who was also called to testify for the defense. There was Alex, Myrtie's grandfather, who was a farmer, and Myrtie's twenty-two-year-old sister Elizabeth, who worked as a housekeeper. There was the widow Mary Scott (B), who raised eight-year-old Sylvester and three-year-old Pearl alone. Then there was Samuel C. Fant (B, thirty), the schoolteacher. Everyone working hard, everyone normal, everyone marked B. So some of Tugaloo's most upstanding black citizens, people with jobs and respect, had turned out for Terrell and Lewis.

Soon, though, names turned up from another part of town, and the case took a twist: E. H. Stonecypher. Age thirty-eight, druggist. Marked as W, not B. Then came Frank M. Cross, who sold general merchandise. Also W. He lived a few doors down from the president of the Oconee Bank. George W. Kay, salesman, and the head of his (W) household. W.C. Peden, another white head of household involved in dry goods. Everyone prosperous, everyone W.

And then there were the men who paid bail for the young men. Kay gave $250 for Lewis. Charles G. Jaymes, from the county seat of Walhalla, had chipped in $1,000 for Terrell. He was a (W) wholesale merchant, aged thirty-seven. Jessie M. Carter, forty, was another wholesale merchant (W), and he chipped in another grand. James G. Breazeale and John W. McClain, white men in their upper thirties with white families to support, laid town $250 each for Jim Lewis.

And as I drew the last detail out of the last page that time was likely to ever gift me on this matter, it dawned on me that this murder was not what it seemed at first. As much as my modern-day, Hollywood-fed cynicism—Southern shame? Yankee smugness?—led me to believe I was uncovering a personal version of the Scottsboro Boys, it wasn't coming true. These kids were loved. They had friends everywhere in town. A wide cross-section of Tugaloo—black and white, rich and poor, young and old—had come together to vouch for Terrell and Lewis. It's as if, as one, they saw an injustice about to happen and banded together to fight it.

All of it over my own bloodline. Me, by extension.

I was feeling as I did when I gazed out over the bewildering jumble of competing state markers at the battlefield of Chickamauga: what to believe? It's a sobering thing when you can look out at something as unquestionably tragic as a place of bereavement, but you can't take at face value a single monument in the panorama.

It started, as all stories do, with what I didn't know yet. I wasn't there, and neither were you, but this is how it happened.

Tugaloo, it turned out, wasn't just any town. It was one of the most ancient and significant communities in America—except we forgot to remember that.

It was settled in about 500 AD and maintained importance off and on for almost a millennium and a half. In fact, the town of Dugilu´yî, later shortened to Dugilu, and then called Tugaloo ("*TOO*-ga-low"), was so important as a hub for trading trails that it's said that when British colonial explorers first began making contact with the

Cherokee out of Charles Town (now Charleston), they thought Tugaloo was the capital. Others think it was a vital regional capital for centuries before that. In the 1720s, an adorably named Scottish colonist, Col. George Chicken, described it as "the most ancient town in these parts," and the ethnographer, John Mooney, catalogued Tugaloo as one of the greatest towns of the Cherokee nation—centuries before the land was stolen by Georgians for its gold lode, in defiance of Supreme Court orders.

There's a big rock lying behind a mostly forgotten wooden inn a few miles west of the site of Tugaloo today, a few miles from Toccoa. The Engineer Will O'Neal was rushed past it in his last moments. If you look at the stone closely, which nearly no one does, since it sulks forlornly in one of the most assertively drive-past-able state parks in all of the South, and I've driven past them all, you may see the faint, badly eroded squiggles of rune-like script. The Cherokee, people forget, were educated—even after the privations of the Trail of Tears, they managed a near-100 percent literacy rate as a group—and the Tugaloo Stone, as it's called, is thought by some to have been a sort of printing press used to transfer that ingenuity among communities. It's been theorized—perhaps erroneously, because nothing loves a vacuum of fact quite like history does—that for centuries, other Cherokee from up river, deeper in the Appalachians, would stop by Tugaloo, press a wet hide against the Tugaloo Stone, and take an impression of the information on it. That, it's been suggested, would have enabled them to share a sort of road map for trading far and wide. Some people, fantasists maybe, have even posited that the Cherokee might have used their knowledge to sail much greater distances across the sea than anyone considers possible today. Like, to Europe.

Whatever its purpose, the Tugaloo Stone had a talismanic power. But it was yet another old stone with a message to impart—this book is full of them. In Dugilu′yî's heyday, it was kept safely at a tall mound that stood in a place of honor in the center of the village. At the mound's peak stood a seven-sided council house, which served as a sort of capital for the seven disparate clans of the Cherokee, and in which an eternal flame burned—Jackie O was not the first. Deceased leaders were interred under the house to imbue it with their greatness, which made Tugaloo itself a pre-America death tourism shrine for exalted politicians. And a target. In one 1717 episode, hundreds of Creek braves came to the house to beg the Cherokee to help them drive the British colonists away. Instead, the Cherokee turned on the Creek and slaughtered them, right there on the mound, kicking off a decade of violence and making their eventual conquest by the British easy. The Tugaloo mound, the symbol of Tugaloo Township, contained some seriously bad karma that ensnared my ancestors as they passed by.

The very summer that Philadelphia declared independence, the new Americans burned Tugaloo to the ground. British cannon and American patriots took turns leveling it, and once the Cherokee were evicted, the incomers turned their backs on the meaning of the old inscriptions. The flame was snuffed, the hallowed mound reduced to nothing more than a bump. The Tugaloo Stone was carted nearby, to the back yard of a coaching inn, as a quaint novelty for white people to ponder. With nothing solid left to preserve the story, no stone to tell future people what to know, Tugaloo vanished. After a while, homes were built there, but this time, the place found itself on the river border of two new states, South Carolina and Georgia.

With Natives flushed out, corporations became the new warriors. By the turn of the last century, the Georgia Railway and Power Company was expanding from electric systems to streetcars to baseball teams (the Atlanta Crackers), and it needed dams to slake a thirst for energy. Tycoons from Atlanta planned new lakes everywhere around Tugaloo. But—and at first this was a curious thing—almost as soon as the dams were announced, rural trains began derailing. In this remote South Carolina backwoods where nothing notable should have been happening, news reports of derailing trains began accumulating in 1902.

Locals tried fighting back. The Battle of Gettysburg's spurned General Longstreet (the proud namesake of the peanut butter burger I ate at the Blue & Gray Bar & Grill near the battlefield) left behind a spirited widow, Helen Dortch Longstreet. Like Julia Dent Grant, she was unafraid to assert herself. She took on the Georgia Railway and Power Company in court over Tallulah Gorge, calling them "commercial pirates and buccaneers" for its intention to impound and flood poor communities. It's thought her campaign was the first environmental protection case ever fought in United States courts.

She failed, badly. By 1909, as Will O'Neal was making what would be his final nightly mail runs, Georgia was finishing Lloyd Shoals Dam, the largest in America at the time. Tugaloo found itself in the crosshairs. The residents, John Terrell and Jim Lewis among them, must have known the mystical 1,500-year heritage of their little hamlet; after all, there was a sacred mound standing above them, filled with departed Cherokee elders, and the ultimate forced removal of the Cherokee people had happened within living memory of some of the older people in the village. This was the last gasp for the Cherokee in this part of the South—the last chance to retain their ground, or at least strike a blow defending it for the final time. Terrell and Lewis knew that the heedless puppeteers of profit and industry, including the Southern Railway, were impounding and devouring towns all around them. Their way of life, their home, was on the brink of permanent inundation.

So they struck back in the only way they could. They hadn't meant to kill Will O'Neal. They liked him. He brought their mail to the station every night. He threw them oranges. They meant to derail the freight train that came before him. It all went so wrong.

Everyone knows that things are often not what they appear to be. If my journeys through America's misery lands taught me one thing, it was that. But I had no idea the biggest discovery would be about the kids who were held for my great-great-grandfather's murder.

I was in the Walhalla courthouse. It's a glassy, contemporary riff on the penchant for Greek Revival, the South's peculiar architectural fetish that overlooks some of the other things Ancient Greeks were famous for, like pederasty and infanticide as entertainment. The courthouse was deserted; I was the only civilian. I guess nothing much happened here now that my ancestor was dead.

I told a sweet-faced reception girl that I was here to research a court judgment, and she gestured me to see a record keeper she called "Miss Gloria," who could help me.

Miss Gloria was skinny and unsmiling, busying herself alone behind a counter for many minutes even though there was no one else seeking her services. "Help you?" she finally said, with no glance my way.

"Hello there!" I sang. (In the South, exaggerated good cheer is always the last step before an explosion of exasperation.) "I'm here to find out the verdict in a murder trial that happened here in 1910. I'm hoping you can help me."

I expected her, as someone who tends to archives, to be fascinated by this unusual inquiry into the obscure past from an enterprising and moderately attractive stranger.

Instead, she said, with acute weariness, "That's going to take a lot of digging."

"Oh," I said. "I don't mind. I have lots of time."

"No," she said. "I mean, *I* have to do it. *I* have to go and look."

"Well, I'd be grateful," I said. "This is an important family matter."

She sighed as she put down the file she was holding. I gave her the details, but then, in a classic social miscalculation of the sort I'm so good at, I continued gushing in a nerdish hope that she'd get as hooked on my family story as I was. "Two guys who were described as 'colored' were accused of murdering a white man!" I said, before apprehending midsentence the words I was relaying, that Miss Gloria was African-American, and let's not get into any more of that. Wisely for once, my shut-up meter was triggered and I went to sit down. Miss Gloria trudged out a side door.

I waited. I palpitated. I was finally about to nail down some truth. I hadn't been able to find newspaper reports of the trial, only the arraignment, but now, finally, there would be truth. We're talking about two poor black kids in rural 1910 South Carolina who were accused of murdering a well-placed white man from Atlanta. I had already scheduled a few hours in the afternoon to go looking for their graves. The deed was long since done, and I was probably the first person to invoke their names ninety or more years after their executions, which made me feel magnanimous.

I didn't have long to meditate on the shortened lives of poor Terrell and Lewis. Despite Miss Gloria's protest, it only took about three minutes for her to return with a slip of paper.

Miss Gloria, of the pinched face and sullen resistance to clerical duties, held the verdict in one hand.

"Here," she said. "Found it."

She slapped it on the counter.

I read it.

Not guilty.

I looked up at Miss Gloria, speechless.

"That's our justice system," she said, and turned her back on me.

When I was in high school, I memorized, among other useless obsessive things, the CD for a Broadway musical based on Charles Dickens' unfinished *The Mystery of Edwin Drood*. There's a song near the start of the second act when the entire company is singing and dancing away, absorbed in momentum and merriment, when suddenly, the music cuts off and everyone halts midkick. The narrator, played by an English actor named George Rose, looks at the audience and informs them, "It was at this point in the story that Charles Dickens laid down his pen and died." Everyone tentatively regains their balance and stands around, wondering what to do next. For the rest of the show, the audience votes on who they think done it. The results differ each night. We decide the legacy by consensus.

That's what death does. Halts us midkick, leaves everyone else wondering how the song should end. Pretty much none of the people who died to inspire these death attractions was supposed to go that early, but they did. And so did *Drood*'s George Rose himself a year later, when his car plunged off a cliff during a trip to the Dominican Republic. At his funeral, they mourned a car accident. Much later, police realized his adopted son had teamed up with his biological father, beaten Rose to death in a homophobic rage, and planted his body in the car. Rose's true end bore no relation to his mourning. On my travels, I had found very few examples of mourning that matched the gritty ugliness of the circumstances that caused them.

The boys didn't swing.

They lived on. They left more stories behind somewhere.

I tried to track them from that point. From his draft cards and other scant minor paperwork left behind by people who had processed them over the course of their lives, I learned that, after escaping the noose, John Terrell moved. He was reinstated as a railroad laborer—all had been truly forgiven, at least by the Railway. I can't imagine he was ever the same. I can't be positive. I do know that he went on to serve in World War I—incidentally, hundreds of thousands of young black men raised their hands for that war because it was a chance to prove themselves to a society that insisted on to degrading them despite the Fifteenth Amendment. Later, he became a farmer near Macon. He stayed married to Beaulah, the sixteen-year-old girl who was at his side even as his neck was being measured for a noose on behalf of my family.

The paperwork had Terrell as a hard-working man. At age fifty, he volunteered again, this time for World War II as part of the "old man's draft." He wasn't called up because, as evidenced by the registrar's notation, "finger on right hand cut off" (a railway injury?). By the middle 1940s, he was living (without a home phone) in Gilpin, Pennsylvania as a coal loader for the Maher Coal Company.

He lived a life. He died, as far as I can tell, in 1964, more than a half-century after the trial, in Cleveland. He and Beaulah had no children. But I'm working on scraps here. The libraries of the South had swallowed him up for good.

The fate of Jim Lewis is unknown—at least, so far and by me. Someone didn't write him down, or someone misplaced the receipts.

But then, look at the precious few documents again.

Comb them to reach for a new angle using the tiniest ignored detail. This is what historians do.

Terrell's draft card. Although the census had marked him with a B for black, the draft registrar had marked his complexion as "light." Even my own grandfather's draft card was marked "dark," and let's just say my entire family ate a lot of mayonnaise. That "light" opened a door in my understanding. In 1910, some census takers in South Carolina would mark people of Cherokee descent, regardless of their complexion, as B for black on the Jim Crow logic that they weren't pure white. Half of Tugaloo was marked B, actually. The other half was MU, which proves there was a distinction being made for mulatto. The folks with money in Walhalla were W.

Terrell, a young Cherokee man?

Just one word on a draft card, so easily overlooked, changed him for me into a secret hero, a vindicator, the young man who would save his community. Like on an epitaph, just a few letters can carry an entirely new story forward.

Perhaps he really did sabotage the train. He had to. As the last in the line of the Tugaloo Cherokee, he had to fight back for his doomed homeland. He had to protect the precious burial mound, the irreplaceable artifact of a lost culture that predated the United States by centuries. He had to kill to preserve his ancestors' hallowed death site.

My own ancestor had been murdered to preserve a death attraction.

The plot was much bigger. As I had seen in the paperwork, townspeople must have grasped the threat to their village while the power company plotted to wipe out a half-millennium of proud Native history, just for the sake of modern greed and Cracker games. After all, the evidence shows it: Together, they united to cover for the boys. The townspeople, white and black, rich and poor, must have gotten together and decided the lads would never be convicted if everyone agreed to protect them. They couldn't thwart the evil Southern Railway before it had a chance to flood the only home they knew together, but they could save the lads who at least had tried.

Or maybe the two kids really had nothing to do with any of it. They wouldn't be the first young black men to be blamed for something they didn't do, or the last.

People told census takers they were Cherokee all the time, sometimes to hide slave blood, sometimes to hide white blood, and sometimes because grandma had simply told them they were once.

And maybe Will's own survivors knew about the arrests but sealed their lips against the event forever since the damned kids had gone free. Maybe thinking two black kids had killed his dad made Tracy O'Neal eager to help the KKK grow through his photographs at Stone Mountain. Maybe he was so furious he buried his rage in the way he chose to record other people, the way the Lost Cause statue builders did.

Or maybe no one in my family ever knew about any of it. No one wanted delicate, unstable Rosa to find out lest she go on another opium binge, and they weren't about to burden her young, fatherless sons with what was going on in South Carolina. So the deeper story never made it to Atlanta.

None of it matters. The dead all died.

After wartime delays, construction on the dam began in 1917. Today, Tugaloo is gone. It's under water. Even lifetime South Carolina locals have never heard of it. Thirty feet above the streets where John Terrell and Jim Lewis walked, you will now find a quiet place to fish. When the level's low, the sacred Tugaloo burial mound can be seen cresting a few yards from where Will O'Neal's old train line crosses the water on a trestle. The ancient mount sometimes appears as a mud bump. A nondescript and distantly placed metal sign on the Georgia (wrong) side begins, "North of this marker, in the center of the lake, once stood an important Indian town."

The Cherokee built a mountain so the legacy of their ancestors would last forever. Now that mountain is a hazard to motorboats. The largemouth bass and black crappie that swim around it contain so much methylmercury that two states warn they're unsafe to eat.

The term *generativity* was coined by lifespan theorist Erik Erikson in the 1950s. It's a lot like the Memorial Impulse, resplendent with the latent terror of death—generativity, in its classroom form, is about sending good vibes to those who will succeed us. It's about that moment when a father dances with his daughter at her wedding, as if to pass the baton of life to her. It's about leaving inheritances in the form of double family portraits, or writing a check to Hubert Eaton for "before-need" funeral services. It's about suddenly getting into genealogy when you hit middle age. It's elders taking care of their own.

It sounds nice, this self-perfecting Darwinism through Hallmark card moments. The more I explored, though, the more I had to embrace the fact—both disheartening and sweet—that historic sites and family gravestones don't hand off anything to the next generation except a heightened version of make-believe. Generativity, once it has been manipulated by the inescapable human impulse for bending reality, means we leave the next batch of people with more idealism than we could ultimately muster through the headwinds of difficult lives.

And now, just like a monument after the ribbon has been cut, I can summarize in a few words the moral of a bad situation. If I were installing one like those at Gettysburg or Andersonville or Oklahoma City, I would choose to tell Will's story—which I now know is James' story and Jim's story, too—as a stirring Hollywoodized fable, our secret formula for a poison that the entire world gulps. I have scraps of detail to prove the central points. Will was a dutiful, hard-working family man who fell victim to an act of vengeance perpetrated in the defense of an ancient Cherokee sacred site. For a colorful supporting cast, there was his opium-addicted housebound wife and quietly vengeful son, and for comic relief, the dainty, but feckless vaudeville actress smeared with makeup. Our hero is the town's beloved mail carrier, but he's also an innocent bystander in a star-crossed rebellion against Gilded Age rapaciousness. He is trapped as a pawn in a game to destroy the railroad, but raise the village.

This scheme goes awry. The wrong man, our hero, pays the price. Devastated to have killed the kindly train engineer they all loved, the competing classes of the village, regardless of their differences, must band together to salvage the situation. If they lose, their town will break under the weight of even more tragedy. They already have little chance of toppling the corporate plot to destroy it. White and black South Carolinians, all citizens of a town the railroad has condemned to die, hatch a clandestine plot to testify together, rebel against the lethal pull of Jim Crow, and save the necks of two young accused black boys. To right the wrong of my grandfather's murder, to rescue two well-meaning social justice warriors from execution, they must overcome what divides them. And they get away with it. At the very moment of their home's annihilation, the town finally stands as a unified community, hand in hand for the first and last time as the water floods in.

But there's a twist. In an epilogue that unravels all the gains, the bereaved son of the engineer vows to make segregation his champion cause. The price of the newly forged love of Tugaloo is the hate the son carries forth. We gain a town, but still lose one man. Because in America, the seed of hate is forever planted, waiting to sprout again, like Jack's beanstalk.

It's such a story I could sell the movie rights off this page.

Given the available facts, it could very well be true. Hell, if I solidified my version by making a movie, it would be as good as fact.

It's telling that in my preferred version of the story, I identify a lot more with the two boys. In fact, in nearly every killing spot I had visited, I suddenly realize, I had a softer spot for the victims than the victors. It's a sign, perhaps, of what this nation has done to me. I have come to see through its assertions of being a fair society.

Then again, given the same details, I could settle on a more mundane explanation: Will died in an accident, no one figured out who caused it, and my own family didn't even care enough to pass word down to a single generation. Two young men's lives were changed forever because of it, but we'll never be sure of the extent of it, because they were as forgotten as the rest of it.

My embroidered version is better. Unlike the rest of history, its meaning is obvious. It codifies Will's death as a symbol of the transition of an American age with plenty of juicy courtroom drama, and it weaves in the subplot of Rosa's drug addiction and a daffy, but kindly vaudeville actress. And as a meaningful coda, it ends with a warning: my great-grandfather's dark sense of revenge against an entire race. It has lies and deception and subverted shame—don't all good stories of Southern families? My version is one worthy of Tennessee Williams or Flannery O'Connor because it comes freighted with metaphor, underdogs, decay, redemption, and vindication for the innocent.

It may be false, but no one can prove that. The things that happened in the past never change. They all happened. But the way we think about them constantly does change. Shifting evidence and evolving worldviews always toss the past into flux. The problem is simple—we can never know the truth. America has no truth. A cemetery full of gravestones is just a field of names, and we fill in the details. If I carve my preferred version in marble to carry the tale forward, the message will stick. That's how you win the story wars in my country. America's entire ethos is about bending the story. Everyone who got off at Ellis Island intended to redefine their lives.

My original hope in visiting these death attractions was that I might find a thread of American values in American sadness. Nowhere on my travels to sorrow had I seen tears. Nowhere except for the very few places that touched us in our own lifetimes, the ones that selfishly plucked memory instead of ideology. Mostly I saw only theoretical emotion: wrinkled brows, like tourists doing math problems, failing to compute true loss or recognize warnings. Like Clara Barton, I had wandered from death field to death field, picking up a little piece of each one, collecting woe in my knapsack. Everywhere I went, the blood from America's grinding fractures bleeds all over everyone, yet our hands remain clasped in an immobilized routine of prayer. We are good at pretending we mean it. I wish we understood that America actually has no sides. There's no point in joining one team because no team stays on top for long.

I feel the faith of capitalism dying, idols cracking, our future withering, and the creeping possibility that our claim to being the best country in the world was held together only by our ability to shout it louder than last time. My birthright has drained away. I was raised to inherit a treasure that never actually existed, not in the form they told me. The nation in which I live is a battleground for a never-ending battle of supremacy, a perpetually swinging scythe, a false smile with a handshake from a greased palm. The melting pot was never our natural way; instead, we mastered simmering subterfuge and ways to erase our enemies before they erased us. This wrestling match didn't start with our lifetime.

In America, none of us is really here. Our proclaimed shared values are fugitive. Countervailing forces are always waiting, biding time until the pendulum swings back, hungry to erase the other side once powers shift. My own family's story was missing and I went looking, but it was in vain, hampered by the broom of history that in America keeps sweeping the past away because our entire system is built on cycles of supremacy.

And the loss. My God, my God, all the loss. All those

places, so many lives. So many futures that never grew to shape this world. Behind every digit in the endless tally of victims across this nation, there lies a fading roar of immeasurable pain and grief that can never be understood. My journey should have been a reckoning with connection and remembrance. But here, at the end of it, I still cannot grasp the weight of these disastrous events. I am, ultimately, alienated. Our eyes shall never be truly opened to the lives we have wasted. And America is still relatively young, if we're lucky. In the historical perspective, if we survive, the violence has only begun.

You may spill your guts in the street, but it won't matter any more than one more death by locomotive steam, or more than one more sacrifice in Antietam, or one fewer victim in Johnstown. We will all be swallowed by the Great Myth. Completely unknown to me at this moment, I may die in a manner that will be wielded to motivate armies. Or I may vanish, unremarked. Either way, it will be up to future Americans to weaponize my existence, to use me in ways I cannot control. Mankind will survive. I will not.

You and I have survived every calamity in human history. Our DNA descended through the ages in snippets that were carried by thousands of faceless ancestors who came before us. In a way, parts of you were here during every world event you ever heard about, embedded in some forgotten forebear, persisting through numberless wars, disasters, childhood mortality, broken treaties, and famines. We fluttered somehow across the millennia, smuggled inside survivors, fishing on the Red Sea or marching with the Romans and winnowing to the living side of the Black Plague, the Inquisition, the famines, the crack of slave whips, the sizzle of Civil War shells, the cheering of Lindbergh, the hissing of Hitler, until our present bones. The dead own what's in this world as much as we do.

Our bloodline was not distilled as the family tree reached from the past to meet us. It expanded exponentially by experiences we'll never know about, but which bore us here nonetheless. Gradually, we pooled. You yourself have been roaming this planet for much longer than your birthday suggests—you've been here since the moment your mother was born, carried inside her infant abdomen as a dormant egg, waiting for the spermatozoa that would someday bear the other half of your ancestors' legacies to finally meet, coalesce, and form. We are travelers who know nothing of how we arrived here.

We arrived from the past in pieces—so we can only glimpse the past the same way. No matter how vivid your imagination, the big moments of history will elude you. Unless you were alive to see it, the image of the bullet's impact, the building's collapse, the locomotive's somersault, the ship's foundering, will always be your personal imaginative creation. Other people will shape your vision. It has been happening all along, but you barely noticed. Every history lesson was planted in your head. Someone told you, and they had motives for telling you the way that they did. When you come down to it, all history is theory.

Let it power you to hate an enemy if you must. The facts of American history—this group collaboration of accidents, this tumultuous opus of us—cannot exist without artifice.

So did I get some facts wrong in my stories? I probably did. So sorry. Or probably I just didn't sell them hard enough. Or maybe my version is the first one that has ever been correct. Discussing the history of the common man is not just a game of telephone. It's also a guessing game, and usually a game of beliefs.

So there I was, right where we began, at the terminus of the overgrown lane marked ROAD CLOSED, stranded in the wilds of South Carolina, desperate to fuse with the memory of the planet. I was trying to conjure the essence of my story so that I might find the warnings I need to survive in my own travels.

This is where America finds itself, too. Time and again, my people have charged in fury down dark roads, howling for vengeance, not grasping until too late that the path would culminate in no victory at all. The fury takes many forms, but always, in my Christian nation, even the hands of the penitent slowly leave the steering wheel to reach for the most convenient weapon. Time and again, we race down a road with no destination. We are convinced that we were on the cusp of outrunning everything that holds us back, and we never realize our uncontrollable velocity until it is too late.

I could have pressed deeper into the forest, but then, no matter what I might find there, it would not teach me anything. There is no destination to this dead end.

Even if I found the right place where his disaster happened, I would never feel Will O'Neal's personality, or hear the sound of his voice, or discover his mannerisms were like mine, or know if he was to blame for any of my good or bad traits. I might have detested him, or I might have recognized in him the first glimmer of myself that this world would get to see.

I will never hear the screech of the train metal. I will never know who sabotaged the switch—and he didn't either. I will never know how the lives of two young men were contorted just as surely as the rails that twisted in the dark that night. I will never know if they really did it, or if they meant for it to go so far, or if they carried that torment with them forever. I will never know if it was done to avenge the Cherokee. I will never know if my life would have been different had his locomotive leapt securely over the faulty switch and continued onward, had the percussion of the wheels faded into the silence of the farmland at night, and had Will crawled back into his bed with poor Rosa in Atlanta at daybreak to send his family's lives in more stable directions.

Ultimately, I only have this present moment. But a piece of me was aboard that railroad through South Carolina and Georgia. A speck of me, me before me, rode the line for decades, heaving bales of Sears & Roebuck catalogs onto platforms and tossing oranges to children who carried forth my memory, until one day I stopped short, spilled, and seeped into the gravel. I am now in that land, too, pieces of who I am, yet the ground has nothing to say to me.

Melt down the statues if you want. Melt them all down, and turn the sculptures to gravel, because they are merely posts beside the road that led us to nowhere once already. Break the figures to match our shattered nation. America, the land that never truly learns, is always being built upon the ruins of itself. Its appetite for ruins cannot be satisfied.

I started my rental car, eager to depart this overgrown homeland.

Perhaps I could have left flowers. I could tearfully pay my respects to my ancestors, tell it to the air how they matter, and I could speak with them in monologue about how I had not forgotten them and how proud they must be of me for the pains I took to make the trip and revisit them. But they're not here. They can only speak with the words of others, whether it's by stone inscription or claims of kinship. My demonstration would be met only by the usual patter of trains, the breeze weaving through trees like mourners through gravestones. My grief, like all grief over history, is only a flailing hunger to feel something. So it will come to nothing. I stand near the road that veers into parts unknown, listening for ghosts that will not appear, weeping for an imaginary life lost.

Will O'Neal (1859–1909)

ACKNOWLEDGMENTS

IT'S A DAREDEVILISH THING TO SAY, "I'M GOING TO write a pop history book," rent a car, and take off across the country without knowing how any of it will end. It's even more hazardous to decide the book should span the entirety of American history. It was a long journey in more ways than one. Many times, I envied the authors who can set up camp in a cushy university library to leisurely find everything they need under the warm glow of pretty green lamps. My idea required mileage in more than half the states, motels in asphalted places, fried food and filthy restrooms, and lots of bizarre questions posed to suspicious rangers.

I didn't map this journey to comment on America's present political knot, but to interrogate its origins. I never mention the current presidency because this book isn't about it. At its core, it's about our mostly unacknowledged habit of using idealism as a weapon, which is perhaps one of our last shared national traits. It's about a country that was established on idealism, and how Americans still default to thinking in terms of it. It's about the voices that we smother and the voices that chose to remain hidden. It's about a battle for our souls that has been going on for as long as we've been losing them. We got here this way.

There is no way to thank all those park rangers, archivists, docents, librarians, and bobblehead salespeople who guided me to glory. These will do as a start: the custodians of the Tracy W. O'Neal Collection at Georgia State University Library; John Bentley at the Brotherhood of Locomotive Engineers and Trainmen; Andrew Jones at the Windsor Hotel in Americus, Georgia; Kerry Adams at the Old Red Museum of Dallas County History & Culture; the Cherokee Heritage Center in Tahlequah, Oklahoma; the passionate women at the Stephens County Historical Society; Aaron Goodwin; Steven D. Tuttle at South Carolina Department of Archives and History Center; the New York Transit Museum Archive; and Sallie Loy at the Southern Museum of Civil War and Locomotive History. A special thanks goes to the National Park Service. All of it. You're doing the Good Work that will outlast us all, and I take my Smokey Bear hat off to you. May you continue to protect and illuminate, and may you never be starved of another nickel. To the junior ranger at General Grant's tomb who responded to my historical question by writing "Google" on a piece of scrap paper, I show my gratitude by not publishing your name.

When you're a writer, your work happens alone. Some people, though, were kind enough to either join me for part of the research journey or nourish my inner one as it related to *Here Lies America*, including Ken Klieber, Curtis Moore, Kristin Harmel, Bryan Anthony Snyder, Zac Bissonnette, Phil Jimenez, Anton Kawasaki, Sion Fullana, Robert Samala, Jeff Kurtti, David Landsel, Andy Parker, Henry Roux, Valarie D'Elia, Jennifer Jellicorse, Doug Lansky, Julie Morris, and my mother, Tracy Temple. For a writer, there's always that nerve-crunching moment when you take your words off your desktop to show them to a peer. Thank you, Becky Sweren at Aevitas Creative Management, for understanding what I was constructing in the earliest days, for helping me clarify my arc and weed out the dad jokes (well, some of them), and most of all, for insisting it should be published—for a solo act, hearing that from someone you respect is the most crucial encouragement of all. Thank you. I wish I could have been a Kardashian. Thanks as well to my sharp-eyed, but sensitive developmental editor, Aja Pollock, whose ability to gently help writers navigate away from rocks without taking the wind out of their sails must be some kind of supernatural gift.

I contended with a discouraging amount of travel, an unadvisable number of facts, and a daily onslaught of decisions about how to distill everything I was seeing and doing into a fast-moving story capable of carrying some heavy metaphors without buckling under the weight of self-indulgence. How much should I assume readers already know about history? Am I treating the casualties with respect? Did I compress the complexity of events effectively enough so that every academic won't want to burn me in effigy? It left my psyche gasping at times, but ample oxygen came from all the friends who discussed this book with me as it evolved. Thanks (apologies?) to the people at the cocktail parties I ruined by talking through the little-known trivia that was on my mind. When a friend is hopping up and down, ecstatic that he has connected dots that prove U. S. Grant's body rode on a beer cart decorated by the Star of David—again, I thank you, every single unlucky one of you, for humoring me and telling me to keep going. I hope your eyes have unglazed enough to absorb the heartfelt gratitude written here. I need to especially thank the trusted friends who read early drafts, including (but not limited to) Brendan Milburn, Heather Taylor Pires, Eve Boissonnault, Jason Young, Curtis Moore, Josh Koll, and others. You were my most valuable preview audience. Special gratitude to Dr. Dwayne Mann for the academic/sensitivity read and for always telling me the truth like my life depends on it.

The delights of travel do not always translate into manageable books. I went to dozens of attractions in pursuit of this work, but as my arc unfolded, many worthy ones had to be pruned dramatically or eliminated from the final manuscript, sometimes for thematic reasons, but just as often because I had to draw a line somewhere, for your sake. Turns out America produces more mass misfortune than a single book can fit. I still lost sweat and frequent flier miles for them, so here's where I get my money's worth: The Alamo, Harpers Ferry, Guilford Courthouse, the Lorraine Motel, Salem, Pulse Orlando,

James Buchanan's Wheatland, Alcatraz, the Burroughs Plantation, Manzanar National Historic Site, Jamestown, Minute Man National Historical Park, Westwood Village Memorial Park and Hollywood Forever, the Old Slave Mart Museum in Charleston, the De Soto National Memorial in Bradenton, the Confederate White House in Richmond—I saw them all (and more) and wrote chapters about many of them (and cut them). If you ever meet me out and about, I encourage you to introduce yourself, buy me a beer, and ask me about them. Or just do that middle thing.

The descriptions of the places I went were true at the time I visited them. This book was made without Wikipedia.

JASON COCHRAN
2019

ABOUT THE AUTHOR

Georgia-born **JASON COCHRAN** (@JasCochran) has been a travel authority and consumer expert for more than twenty years. He's been a regular writer for publications including *Travel + Leisure*, the *New York Post*, *USA Today*, and the *New York Times*, and he has been on staff at *Entertainment Weekly*, *Budget Travel*, and AOL Travel (as executive editor). Jason has twice won Guide Book of the Year in the Society of American Travel Writers' Lowell Thomas Travel Journalism Competition, and once from the North American Travel Journalists Association. He is currently editor-in-chief of Frommers.com and cohost of the weekly *Frommer Travel Show* on WABC in New York City.